The Making of
YOSEMITE

To Ada Kathryn and Sophia Louise,

my amazing daughters;

to Susan and Mallard, my beloved parents;

and

to Jim Snyder

The Making of

YOSEMITE

James Mason Hutchings
and the Origin of America's
Most Popular National Park

Jen A. Huntley

UNIVERSITY PRESS OF KANSAS

Published by the University Press of Kansas (Lawrence, Kansas
66045), which was organized by the Kansas Board of Regents and is
operated and funded by Emporia State University, Fort Hays State
University, Kansas State University, Pittsburg State University, the
University of Kansas, and Wichita State University

Library of Congress Cataloging-in-Publication Data

Huntley, Jen A.
 The making of Yosemite : James Mason Hutchings and the origin
of America's most popular national park / Jen A. Huntley.
    p. cm.
 Includes bibliographical references and index.
 ISBN 978-0-7006-1805-7 (cloth : alk. paper)
1. Yosemite National Park (Calif.)—History. 2. Yosemite Valley
(Calif.)—History. 3. Hutchings, J. M. (James Mason), 1820–1902.
4. Nature conservation—Government policy—United States—
History—19th century. 5. National parks and reserves—
Government policy—United States—History—19th century.
I. Title.
 F868.Y6H897 2011
 979.4'47—dc23
                          2011031526

British Library Cataloguing-in-Publication Data is available.

Printed in the United States of America

10 9 8 7 6 5 4 3 2 1

CONTENTS

ACKNOWLEDGMENTS

Like every publication, this book reflects the support, encouragement, patience, and cajoling of an almost infinite network of friends, family, and colleagues. *The Making of Yosemite* is an adaptation and extension of my 2000 University of Nevada, Reno, dissertation, and therefore my debts of gratitude extend back over the past decade and beyond.

I have been blessed through the years with a network of incredible mentors, both as a graduate student and as a young academic professional. These mentors, many of whom were teachers during my graduate years and became colleagues after, deserve the lion's share of credit for their support of me and this project. For their insightful criticism, for challenging my ideas, and for innumerable acts of kindness, generosity, and collegiality I am profoundly grateful. My dissertation advisor Scott E. Casper exposed me to the nuances of cultural history and history of the book, central ideas in this work, and provided me with countless gifts of excellent advice and connections to a wonderful network of scholars, including the American Antiquarian Society, the Society for the History of the Early American Republic, and the Society for the History of Authorship, Reading and Publishing during the early years of my scholarly career. William D. Rowley of the UNR History Department deserves credit for convincing me to make James Mason Hutchings the focus of my dissertation, and thanks for his many years of friendship. I learned to appreciate the value of landscape studies from C. Elizabeth Raymond of the UNR History Department and Paul Starrs in Geography. Martha Hildreth was the History Department chair who hired me for the wonderful Visiting Assistant Professorship in History position, from which I was able to design and teach the field-based seminar "Yosemite: Issues in Environmental History," funded in part with a grant from the Woodrow Wilson Foundation "Imagining America" series. Dennis Dworkin's contagious fascination with cultural theory, class, and the process of modernity forms a key component of this book.

Jim Snyder, former Yosemite National Park historian, is the true expert on James Mason Hutchings, and it is no exaggeration to say that without his unstinting efforts this book simply would not have happened. He has been endlessly generous in sharing insights, drafts of his own manuscripts, documents from his own collection, generous gifts of books and documents, and access to Yosemite Research Library holdings. In addition, he devoted countless hours to conversation, tracking down random bits of information, and deeply thoughtful email exchanges, all of which have been invaluable contributions to this project, from the earliest days of research to the throes of the final manuscript draft. It is not only that Snyder knows so much about Hutchings—he has also been one of the few historians to share the conviction of the broader historical value in telling Hutchings' story. I am eternally in debt to Snyder not only for his intellectual support for this project, but for his good humor and friendship over the past twelve years.

Both my dissertation and subsequent research were underwritten with generous grants from the American Antiquarian Society (AAS), the Huntington Library, and the University of Nevada. The American Antiquarian Society's Stephen Botein Fellowship supported a month of dissertation research in the AAS library in the fall of 1999; the Huntington Library's William Keck fellowship gave me a month of research in San Marino during the summer of 2004; and the University of Nevada dissertation year fellowship funded an entire year of dissertation research and writing in 1999–2000. In 2005, the University of Nevada Special Collections department gave me office space to pursue research and writing there. These fellowships, together with the ongoing support of the University of Nevada Department of History teaching assistantships during my graduate study, provided critical research and writing time to draft the early versions of this project.

I also want to thank the many archivists and librarians for their generous and patient contributions of time, energy, and insight: at AAS, Georgia Barnhill, Joanne Chaison, John Hedges, Tom Knoles, Russell Martin, and Caroline Sloat; at the University of California Bancroft Library, Susan Snyder and Anthony Bliss; at the California State Library in San Francisco, Pat Keats; at the Huntington, Peter Blodgett; at the University of Nevada Special Collections, Bob Blesse and Kathryn Totton; at the Yosemite Research Library, Jim Snyder and Linda Eade. Gary Kurutz at the California State Library has been a great advocate of Hutchings' historical recovery. Dennis Kruska's 2009 *James Mason Hutchings of Yo Semite: A Biography and Bibliography* was a tremendous motivator to finish this project and provided great material to fill in the gaps of my own research.

I am grateful to many friends and colleagues for providing the variety and strength of the scaffolds I've needed to see this project through to completion. Nancy Scott Jackson was the original acquisitions editor at the University Press of Kansas who took on this project ten years ago. I am grateful to the University Press of Kansas for staying with this project for such a long time and to current editor Ranjit Arab for motivating me through the completion of it. I would also like to thank David Wrobel and Mark Fiege for their comments on the initial proposal and amazing peer review on the next-to-final manuscript. Caroline Sloat of AAS encouraged and patiently edited my article "'Such Is Change in California': James Mason Hutchings and the Print Metropolis, 1854–1862" for the *Proceedings of the American Antiquarian Society*. I was motivated to return to this project after it languished for many years through Meggin McIntosh's "Thirty Articles in Thirty Days" teleseminar, and I thank Meggin as well for her personal encouragement of my professional writing. Gini Cunningham offered insightful editorial feedback on the final manuscript. I want to thank the director of UNR's Oral History Program, Alicia Barber, for another terrific reading of the manuscript that really helped to shape the final version. For years of friendship, and collaboration, I wish to thank Scott Slovic of the UNR English Department, Stacy Fisher of Political Science, Kate Berry of the Geography Department, and Shaunanne Tangney of Minot University. Also Linda Curcio, Jenni Baryol, Phil Boardman, John Sagebiel, Derek Kauneckis, and Sue Davis. Finally I wish to thank Mike Collopy of the Academy for the Environment, for putting me first when the chips came down.

I am also grateful for the support of my family and close friends. My sister Erin Castle has been my closest confidante and never lost faith in my ability to finish this. My mother, Susan Burke, shared with me her love of the Sierra Nevada and took me to Yosemite for the first time when I was a teenager. My father, Mallard Huntley, instilled in me the love of words, history, and books as objects. He also contributed materially to this project with annual gifts to my collection of Hutchings ephemera and a month of writing time in our Connecticut family home. I am grateful to Mark Smith for his many years of material support and for being such an excellent father to our two children, Ada and Sophie, who have grown up with this project like another sibling; and to Claude Cole for being such a good friend and devoted member of our family. My fencing coach, Eric Momberg, and fencing buddies Andy Robinson, Ric Kulik, and John Springgate gave me a much-needed outlet during the many years of this project. I thank Donna Andrews, Anna Bernard, Susan Coats, Amelia Currier-Dworkin, Sherman and Kathy Lam-Guarneri, Melanie Mathews, and Bruce Rehm for all the cheerleading, coaching, and listening to my rambling. Finally, I am deeply grateful to my partner and muse, Jim Meiklejohn, for inspiring me to be a writer again.

While this project would not exist without the support of all these friends, colleagues, and family, any errors of research or interpretation are wholly my own.

The Making of
YOSEMITE

"General View of the Great Yo-Semite Valley, Mariposa County, California," by Thomas Ayres; James Mason Hutchings lithographic print, 1855. Hutchings commissioned Ayres to sketch the panoramic view from Inspiration Point in 1855. The resulting lithographic prints gave the public its first visual images of Yosemite Valley. (Courtesy Bancroft Library, University of California, Berkeley)

INTRODUCTION:
YOSEMITE AND THE TIPPING POINT IN AMERICAN ENVIRONMENTAL THOUGHT

Standing in the chill, rarefied air at the summit of Mt. Whitney, James Mason Hutchings surveyed the country around the highest peak in the contiguous United States, while his hired photographer, W. E. James, mixed chemicals for the images he would take from the summit. Unbroken chains of granite peaks, some still lined with snow even late in the season, ran as far as the eye could see to the north and the south, while Owens Lake glimmered in the shadowy valley thousands of feet below to the east. Beyond more peaks to the west, California's Central Valley was a barely visible blue shadow on the horizon. Wind whipped around Hutchings and James as other men from the party stomped their way to the rocky summit, and James began the laborious work of making his wet-plate exposures, the first photographs ever produced from that peak.

It was October 3, 1875, a tumultuous year in Hutchings' life. Twenty years before the Whitney expedition, Hutchings had organized the first tourist party into Yosemite Valley, when he began his life's work of depicting, interpreting, and publicizing Yosemite to "the public eye." He did so by publishing lithographs, magazine articles, and tour guides; by opening and running a hotel in the valley; by hosting scientists, editors, and religious thinkers; and by hiring artists and photographers and publishing their works. His efforts quickly spread through California and to the nation beyond, culminating in the Congressional act of 1864 to set aside the Yosemite Valley as a public park, "inalienable for all time." But Hutchings had filed preemption claims on the valley floor, and his efforts to defend those claims in court arrayed him against the Yosemite Grant's administrators, the national government, and, in the lens of history, against those who would protect the environment from "spoliation" by selfish, profit-seeking interests. In 1873, the long legal struggle finally came to an end with the U.S. Supreme Court decision against Hutchings' claims. Though Hutchings strenuously resisted his eviction notices, the 1875 tourist season was his last. His expedition to Whitney with the first photographer to ascend it was Hutchings' final flourish after a dozen years of building a home, raising a family, and running a business in Yosemite Valley.

Hutchings' notes of the expedition do not record whether he contemplated his personal life while surveying the summit. His wife, Elvira, had turned back from the expedition a month earlier. The same year as his court defeat she had confessed to him her deep attachment to his erstwhile employee, John Muir, and the couple had begun discussing separation. Elvira would soon move to San Francisco, and their marriage would continue to unravel over the next few years. Their three children, all born and raised in the mountain valley, were also to be evicted from their childhood home and community. And yet, Hutchings was a resourceful and entrepreneurial man of immense energy. After his Whitney expedition he would launch a new phase of his career to advocate for protection of the Sierra high country through guided tours, traveling illustrated lecture series, and political lobbying.

Despite Hutchings' lifelong dedication to Yosemite and the high Sierra, history has reduced him to an emblem of the selfish, narrow-sighted businessman; a "short, bald-headed and temperamental entrepreneur." In his 2009 documentary series *The National Parks: America's Best Idea*, Ken Burns blasted Hutchings for "illegally" squatting on public land. In Hutchings, Burns found the model antihero to provide the narrative structure of his entire story: each sacred place that would become a park faced a threat from developers, a threat that only the concerted efforts of passionate nature lovers and the federal government could defeat. While elements of this narrative are indeed true, the tale leaves out the messy complexity of historical context, while reducing the history of the national parks to a simplistic account of heroic nature lovers joined with a benign government to defeat the selfish entrepreneurs standing in the way of enlightened progress. The dualistic quality of the story reinforces other dualisms in American environmental thought: particularly the binary opposition between human civilization and Nature, the problematic fiction at the core of the idea of "wilderness," as described in William Cronon's 1994 critique, "The Trouble with Wilderness."[1]

For Hutchings, there was no contradiction in the idea that one could simultaneously feel a deep, spiritual connection to a place and seek to make a living in and from that place. The notion that those two kinds of experiences oppose each other belongs to a later, more modern time. Hutchings' career illustrates the way that the Yosemite Grant and the environmental conservation movement it launched were integrally connected to and interdependent upon the consumer tourism that would be his bread and butter. Indeed, in establishing that the Yosemite park be managed through a system of leases, Congress itself legislated that Yosemite would be a consumer commodity. The twin forces of conservation and consumer tourism have continued to be intertwined and interdependent in the subsequent 150 years of American conservation history.

The same media processes that advertised Yosemite to tourists stimulated the necessary public perception that certain landscapes needed to be set aside. Without protection from industry and resource exploitation, Yosemite and later national parks like Yellowstone and the Grand Canyon would have never attracted and sustained the tourists who flocked to their hotels and campgrounds. Many of these were individuals whose experiences in these landscapes led them to become activists for the emerging conservation movement at the end of the century. Yet, neither would those places have continued as tourist destinations without the urban industrial infrastructure of transportation networks, capital investment, and labor systems that have made consumer tourism an industry. Not only are the two forces linked through the nineteenth-century developments at Yosemite, this interconnection is a dynamic and creative force that has charged conservation politics in the twentieth century and beyond with much of their driving force.

However, these connections in many ways belied some of the most important nineteenth-century notions about sublime landscapes, especially that such landscapes were sites of divine redemption and antidotes to the problems and stresses of modernization. Therefore, the dynamic interconnection between consumer tourism and preservation paradoxically depended on people's willingness to *not* recognize the interdependence upon the two. That is, for Yosemite and other scenic destinations to continue to function as sites of escape from and restoration for the ills of urbanization and modernity, visitors had to be able to avoid recognizing the fact that these sites were themselves *products* of urbanization, industry, and modernity. The paradox at the heart of the interconnection between preservation and consumerism gave rise to the fiction that preservation of scenic landscapes was itself an antidote to modernization rather than a product of it. By restoring Hutchings to his rightful role in the creation of Yosemite, the history of this paradox becomes visible: throwing new light on the complex cultural, economic, political, and legal processes that produced America's "best idea."

Hutchings' journey to Whitney's summit had begun a half century and half a world away, with his birth in the English midlands, and his early adulthood among the nascent cultural institutions of the middle class as the first industrial revolution reached its apex. Educated at Edgbaston, Hutchings developed appreciation for science, landscape aesthetics, and a "seeing eye for beauty." He was also surrounded by the rapidly expanding print culture of early nineteenth-century England. The twin forces of print culture and landscape ideology were important bourgeois cultural expressions of the value of order and hierarchy and would become critical tools in Hutchings' efforts to adapt to and shape California society in the post–gold rush era. Part 1 of this book, "The Mountains of California: Gold, God, and the Quest for Social Order, 1848–1855," explores the cultural context of Hutchings' early life in England and the influence of the gold rush on his early publishing career. For Hutchings, the gold rush was the key event shaping his approach to California landscapes, as developed in chapter 1, "'To Cheat Ourselves into Forgetfulness of Home': From the Middle of England to the Rim of Civilization." The gold rush not only brought him, personally, to California, but was also a chaotic and unruly society of single white male miners that reinforced Hutchings' bourgeois assumptions about the need to create a stable, moral social world through landscape imagery and print culture. In chapter 2, "'Such Is Change in California': Technology, Violence, and Race in Post–Gold Rush California," Hutchings' evolving publishing work reveals interconnections between society, technology, and race in the volatile era when California transitioned from the gold rush to industrialized hydraulic mining.

Hutchings' famed 1855 trip to Yosemite inaugurated the second stage of his journey, when he witnessed the ultimate sublime landscape: "The truth is, the first view of this convulsion-rent valley, with its perpendicular mountain cliffs, deep gorges, and awful chasms, spread out before us like a mysterious scroll, took away the power of thinking, much less of clothing thoughts with suitable language."[2] The Yosemite that Hutchings and his party saw in 1855 was the very image of John Milton's *Paradise Lost*, a deeply familiar text to middle-class Americans steeped in Protestant faith and Romantic perceptions of nature. Surrounded by the "steep wilderness" of high, impenetrable cliffs, a series of "murmuring waters fall[ing] down the . . . hills," to join the Merced, a "mazy . . . river" winding through meadows or "level downs," Yosemite Valley even contained a "crystal mirror" lake that reflected the surrounding scenery. The clearly recognizable vision of Eden in Yosemite's landscape carried powerful symbolic content to midcentury Americans.[3]

To Hutchings, it represented a vision of order to replace the chaos and confusion of the gold rush. Part 2, "The Church of California: Yosemite and the Regional Sublime, 1855–1860," explores Hutchings' work to promote Yosemite as an icon of divine sanction supporting the consolidation of elite and bourgeois Anglo economic power in the financial districts of San Francisco in the 1850s and early 1860s. Chapter 3, "'Opening the Sealed Book': Making Yosemite Known to All," clarifies the role of technology, economics, and urban development in fostering Yosemite as a scenic destination for Californians. After his first trip to Yosemite, Hutchings moved to San Francisco, and chapter 4, "Hutchings and Rosenfield in the Print Metropolis," explores Hutchings' works in the context of San Francisco's imperial expansion into the western hinterlands and out to the Pacific. Tracing the interlinked quality of Yosemite's iconography and San Francisco's expanding metropolis demonstrates how Yosemite was very much a product of urbanization and industrialization, even as it came to be seen as the antidote to such processes.

Hutchings popularized images of Yosemite-as-Eden through lithographic prints like "The Yo-Hamite Falls" and "General View of the Great Yo-Semite Valley," through articles he wrote for his own *Hutchings' California Magazine*, and by giving lectures illustrated with the latest in photographic technology. In the decades after his visit, hundreds of other writers, artists, and photographers proliferated visions of Yosemite until it became an icon of sublimity, familiar to most Americans. Though few in the twentieth century recognize the Miltonian echoes in Yosemite imagery, the power of the sublime landscape to transport us away from daily stresses has remained a core assumption of environmentalist aesthetics.[4]

But the appeal of Yosemite's powerful symbolism stretched beyond California's borders as the nation fell into the Civil War in the 1860s. Images of Yosemite displayed in eastern galleries spoke to war-weary Easterners of a redemptive space, and in the midst of America's most violent war, Congress passed the act designating Yosemite Valley as a public park "inalienable for all time." Hutchings had just purchased a hotel and moved his family into the valley to start his career as hotelier. In part 3, "Yosemite and the National Sublime," the role of Hutchings and Yosemite in the creation of the Yosemite Grant and Yosemite's growth as a tourist destination is juxtaposed against evolving American ideas about the environment. Chapter 5, "Yosemite and the Crucible of War," explores how the Civil War transformed Yosemite from a regional icon central to the consolidation of bourgeois Anglo cultural identity during San Francisco's early stages of metropolitan imperialism to a national symbol of postbellum redemption and sublime sanction. Congress's act of appropriation set the stage for conflict between the local/regional and national values—a conflict that played itself out in Hutchings' own legal struggles to retain his preemption claims in the valley, but was also reflected in broader struggles throughout western lands between local interests and national corporate designs in the wrenching postwar era of Reconstruction, incorporation, and the second industrial revolution to follow.

Like Hutchings, the United States on the eve of its centennial was a land in turmoil. The victorious Union had aggressively expanded the industrial machine developed in wartime and sought to bind distant regions more tightly to the economic, political, and cultural cores of power along the Atlantic, but these moves generated conflict in the affected regions. Furthermore, class and ethnic unrest, combined with a dramatic economic recession, continually challenged the efforts of elites to organize society into tidy, obedient hierarchies. Yosemite's Edenic scenery offered respite from the worries of the modernizing society, especially as photographers and other artists generated images of a pure landscape, devoid of humans and human artifacts: eternal images untroubled by history.

Hutchings may have gained a new perspective on the high Sierra in his journey to Whitney's summit and the mountaineering expeditions he led for several summers after that. The final chapter of this book, "Hutchings, Muir, and the Modern Paradox of Wilderness," explores Hutchings' own changing perceptions of the role of government in land disputes and the emergence of John Muir's wilderness philosophy. The conclusion, "Discovering Our Place in Nature," offers some reflections on the twenty-first-century implications of the more complex historical understanding of Yosemite that Hutchings' story reveals.

Yosemite: The Tipping Point

The story of Hutchings' career restores history in all its messy, contradictory complexity to Yosemite. Contrary to the dualistic myth of the Yosemite Eden, since Hutchings' first visit in 1855, the place has been deeply interconnected with the dramatic transformations in American technology, economy, power politics, and sense of national identity. Hutchings first "discovered" Yosemite in the aftermath of the California gold rush, and Congress passed the Yosemite Grant Act in the final months of the Civil War. In the fusion of cultural, ideological, nationalist, and economic forces that produced the first government-sanctioned "sacred" landscape in America, midcentury Yosemite represents a powerful tipping point in American concepts of land use, with widespread ramifications. Malcolm Gladwell defines the "tipping point" as "that magic moment when an idea, trend, or social behavior crosses a threshold, tips, and spreads like wildfire." Yosemite, in the contexts of the California gold rush and the American Civil War, became just such an idea, one that tapped into multiple midcentury American hopes and anxieties. In the fusion of consumer tourism and Congressional appropriations of land for nationalistic purposes was born a powerful dynamic that recognized the cultural significance of landscape in ways that allowed it to be connected to and fostered by the economic power of expanding industrialization and urbanization as well as the political power of a unifying postwar national identity.[5]

Gladwell's tipping point rests on the interlocking forces of key individuals, changes in context, and transformation of the idea itself. Just as a biological epidemic depends on multiple forces for an otherwise benign virus or bacteria to become virulent and spread, ideas also require the right conditions to transform. In the origin and proliferation of the images and text constituting Yosemite's iconography, tipping point qualities clarify the interlocking historic forces driving the process. Yosemite's rise as a national icon was contingent on midcentury developments in media technology and on key national turning points that charged the place with meaning.

The 1864 Yosemite Grant initiated more than just the federal infrastructure for later land set-asides. American ideas about landscape, nature, and environment have evolved dramatically since the grant and in many respects because of it. When Hutchings proclaimed the wonders of the "Yo-Hamite Falls" or landscape architect Frederick Law Olmsted praised the valley's holistic beauty, they were not thinking of the place as a delicate ecological system in need of preservation, as the American public would learn to do with the Wilderness Act a century later. Rather, they valued Yosemite as *scenery*: a highly visual, even pictorial approach to the landscape that apprehended it almost exactly as a three-dimensional work of art, a spectacle. Just as with a painted landscape, the scenery of Yosemite carried, in the eyes of its promoters, intrinsic coded messages about society, power, God, and morality that only needed to be "revealed" or clarified to audiences. Hence arises Hutchings' self definition as the one to "open the sealed book . . . to the public eye." At the same time, the act of viewing scenery not only infused a physical space with cultural meaning, it also created a sense of identity for the viewers. The act of viewing scenery, whether in a gallery or on a precipice, tended to be a communal experience; one that contributed to a united sense of "we." It also contributed to the divide between the viewers and the subject of their gaze.

After the Civil War, Americans began to shift their understanding of the value of landscape. The visual, pictorial, and communal experience of scenery began to be replaced with a more intensely individualized, experiential *relationship* with "nature." John Muir was the key author of this new relationship, and articulated it in terms simultaneously sensual, religious, and intellectual. Working as a high country shepherd and then manager of Hutchings' property from 1869 to 1872, Muir quite literally developed this next generation of American environmental philosophy within the architecture of the Yosemite

Grant. Muir's *wilderness* was a much more immersive experience for those who would adopt it, replacing the act of viewing and "reading" landscape scenery for its "intrinsic" messages with the act of toiling in high mountain places to cultivate a relationship with the sacred embodied in highly specific wilderness contexts. Where the spectacle of scenery was a communal experience, Muir's nature exploits were solitary, constituting the relationship with the environment through individual, not group, identity. This shift in consciousness, from a communally based identity to one rooted in individual psychology, is one of the characteristics of modern societies, where autonomous individualism replaces social conformity as the behavioral ideal. At the same time that Muir developed this more modern notion of the relationship between Human and Nature, he contributed to the widening opposition between the two. Materialism and all the trappings of society were anathema to Muir. In his eloquent and ecstatic celebrations of the high Sierra, Muir taught generations of readers to seek solitude in Nature and to understand wilderness not only as separate from but morally and spiritually superior to "base" human activity.

John Muir's vision of wilderness has been a poetic inspiration to environmentalists around the world for over a century. As testimony to his enduring association with western wildness, Muir's name adorns five mountains, a beach, a glacier, an inlet, a gorge, a lake, a snowfield, a wilderness, and a national monument, and governor Arnold Schwarzenegger chose his image to grace the California Quarter.[6] However, as William Cronon argues in his pathbreaking essay "The Trouble with Wilderness," the romantic dualism of Muir's wilderness is as problematic as it is inspirational. Cronon's critique of the idea of wilderness exposed the culturally constructed nature of the concept and the troubling impacts of this idea on American environmental culture. "Wilderness presents itself as the best antidote to our human selves," Cronon writes, "an island in the polluted sea of urban-industrial modernity." But this dualism carries a cost: "To the extent that we live in an urban-industrial civilization but . . . pretend to ourselves that our *real* home is in the wilderness . . . , we give ourselves permission to evade responsibility for the lives we actually lead."[7] This evasion and the dualism that underpins it are both products of the simplistic vision of Yosemite's history that fails to accurately analyze its multiple contexts. But a new understanding of Yosemite's history, complicated through analysis of Hutchings' central role in its development, can offer some insights into a different vision of modern Americans' relationship with the environment, one that embraces politics, economics, and the working landscape where humans dwell along with the spirituality and artistic inspiration of purified imagery.

Yosemite and History

Restoring the complexity of historic context to Yosemite, including the contradictory and conflicted process by which Americans sought to preserve sacred landscape, brings into focus Yosemite's central role in the development of American national identity in the second half of the nineteenth century. Beyond its role as the first expression of the national park idea and wilderness, Yosemite was a crucible in which Americans worked out contentious questions of power, place, and identity. Though many interpretations of Yosemite upheld existing values, occasionally a flash of insight, such as Muir's, would transform old ideas into new forms. In this way, Yosemite was not merely a reflective surface but a creative and dynamic force in the evolution of American environmental attitudes and policy. Hutchings' experience in promoting, living in, and advocating for Yosemite and the high country provides dramatic illustration of the dynamic role of Yosemite in the creation of modern American identity.

Whether through national parks, landscape paintings, scenic highways, photographs, novels, or consumer images, Americans have a long and dense history of working out our identity through the environment. As an icon that continues to resonate with cultural power centuries later, Yosemite's cultural origin is an important piece of American history. However, precisely *because* of that continued cultural power, certain aspects of Yosemite's origin have traditionally been difficult to interpret and understand. James Mason Hutchings—publisher, writer, hotel manager, public speaker, amateur scientist, and mountaineer—was a unique and powerful force who helped to forge Yosemite's iconography. His career illustrates the multiple forces involved in the creation and production of iconographic landscapes: the way to frame images, how to define their significance, who to bring into the valley, and how to accommodate them once there. In other words, he initiated the physical and cultural apparatus necessary to craft the apparently "natural" response of wonder and awe of Yosemite's spectacle.

Restoring Hutchings to his place in American environmental history does more than mitigate the notoriety and disdain heaped upon him by modern historians. In his best moments, Hutchings' work offers a potential alternative perspective for Americans wishing to construct a more sustainable relationship with their environment. Although he expressed many of the racial, ethnic, and class biases of his day, Hutchings sincerely sought to mitigate the social and environmental violence wrought during the gold-rush years by creating a sense of place for California residents. Seeking to transform transient capitalists as well as miners into stable residents, Hutchings emphasized the redemptive qualities of nature, encouraging his readers and guests to see beyond their material lives and draw out their own best qualities in the context of spectacular scenery.

Exchanging our romance of the wilderness with a deeper knowledge and affective relationship with our local environmental habitats is a widely acknowledged first step toward building an environmentally sustainable society. Looking past his legal battles with Yosemite commissioners, we find that James Hutchings' lifelong project was to build a livelihood around his passionate attachment to the mountains of California, and to freely share the sense of place he constructed in that process. His quintessential "live-work" residential project was to live sustainably within the confines of Yosemite's walls. It is my hope that in recovering his story and the new understanding of America's relationship with place that Yosemite reveals, we can begin to imagine anew a healthier environmental future, one that starts with we humans embracing our status as indigenous residents of our specific homes, and all the humbling rights and responsibilities that come with that understanding. Hutchings had an inkling of those things, but the wheels of modernity sped past him, flattening him into a caricature of his (and our) worst qualities in the process. In recovering his story, I hope to help others write a new one for the rest of us.

Part I

The Mountains of California: Gold, God, and the Quest for Social Order, 1849–1855

After months of exhausting overland travel from New Orleans, James Mason Hutchings struggled against time and snow-laden storm clouds to finally reach the summit of California's Sierra Nevada mountain range in October 1849. Although just four years earlier autumn snowstorms had visited tragedy upon the Donner Party, Hutchings' response to the mountains was one of admiration, not dread. Pausing on the 9,000-foot pass near Caples Lake to notice the "view of the beauty, clouds rolling among the snowy peaks and pine-studded sides of the distant mountains," Hutchings concluded in his diary, "The scene was grand."[1] The man gazing out at his future home was tall, with dark-brown hair and beard, jutting chin, and laughing eyes. "Eminently adapted to the matrimonial relations," wrote an admirer several years later. "Well-proportioned . . . nearly six feet tall, tough, wiry and enduring, if not athletic. His complexion florid; eyes black, features regular but striking. It is a head, face, and character once seen, not to be forgotten."[2]

Hutchings had traveled to California to make his fortune in the gold rush, but it was in the high mountains of the Sierra that he found his calling. Returning repeatedly to these mountains over the next decade, in 1855 he found his way to the Yosemite Valley that would become his life's passion. The "scenes of wonder and curiosity" that he observed there spoke powerfully to the aesthetic tastes, religious sensibilities, scientific curiosities, and social anxieties he had developed during his upbringing in middle-class England. As the organizer of the first tourist party to Yosemite, the chaotic and violent social world of the California gold rush and its aftermath had impressed Hutchings with the need to give California residents an uplifting symbol that might encourage residents to settle in the state and invest in its future rather than plunder its riches and leave.

The story of Yosemite's emergence as an icon begins many decades before Hutchings' initial 1855 visit. It includes the cultural history of values and aesthetics that stretch back to the end of the eighteenth century in Europe and England. It encompasses cultural responses to the first stage of industrialization and the massive social transformations it wrought on both sides of the Atlantic. It is also a story of the particular circumstances of the California gold rush and the specific opportunities and challenges that era posed to Hutchings and like-minded Atlantic bourgeoisie.

Prior to encountering Yosemite, Hutchings spent six years working in various California enterprises: as a miner, a newspaper correspondent, land speculator, and finally, as one of California's most prolific midcentury publishers of ephemeral literature such as letter sheets, almanacs, and periodicals. When Hutchings began publishing images and text about Yosemite in 1855, he was in the midst of expanding a fairly successful venture in letter sheet publishing to include a variety of other formats like *Hutchings' Illustrated California Magazine.* Hutchings was one of California's most prolific publishers when he decided to move to San Francisco and expand the business. The early Yosemite iconology was therefore the product of a particular matrix of social, technological, economic, and ideological forces born from the collision between the English midlands and California's gold-laden mountains.

"To Cheat Ourselves into Forgetfulness of Home": From the Middle of England to the Rim of Civilization

The mountains that shaped the last half-century of Hutchings' life were the Sierra Nevada (Spanish for "snowy range"), one of the more dramatic mountain chains in North America.[1] Fairly young by geologic standards, the Sierra is a granitic uplift running on a north-south axis with a dramatic eastern scarp and gradually sloping western flanks. The mountains rise in elevation the farther south one travels among them—barely reaching 9,000 feet at the northern end, they are capped in the southern reaches by Mt. Whitney at 14,505, the tallest peak in the contiguous United States.

The Sierra shapes the climate, flora, and fauna on both sides of the range. With these mountains as a barrier, California to the west evolved a unique series of complex ecosystems, including endemic species of plants and animals found nowhere else on the planet. Storms cycling inland from the Pacific Ocean drop their moisture on these mountains, creating a rain-shadow effect defining the aridity of the Great Basin high deserts to the east, while watering the subtropical savannahs of California's lowlands and valleys to the west. Although indigenous people communicated and traded across this barrier, it effectively worked to isolate humans as well as other species. California was home to over 250 mutually unintelligible language groups prior to European contact. These people evolved "luxury subsistence" ways of life, using fire, intentional pruning, seed scatter, and other means to manipulate the landscape to produce a wealth of food sources as well as raw materials for tools, shelter, clothing, and other amenities.

"The Miners' Ten Commandments," Hutchings' first letter sheet publication, 1853.
(Courtesy California State Library, Sacramento, CA)

In addition to the mountains, the Pacific Ocean shapes California's climate and seasons. Fluctuating between wet and dry seasons, the California lowlands historically experience periods of drought and flooding over multiyear (rather than annual) cycles. In the Great Central Valley, the 800-mile valley fed by numerous Sierra rivers and enclosed by coastal ranges to the west, wet cycles led to the creation of a very large intermittent lake that would slowly drain out through the San Francisco bay. Only decades of massive hydrologic engineering would render this valley habitable year-round. Relatively few California indigenes settled into large agricultural societies like those that inhabited the Mississippi river drainage and southeast woodlands areas. Instead, like their cousins in the Great Basin, California groups adopted migratory seasonal rounds, exploiting resources between valleys and mountains, avoiding the flooding in the wet winter months in the middle elevations, escaping the summer heat in the higher elevations, and capitalizing on the wealth of game and plant life in the central valley as the lake waters receded.[2]

"Seeing Eye for Beauty": The English Search for Order

In stark contrast to California's prehistoric landscape, Hutchings was raised in a more humid, temperate zone with gently rolling hills and a four-season annual cycle conducive to settled agricultural practices. He was born in Towcester, the geographic center of England, on February 10, 1820, the sixth child of William, a carpenter, and Barbara, a paper lace maker. Towcester was a midsize town of nearly 3,000 inhabitants. It was the oldest town in Northamptonshire, settled on what had been for many centuries the main turnpike road from Dover to London to Chester. Throughout the eighteenth century, Towcester was an important way station, with numerous inns for travelers. In the 1790s, the construction of a nearby canal route provided an outlet for locally manufactured goods.[3]

During Hutchings' childhood, Towcester's importance as a communication hub and transit center increased. Travelers by coach passed through on their way between Peterborough and Oxford as well as from London to Birmingham. Horses were kept as relays for the coaches, "every third or fourth house was a public-house or inn," and Towcester was the sorting office for all mail traffic from London, Birmingham, Liverpool, Dublin, Northampton, and Oxford. So familiar would this town be to English travelers that Charles Dickens staged a delightful satire on editorial rivalries in *The Pickwick Papers* in the kitchen of Towcester's Saracen Head Inn. Dickens might have chosen any number of inns in any number of towns along the Dover road, but the scene of two well-known editors meeting in Towcester suggests the town's importance in the communication circuits of the day. The countryside surrounding the town contained the country seats of nobility and gentry, while the town itself housed a wide diversity of professionals and artisans, including attorneys, wool staplers, chemists, ironmongers, surgeons and lace makers. Thus, though Towcester may have been a rural village, during Hutchings' childhood it was certainly no cultural backwater. Its role in mail distribution networks meant that James would have easy access to the London newspapers and magazines that flowed through Towcester's post office on their way to subscribers and distributors, and the important literary and political figures passing through would have reinforced Towcester's connection to metropolitan culture.[4]

As if his early life in Towcester were not enough to steep Hutchings in the values and institutions of England's bourgeois culture, around the age of ten he was sent to live with his married older sister Charlotte in Birmingham, where for six years he attended the Edgbaston proprietary school. Edgbaston was one of the first suburbs designed to house the emerging bourgeois elite whose identity is suggested in this possibly satiric poem:

> See Edgbaston, the bed of prosperous trade,
> Where they recline who have their fortunes made;
> Strong in their wealth, no matter how possessed,
> There fashion calls, and there at ease they rest,
> The beauteous suburb swells with lofty pride;
> The vulgar poor are there forbid to hide.
> With longing eye, the favoured of the day
> Towards the loved purlieu make their eager way;
> And as their broughams by our dwellings wheel,
> We think how nice it is to be genteel.[5]

At the Edgbaston Proprietary School, Hutchings claimed to have been "steeped in English Literature and had an inherent interest in the Natural Sciences cultivated and a 'seeing eye' for beauty fostered."[6] The three institutions of literature, natural science, and landscape aesthetics that drew Hutchings to Yosemite in the 1850s were powerful forces that combined in the first half of the century to uphold and extend Victorian English bourgeois values in several interlocking ways. Analysis of the ways that these powerful ideologies served middle-class interests in consolidating social order in the middle-class

England of Hutchings' youth sheds light on his own publishing efforts to shape California culture and society in the decades following the gold rush.

The Cultural Milieu of Victorian England

The middle class in England rose to social, political, and economic importance with the expansion of imperial, industrial capitalism during the generation prior to Hutchings' birth. Educated and ambitious, middle-class men desired political power commensurate with their economic status and chafed under what they considered to be the oppressive political regimes of the landed aristocracy. Similar ambitions fueled the two bourgeois revolutions of late-eighteenth-century America and France. Although the English bourgeoisie may have sympathized with their Atlantic counterparts, they were dismayed by the loss of the American colonies and the outlet that France's radically violent Thermidorean reaction gave to the working-class and peasant discontents. Because of this, English middle-class culture in the early decades of the nineteenth century was marked by two impulses: ambition for the political power still associated with the landed aristocracy and anxiety over the potentially insurgent working classes at home and colonial unrest abroad.[7]

In the small-town and suburban bastions of Victorian respectability where Hutchings lived his early years, these middle-class ambitions and fears were expressed through values, institutions, and assumptions. Ideas about family life and domesticity, the respective roles of women and men, work and leisure, Protestant Christianity, science, industry, and the English landscape served to mark and strengthen bourgeois identity. This identity was formed in opposition to the perceived "extravagant" nature of the aristocracy and the "profligate" lower classes and colonial subjects, but was never wholly cohesive. Nevertheless, the ideological implications behind Hutchings' "inherent interest in the Natural Sciences . . . and 'seeing eye for beauty'" suggest his strong identification with the fears and aspirations of the Victorian bourgeoisie.

Christianity and science worked in ideological tandem to further visions of nature as a highly organized, interlocking system in which each piece played an important role, mimicking the bourgeois desire for an orderly social system to underpin industrial production and imperial trade. Scientific societies such as the Manchester Literary and Philosophical Society were often linked to Nonconformist and Dissenting churches, which sometimes lent institutional support. Membership in both provided aspiring middle-class men social and political support and helped to solidify middle-class professional and political aspirations. Middle-class men joined literary and philosophical societies not only to pursue amateur scientific studies, but also to make business contacts and further their careers and status.

Additionally, the sponsorship of factory schools and Mechanics' Institutes fostered the spread of middle-class worldviews by preaching stability, containment, and individual improvement to the working class.[8] Working-class slums were the targets of Protestant domestic missionary activities in the 1830s where volunteers like Hutchings (who taught Sunday school in Shirley and Kings Norton) hoped Christian values would reform the "unchurched masses" from within. After visiting services at the Baptist Colored Church in New York in 1848, Hutchings wrote of "the time when my heart was in Africa and my body about being sent there," suggesting that Hutchings' participation in the domestic visiting movements had primed him for imperial missionary activities in the colonies.[9]

Ideologically, "the Newtonian model of science . . . was a subtle creature capable of answering soothingly to the two most basic middle-class concerns" of desire for political authority and anxiety of class unrest. The Newtonian vision of the natural world promoted the idea of inevitable, evolutionary change, implicitly challenging aristocratic claims to legitimacy rooted in a static past *and* working-class revolutionary impulses. The literary and philosophical societies cast scientific pursuit as meritocratic, rational, and progressive, practiced by talented men who transcended the social limitations of their station, just as the politically ambitious bourgeoisie hoped to do. At the same time, science justified the value of the status quo to the lower elements of society by characterizing the natural world as a complex and delicate system, dependent upon the controlled cooperation of all its parts. In the nineteenth century, scientific interest focused on geology and botany, two branches especially suited to the notion of evolutionary change and the importance of interlocking parts in an overarching system.[10]

The Romantic notion of nature as a source of divine inspiration and an escape from urban stresses that fueled the rise of consumer tourism and landscape painting simultaneously elaborated upon and altered many of the assumptions behind the scientific study of natural philosophy. In their critique of modern industrial society, Romantics developed the idea of the sublime to frame their response to nature: in the mountains, thundering cataracts, and stormy sea, Romantics sought the thrill of proximity to danger. For Romantic poets, essayists, and painters, the sublime experience in nature brought humans to their closest contact with the divine. Edmund Burke in the late-eighteenth century first explored this idea that was later developed through the poems of Percy Shelley, William Wordsworth, and Lord Byron and the landscape paintings of J. M. W. Turner and Caspar David Friedrich. In America, the Hudson Valley School of landscape paintings celebrated the Romantic sublime in American landscapes in the early decades of the nineteenth century.[11]

In contrast to science, Romantic nature was accessible to women as well as men. However, like natural philosophy, the Romantic vision of nature also underpinned middle-class desires for order. Victorians expressed their vision in numerous ways: through the landscape design of estate parks, in tour guides and literary descriptions of scenic beauty, and in landscape painting and art criticism. Additionally, landscape aesthetics were materially linked to *both* bourgeois and aristocratic power, as well as empire: estate parks frequently occupied lands once populated by tenant farmers and then enclosed, while many of the estate purchases and renovations were financed by colonial ventures.[12] Landscape rhetoric was closely entwined with bourgeois political philosophy. Uvedale Price wrote in 1794 that "a good landscape is that in which all the parts are free and unconstrained, but in which, though some are prominent and highly illuminated, and others in shade and retirement, some rough, and others more smooth and polished, yet they are all necessary to the beauty, energy, effect, and harmony of the whole. I do not see how good government can be more exactly defined."[13]

Thus landscape aesthetics in gardening, painting, and tourism were closely aligned with bourgeois and aristocratic ideologies of society as an organic whole, subject to evolutionary change. Critics' insistence on the artist's responsibility to follow nature's details as closely as possible reinforced the ideology of natural philosophy as a model for the organization of society: the more attention one paid to the details of the natural world, the more one would recognize the intricacies of a grand system, where each part was integral to the whole design.

By cultivating aesthetic rules for visually pleasing landscapes, Hutchings' own "seeing eye for beauty" would have prepared him to appreciate those elements of the California landscape, such as mountains and waterfalls, that conformed to such rules. More importantly, Hutchings was imbued with the assumption that landscape imagery, connected with scientific study and Protestant ideology, could contribute to creating social order in the construction of cultural identity.

The Romantic approach to nature was born of the stresses of rapidly industrializing and urbanizing England and Europe. Romantics sought escape from the increasingly polluted and congested cities into the fresh air and quiet of rural and mountainous landscapes. Although Romantic philosophy and aesthetics were themselves a more or less direct critique of industrialization, it is important to note that with very few exceptions they did not effectively challenge the fundamental process of it. That is, Romantic poets, philosophers, and painters did not oppose the legal transformations that gave rise to laissez-faire capitalism, did not question the right of landowners to enclose their estates and dispossess residents of their livelihood, did not object to factories dumping pollution into waterways or chaining child workers to machinery. In short, Romanticism was not radical—it offered an escape from the cities, but the escape assumed that the cities would continue. And for those who lacked the means to escape the cities, there was no succor in the sublime.

Voluntary societies, lectures, and tours to the country were important vehicles for conveying ideas about nature and for expressing and reinforcing middle-class culture more generally. But they paled in comparison to the critical impact of printing and publishing. Technological innovation transformed English printing in the Georgian period: mechanized Fourdrinier papermaking techniques, steam-powered presses, and multiple-cylinder stereotype printing, all of which made low-cost, high-speed dissemination of the printed word possible.[14] In the early decades of the nineteenth century, books, pamphlets, magazines, newspapers, and broadsides became much more widely available than before. Various groups, from working-class radicals to conservative Tories, used print culture to articulate and constitute their visions of society. Print culture was never the uncontested tool of any one group to assert social visions, but it was certainly a critical one for members of the middle class.

James Mason Hutchings was born in the midst of a great magazine boom. In the seventeen-year period beginning six years before his birth and ending with his eleventh birthday, seven of the most significant bourgeois Victorian periodicals launched: the *New Monthly Magazine* (1814), *Blackwood's Edinburgh Magazine* (1817), the *London Magazine* (1821), *Westminster Review* (1824), the *Athenaeum* (1828), *Fraser's Magazine* (1830), and the *Metropolitan Magazine* (1831). Each of these periodicals had audiences of from 5,000 to 15,000 readers. Total readership was around 20,000 of the upper gentry and 200,000 in the "middling classes." At the same time, radical writers like William Cobbett created periodicals for the working class such as the *Political Register* (1816). Somewhere in between were illustrated periodicals that appealed to consumers entertained by novelty as well as to the marginally literate.[15]

Periodicals helped to shape middle-class identity and efforts at asserting cultural authority in several ways. First, they helped create "imagined communities" of readers with shared worldviews, and second, they promulgated ideologies of social cohesiveness and control. Indeed the scientific societies and landscape philosophers publicized their ideas in books, pamphlets, and periodicals. Some, including the Society for the Diffusion of Useful Knowledge, pursued an explicit mission of inculcating middle-class values in their working-class audiences.[16]

However, it is important to recognize that the constitution of the groups designated as middle, lower, or working "class" were far more fluid, and the relation between the various social groups far more dynamic, than any simple schema can indicate. In the process of consolidating power and addressing fears about the poor, the English bourgeoisie themselves were frequently divided. Likewise, regardless of the intent of editors and publishers to proclaim certain ideologies, they had no direct control over the ultimate meanings their audiences would take from the printed word or image. Though the English bourgeois classes had many cultural institutions at their command to consolidate political and economic power, their efforts to control the "lower" orders of society were never complete. The importance of print culture in underpinning power and the desire for social order in Victorian England foreshadow Hutchings' publishing efforts in midcentury California.

To California

After his six years in Edgbaston, Hutchings returned to Towcester to take up his father's carpentry trade. He attended services in Anglican churches and taught Sunday school in the neighboring villages of Shirley and Kings Norton; later he conducted Protestant services on board the ship *Gertrude*. In 1841, his father died, leaving James, as the youngest child, the responsibility of caring for his mother. Three years later, during a trip to Birmingham, Hutchings visited a touring exhibit of George Catlin's paintings of American Indians. According to later autobiographical statements, it was this exhibit that inspired James to want to see America. In 1838 the London to Birmingham railway was completed, bypassing Towcester. The town's economic base as a stopover for turnpike travelers was radically reduced as a result: income from tolls alone dropped from £5895 in 1835 to £2702 four years later. Where twenty to forty coaches had passed through the town each day in 1830, by 1849 there were only four. The resulting economic stagnation may explain Hutchings' decision to leave as much as any inborn desire to know "what is around that corner, over those mountains, or across that ocean."[17]

After the family arranged for another sister to care for Barbara, Hutchings took his chance and set sail for America on May 19, 1848[18]: "'Betty is a pretty gal, hey, ho, hey,' is the sailors' chantey . . . 'She's up, sir,' is the cry. 'Set the mainsail'—'foresail'—'flying jib'—'fore-staysail'—then 'main-top' and so on until sails are set and away we go, gently; now faster; now pilot says 'five knots.' 'Hurrah!'"[19] As Hutchings watched the sails rise on the *Gertrude*, his "thoughts took me to the ship's side for a last look at the Fatherland, where I was born and wherein those I loved still lived. Night dropped gently down . . . and then the light-houses and light-ships were looked for . . . as objects of importance in a general attempt to cheat ourselves into forgetfulness of home."[20]

Half a world away, exactly one week before the *Gertrude* slipped out of the Mersey, a blustering entrepreneur with a keen sense of spectacle had marched into the streets of San Francisco holding aloft a bottle of gold dust and shouting, "Gold! Gold! Gold from the American River!" Sam Brannan's announcement jettisoned California, and the world, into a frenzied rush to the foothills of California's Sierra Nevada mountain range in search of instant wealth. Hutchings' trajectory would take him into the heart of that rush and the social and cultural world to emerge from it, but first he spent several months in New York, attending services at various Protestant denominations and visiting Niagara Falls. He then accompanied the *Gertrude*'s captain to New Orleans in the fall. He spent the winter in New Orleans, writing for a local newspaper, before he, too, caught the gold fever and joined the thousands on the overland trek to California in the spring, arriving in Placerville on the American River in the fall of 1849.[21]

It would have been difficult for Hutchings to find a spot on the globe where history and the environment had conspired to create a greater contrast with his hometown of Towcester. Where Hutchings left a centuries-old village, he arrived in a land and a society that had undergone radical transformation in just eighteen months. In 1846, the United States had provoked war with Mexico, and, by January 1847, the military conquest of California was over and a series of military governors was developing the legal and political administrative structure for the region.

During the Spanish and Mexican era from the late eighteenth century to 1847, California-born Mexicans, or Californios, had developed vast cattle-herding empires on large estates for international markets in tallow and hide. This pastoral economy was structured around the Spanish colonial system of mission-pueblo-presidio that connected religious, military, and economic activities. Coastal California Indians had provided most of the labor as "novices" in the mission system and had suffered decimating epidemic disease in the eighteenth century. Prior to the first waves of American immi-

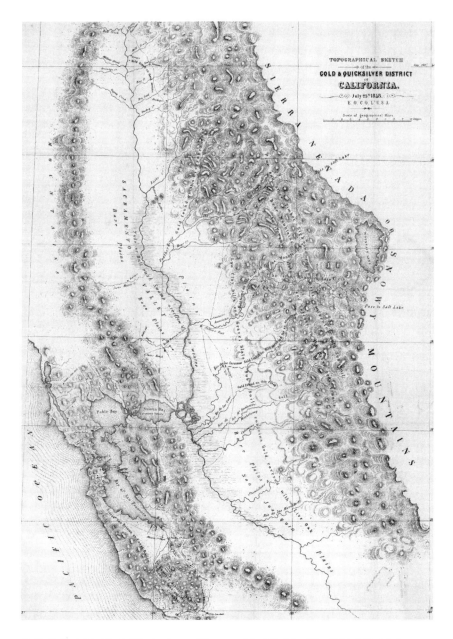

E. O. C. Ord, Lt., United States Army, "Topographical Sketch of the Gold & Quicksilver District of California," 1848. (Private collection)

grants, the Californio economy was mostly geared toward Pacific trade. Indeed, the first generations of Americans in California were "Yankee" traders who married into Californio Anglo families, adopting Spanish names and Mexican mores.

However, in the mid-1840s, a new breed of English-speaking immigrants moved into the region. Thomas Larkin was the first of these. A land speculator from the Midwest, Larkin rejected the idea that Americans should adapt to the Californio economy or lifestyle. Encouraging the overland emigration of farm families to California's Central Valley, Larkin openly advocated war with Mexico and supported California statehood. The first wave of overland emigrants, including the Donner Party, responded to efforts of speculators and boosters like Larkin to increase the numbers of settled agriculturalists in a blatant effort to overrun the Hispanic Californio inhabitants.

California's unique nineteenth-century cultural trajectories pose linguistic dilemmas for historians attempting to describe these shifting power dynamics. Mexico is part of the Americas, even North America, and Mexicans and Californios are descendants of Europeans. Therefore, the term "Euro-American," commonly used to refer to whites in the eastern seaboard, does not adequately distinguish the new generation of aggressive English-speaking immigrants who entered into and came to dominate California's politics and economics from their more easily assimilated predecessors. I prefer to use the term "Anglo" to distinguish this group. Perhaps the most compelling reason for this is that it is a term they used to describe themselves. Secondly, because it refers to language and culture, it more accurately captures the culture and ideology of the Atlantic world, including England and the eastern seaboard of the United States. Anglos came from similar backgrounds and contexts in terms of the temperate environments, shared language, culture, religion, and industrializing, urbanizing economies of their respective homelands. Whether from England or the United States, they and their European counterparts recognized each other in the context of California's intensely international and polyglot gold-rush experience, where much else in the cultural and physical landscape was highly exotic.

The sparsely settled towns and farms emptied out over the summer of 1848 as the first wave of gold-seekers descended on the banks of California's rivers: Feather, Yuba, Bear, American, Cosumnes, Mokelumne, Tuolumne, and Stanislaus. The first gold-rush immigrants were those from the Pacific Rim, closest to California: from Oregon, Mexico, Chile, Argentina, and, by ship, from the Sandwich Islands (Hawai'i). In October 1848, President Polk announced that the fabulous tales of instant and massive riches filtering to the eastern states were substantiated, launching a tidal wave of emigration from the Atlantic and midwestern states. As these Americans made their way by ship or overland routes during the summer of 1849, more than 5,000 Mexicans, 1,500 Chileans and Peruvians, and uncounted Australians already inhabited Alta (upper) California. By the time of Hutchings' arrival in October 1849, California's non-Indian population of approximately 1,500 in 1848 had exploded to over 100,000 with the arrival of overland emigrants from the eastern United States, as well as England, Germany, France, and China. Eric Hobsbawm has termed the California Gold Rush "the first expression of global capitalism."[22]

For most Argonauts the journey to California was expensive, long, and difficult. It took several months for Americans to travel overland or by ship to the Pacific coast. Easterners who came by ship found themselves crammed onto vessels carrying well beyond their passenger capacity. Either the long route around the Horn or the shorter version with a land passage across the Isthmus of Panama exposed passengers to food shortages and disease. Overland travelers had to traverse completely unfamiliar territory as they crossed the mountains and deserts of the west. By the time they arrived in California, many miners (and their finances) were exhausted. Upon arrival most discovered that gold was much more difficult to get than the giddy hometown newspaper headlines had proclaimed, requiring heavy physical labor and the formation of partnerships. The cost of living in California was also extremely high so that within a few months the vast majority of California gold miners found themselves struggling to make a living, much less the fortunes that they had promised their friends and family back home.

The crowding brought troubles for a region without legal, transportation, or economic infrastructure. Disease spread through the crowded mining camps and cities such as Sacramento. One of Hutchings' mining partners was afflicted with severe diarrhea when the pair first arrived in Placerville. "I must tell you," wrote Hutchings to a New Orleans newspaper, "that there has been considerable sickness in the mines, chiefly diarrhea and fever, and more sickness in Sacramento City than here. Many have escaped the dangerous sea, and hazardous land journeys, to lay their bones in California."[23] Writing in December a year later, Isaac Lord observed: "[Sacramento] is one great cesspool of mud, offal, garbage, dead animals and that worst of nuisances consequent upon the entire absence of outhouses."[24]

Disease, disappointment, poverty, and loneliness combined with ready access to alcohol and guns and a complete lack of law enforcement are never a good formula for social harmony. Add to the mix a virtually all-male society steeped in xenophobia yet surrounded by immigrants from around the world, and you have a recipe for disaster. R. B. Mason, the territorial governor of California in 1848, acknowledged his inability to enforce any kind of legal requirements on the gold miners: "considering the large extent of country, the character of the people engaged, and the small, scattered force at my command, I resolved not to interfere."[25] Within a month of arriving in California, Hutchings witnessed several acts of violence, including the spontaneous mob violence that substituted for "justice" in many gold-rush communities.

> On the day of our reaching Hang Town [Placerville], I saw a concourse of people and going up saw a man on his knees gasping for breath. I enquired if he had fallen into the creek! "Oh no," they replied—"he has been stealing a watch and we have just given him a ducking and as he has had a good one we hope that he will either leave this world, or these diggings, for he bears an indifferent character." The man died the next day.[26]

During the early years of the gold rush, more or less spontaneous violence became a tool for asserting Anglo authority in the mines. Homicides and vigilante law terrorized Californios, Mexicans, Chinese, Chileans, French, Native Americans, and African Americans as well as fellow Anglos. In San Francisco, semi-organized bands called the Hounds roamed the Chilean neighborhood in 1849, looting, raping, and pillaging. In 1851 and 1856, "respectable" businessmen countered such violence with vigilante actions of their own, resulting in hangings without trial.[27]

Although all groups suffered in the frays, by far the worst violence was that perpetrated by the whites against the native Californians, for whom Americans had a deep, almost psychotic, fear and hatred. For the California indigenes, the gold rush was nothing short of demographic catastrophe. Coastal Indians had long suffered the impacts of Mission indentured labor and the virgin soil epidemics brought by the initial wave of Euro-American settlers during the Spanish and Mexican period, but in the river canyons, inland foothills, and mountains tribes had remained relatively insulated from the worst impacts. The rush brought epidemic disease, miners who ripped apart the riparian habitats central to traditional food economies, and angry, desperate men whose increasingly fragile moral codes stopped short with the Indians they considered to be subhuman. California Indians were victims of individual acts of violence, including rape, kidnapping, and murder, as well as more systematic efforts by mobs or "vigilante" groups to herd them off their traditional homelands. These "removals" were forced marches often covering hundreds of miles to rancherias in swampy lowlands.[28] The spontaneous actions of individuals, small vigilante groups, and state-supported military battalions resulted in such widespread and rapid decimation of native California peoples that the era has earned the officially recognized term of genocide.[29]

The editors and writers of newspapers and other publications rarely publicized such violence. If they did, they usually cast the Anglos as military heroes hastening the progress of white civilization. Occasionally, one or two California elites might recognize the Indian perspective: "They . . . look upon us as trespassers upon their territory, invaders of their country, and seeking to dispose them of their homes."[30] In the most famous exception to prove this rule, writer Bret Harte condemned the 1860 massacre of the entire Wiyot tribe near Crescent City in the *Northern Californian,* writing that "a more shocking and revolting spectacle never was exhibited to the eyes of a Christian and civilized people. Old women wrinkled and decrepit lay weltering in blood, their brains dashed out and dabbled with their long grey hair. Infants scarcely a span along, with their faces cloven with hatchets and their bodies ghastly with wounds." After publishing the editorial, Harte's life was threatened and he was forced to flee one month later. Clearly, literary men could wield only so much social influence among the Anglo miners, at least where the treatment of native Californians was concerned.[31]

The instability of California's gold-rush society challenged culture makers like Hutchings to find ways to encourage more stable patterns of behavior. In some cases, as with the question of violence, this meant modifying one's personal response into a form that would be acceptable to one's audience. Plenty of his diary entries from 1854–1855 indicate that Hutchings was disturbed by the casual regard for human life that he encountered in his travels. In Yreka, he noted the "singular and painful contrast" of the California Sabbath: "Rodgers and Williams had a quarrel over a Spanish woman . . . Rodgers fired three shots at Williams, and running away as he fired, fell down, and Williams, badly wounded rushed up and stabbed him—four times—drove the knife through his body."[32] In May, Hutchings learned about "3 Chinamen being killed and 2 more dangerously wounded by Americans—robbers—for their money—on Shirt-tail Canyon." The next day, "met 3 Chinamen who asked by counting on their fingers how many killed 'Shirt-tail Canyon?' I said '3.' They shook their heads—said 'bad—bad—goo-bye John.'"[33]

Aside from violence, there were other dimensions to gold-rush California that would dismay a bourgeois Anglo like Hutchings. One was the "plunder" mentality of miners and absentee investors who came to "take, not build." On a very direct and simple level, the effect of such a mentality meant that the markets for entrepreneurs like Hutchings were constantly shifting. Add to this the incredible volatility of California's post-1849 economy, which continued to discourage long-term investment in the state, along with the unraveling of moral fabric and you have a world of chaos for the educated, ambitious, would-be missionary types like Hutchings.

At the same time, however, there was a sense of opportunity. Hutchings may have been devout and dismayed by the lack of moral structure in California, but he was not a prig. He had a sense of humor, tolerance, and sympathy for the hard-working and often unlucky miners, and he could write. There was a market for such writers: for Hutchings and others like him, popular publications became a vehicle to encourage settlement and a sense of residential identity to replace the chaos and violence of the gold-rush era with a more permanent society. Hutchings' early life in the midst of England's industrial revolution gave him many cultural institutions to draw upon as he moved from mining to publishing as the next stage of his California career.

"The Miners' Ten Commandments": Identity, Landscape, and Society in California

When Hutchings arrived in Placerville on the American River, he found, like many of his fellow gold-seekers, "the diggings" crowded and overworked. And, like others, he joined in a company of men to pursue mining in nearby White Rock Canyon. Contrary to the romantic legends of the gold rush, most of those who arrived in 1849 met with failure or only limited success compared to the fortunes made by some the previous year. Hutchings, however, was one of the somewhat successful ones. On his first day of mining with a pan, he made $5.75 and the next day graduated to a loaned cradle, making $10.60, on the third $27.30, "which in New Orleans would have taken me two weeks." Hutchings made enough to purchase property and some equipment, and within a few months he began to search for other ways to make money. Although he would pursue mining again at various points in his later life, he seems to have learned early on that the people most likely to keep their mining fortunes were those who could reinvest them into other business ventures. Despite his relative success in mining, he immediately began searching out business alternatives; including purchasing agricultural property and investing in ditch and canal companies.

Hutchings' own progression in mining technology mirrored mining development on a large scale throughout the mines. In 1848, prior to the first wave of immigrants, most miners worked as individuals panning for gold in a small area. Some did hire or coerce groups of Amerindians to work for them but never for very long. These individuals used the Mexican mining technique of swirling sand or dirt and water in a large pan or bowl, then washing out the lighter particles as the heavier gold settled to the bottom. The process of using water to separate gold from lighter particles formed the basic principle of California gold mining well into the 1860s. From 1849 to 1855, most mining in California was river or placer mining, which involved digging out claims and washing the dirt. As the surface deposits became exhausted, miners dammed and diverted rivers, constructed ditches and flumes to convey water to "dry diggings," and after 1853 used high-pressure hoses to blast soil away from hillsides and run water into sluice boxes. These long boxes were joined together with riffles on the bottom, which would catch gold as it ran through with other detritus.[34]

Whereas individual miners could pan successfully, to work a long tom or a sluice box efficiently, several men had to coordinate their efforts. Miners combined their claims to form associations and divided their labor to increase profit. Members of these small associations frequently lived together and also apportioned domestic duties in the overwhelmingly male population. Miners' associations have been celebrated as folk expressions of the American democratic spirit; however, they overwhelmingly favored white miners and actively excluded the many miners of other races who came to California. Even so, the development of miners' associations in conjunction with the increasing complexity of mining technology represented a social, as well as technological, response to the challenges posed by California's mineral environment.

Having settled for the time being in the foothill town of Placerville, Hutchings spent the next few years mining and investing his profits in other ventures. He purchased farms and town lots, wrote occasional newspaper articles, and participated in the California versions of the middle-class institutions that he had grown up with in England: Protestant services, fireman's balls, and temperance society meetings. He also wandered about; several of his newspaper columns from that time described various localities around central California. Thus began his lifelong passion to describe and promote California landscapes, especially the mountainous areas, in print. Many of Hutchings' activities during 1852–1856 are documented in the scrapbook he kept during this time. The book contains numerous newspaper clippings, copies of Hutchings' letter sheets, and first prints of illustrations, not arranged in any clear chronology.

In the spring of 1853, Hutchings stood in for a friend as editor of the Placerville *Herald* newspaper. While there he published a humorous column lampooning various elements of mining society, entitled "The Miners' Ten Commandments." This column evidently struck a chord among mountain miners as newspapers around the mining camps began reprinting it without attribution. Seeing an opportunity, Hutchings quickly copyrighted the piece and commissioned the talents of illustrator and engraver Harrison Eastman to provide images to accompany the text. Within a month, Hutchings had turned "The Miners' Ten Commandments" into an illustrated letter sheet. Letter sheets combined text, image, and enough space to write and were especially popular in the gold rush as they could be folded and mailed without an envelope. This was not only his most successful publication to that date, but it also was perhaps the most popular and well-known of all the nineteenth-century California letter sheets.

This initial effort launched Hutchings into the career alternative to mining he had apparently been casting about for. Within a year, he commenced traveling about the mountains of California, gathering information and images to form the basis of an outpouring of ephemera over the subsequent decade: letter sheets, almanacs, maps, children's stories, and most famously *Hutchings' Illustrated California Magazine.* What set Hutchings' publications apart from others of the same era were the number and quality of images, most of which depicted California landscapes in great detail. Analysis of "The Miners' Ten Commandments" within the context of its initial production and reception illustrates the multiple cultural strands that Hutchings linked together through his publication efforts: Anglo identity and social order; landscape, environment, and economics; metropolis and hinterland; and Californians (through their letters) with the world.

"The Miners' Ten Commandments" was composed of three columns of text surrounded by eleven illustrations, one for each of the ten "commandments" plus one illustrating the preface.[35] In these commandments, Hutchings combined humor, a biblical style, and the folk rules of mining-camp life, exhorting miners to "have no other claim than one," not to steal from fellow miners, not to gamble, and so forth. Despite the biblical cast, Hutchings lacked the Old Testament's brevity—several of his commandments contained multiple proscriptions. Commandment number six, for example, began with "Thou shalt not kill thy body by working in the rain," and continued, "neither shalt thou kill thy neighbor's body in a duel"; and further, "Neither shalt thou destroy thyself by getting 'tight,' nor 'slewed,' nor 'high,' nor 'corned,' nor 'half-seas over,' nor 'three sheets in the wind.'" What Hutchings sacrificed in brevity he gained with his lightly humorous tone, offsetting the gravity implied by the "commandment" form.

The commandments themselves were a curious blend of moral proscription and tolerance, offset with a satirical humor that poked fun at moralism at the same time. Hutchings seems to have tried to balance his own sense of morality with his understanding of what miners would accept. In commandment number four, for example, he wrote:

> Thou shalt not remember what thy friends do at home on the Sabbath day, lest the remembrance may not compare favorably with what thou doest here. Six days thou mayest dig or pick all that thy body can stand under; but the other day is Sunday; yet thou washest all thy dirty shifts, darnest all thy stockings, tap thy boots, mend thy clothing, chop thy whole week's firewood, make up and bake thy bread and boil thy pork and beans, that thou wait not when thou returnest from thy long-tom, weary. For in six days' labor only thou canst not work enough to wear out thy body in two years, but if thou workest hard on Sunday also, thou canst do it in six months.

Not only does this commandment give a striking illustration of the grinding physical labor associated with California mining, it shows remarkable restraint on Hutchings' part, for whom Sunday church attendance was an important value. Eastman's illustration subtly carries the point by depicting all the activities listed here, but with a church and steeple clearly visible in the background landscape. Hutchings recognized that his audience would probably resist direct badgering, observing in his diary that "'Religious' has become a by-word and a reproach. There are not half a dozen men in the mountains who 'preach the gospel' that are acceptable to an audience and . . . respected by the people."[36]

Despite his restraint on the matter of church attendance and its humorous tone, the "Miners' Ten Commandments" is a moralistic document aimed at both depicting and shaping Anglo mining society, contributing to the creation of Anglo identity in California. In addition to the biblical injunctions, Hutchings modeled his text on variations of the rules and regulations of mining districts and associations in the content of "Commandments."[37] These forms would have been very familiar to most, if not all, of the Anglo miners in 1853, since Anglos had adapted the codes of Mexican and Californio miners as the basis of local legal systems to regulate mining claims and disputes.[38] The resulting miners' codes were established district by district, generally lim-

No. IV.

Commandment Number Four from Hutchings' "Miners' Ten Commandments": "Thou shalt not remember what thy friends do on the Sabbath day." (Courtesy California State Library, Sacramento, CA)

ited individuals to a single claim, controlled the process of formally register-ing claims, and articulated penalties for violations. They usually implicitly or explicitly favored white miners over those of other ethnicities, and clearly formed the basis of *Miners' Ten Commandments*.[39]

Eastman's illustrations extended Hutchings' text in several ways. With one exception, the illustrations corresponding to each commandment portrayed outdoor scenes, usually of mountainous terrain, sometimes forested. Most scenes depicted the action described in the corresponding commandment, packing several points into a very small space. Three of the illustrations sug-gested the violence of mining camp life with images of vigilante action. Min-ers in these illustrations corresponded with the stereotyped convention of the day, sporting the broad-brimmed hat and knee-high boots that had by then become symbolic of the independent and industrious "forty-niner."[40]

However humorous the text of the "Miners' Ten Commandments" may have been, close examination of the illustrations reveals a serious undertone. Most of the illustrations dramatized violent consequences for violation of the commandment described. For example, the illustration for commandment nine portrayed two miners in conversation in the foreground, one presum-ably telling the other "false tales about 'good diggings in the mountains,'" while in the background two figures displayed the consequence: "Lest in de-ceiving thy neighbor, when he returneth . . . with naught but his rifle, he pre-senteth thee with the contents thereof, and like a dog thou shalt fall down and die." Eastman cast these violent scenes in landscapes that may have surprised some nineteenth-century middle-class audiences. In the illustration for "No. II," what appeared at first glance a benign scene of gentle meadows stretch-ing away to lofty, wooded alps turned out upon close inspection to contain a vigilante team driving away an individual perpetrator.

California gold mining took place in some of the state's most rugged, mountainous terrain, so one purpose of Eastman's landscapes may have been simply to convey California's exotic topography to outsiders. However, these landscapes had potent symbolic meaning as well. By midcentury, images of meadows and forests such as these usually denoted peace and tranquility to middle-class Anglos, while mountains suggested the Romantic sublime.[41] The context of the California gold rush transformed these common perceptions of landscape into a framing device for culturally reinforcing social codes rooted in the threat of violence. Evidently, Hutchings was not as offended by the kind of violence that seemed necessary to uphold institutions of Anglo so-cial order as he was by the more spontaneous outbursts.

The combination of social commentary with illustrated landscape imagery

No. IX.

Commandment Number Nine from Hutchings' "Miners' Ten Commandments": "Thou shalt not tell any false tales." (Courtesy California State Library, Sacramento, CA)

linked two areas over which many California Anglos sought to impose order: society and the environment. In attempting to influence miners' behavior, writers and publishers created cultural symbols, perhaps the most prevalent of which was the idealized independent miner. The appeal of the "Miners' Ten Commandments" may lie in the way it simultaneously celebrated this independent miner and expressed many of the norms that underpinned institutions of social control, like the miners' associations.

Because the vision of the independent miner shared many of the aspirations and values of yeoman farmers and working men, I prefer to call this idealized figure of popular California publications the "yeoman miner." Yeomanry was a feature of Anglo-American republicanism, often associated with Thomas Jefferson's "Yeoman Farmer" ideal, which exalted the independent individual's characteristics of honesty, truthfulness, and industry. Like the "Miners' Ten Commandments" itself, the yeoman miner concept was a combination of Anglo-American values and the particulars of the California gold rush.[42] To many of the thousands who flocked to California, the gold rush offered the hope that a man could achieve "wealth somewhat beyond one's basic needs, freedom from economic or statutory subservience" and earn the "respect of society for fruitful, honest industry" with just a few months' work. In other words, a competency.[43] The news of California's gold rush breathed life into the yeoman dream as many men from the eastern United States gambled everything on the hopes of gaining a competence and the independence it would guarantee, in a few weeks of work.[44]

Once in California, the yeoman ideal was adapted to the mining context. In mining communities, made up of men from all nations, regions, and walks of life, familiar markers of class and status gave way to a universal uniform: the "figure of the flannel-shirted miner" with broad hat and denim trousers tucked into boots.[45] To some the almost total absence of social hierarchy meant that the California gold fields briefly represented the freedom and independence so central to yeoman ideals. For others, however, the gold fields represented social anarchy. To those the fluid social world of the gold rush threatened independence by its very lack of structure. Yeoman miner ideology, particularly as expressed in the "Miners' Ten Commandments," simultaneously celebrated the democratic vision of the first group while offering codes of morality and behavior that seemed to contribute to a more orderly society, thus mollifying the fears of the second.

The ideals of yeomanry were also valuable to a more corporate life, one in which individuals had to work together, often sacrificing dreams of individual success in favor of more modest gains. Thus, the emphasis in "The Commandments" against forms of cheating other miners. Even the exhortations against drinking and gambling can be read in this light: the member of the association who failed to work due to a hangover or who gambled away his portion of the group's profits would be a liability to the association as a whole. The illustrations of vigilante action and lynch law served as reminders of the violence and chaos that could erupt as a result of failure to live up to the yeoman miner ideal.

At the same time, California's environment also seemed to be a fickle and volatile factor in the fortunes of miners. Looking back from our postindustrial vantage point, it is difficult to sympathize with the fears of miners who, after all, wreaked a great deal of environmental havoc in a very short period of time.[46] Just as violence, drunkenness, and other forms of antisocial behavior could undermine the cooperative efforts of mining associations, California's apparently erratic (especially to the new arrivals) climate patterns could ruin months of hard work, as Hutchings observed in October 1854: "Down the north fork this morning, from Downieville, the whole course of the stream was floating, spans, lumber, wheels, flumes, tools. Men . . . with hands in pockets, were looking upon the havoc and ruined prospects."[47] In the second half of the century, miners rechanneled rivers, dug drainage tunnels through mountain bedrock, and sluiced, washed, and "hydraulicked" whole mountains into oblivion in their search for gold.[48]

These energetic attempts to control and manipulate the environment did not change the basic fact that miners were deeply dependent upon it: on the rains coming at the right time and in the right amount, on the presence of gold at all. The prominence of landscape imagery in popular California illustrations such as the "Miners' Ten Commandments" subtly reflected such tensions in the yeoman miner's relationship to the environment, while reinforcing the social codes of mining camp life. In a world of unpredictable geology, where luck played as significant a role as any other factor, this vision of individual accountability offered a reassuring illusion of human control over both environment and society.[49]

While broad features of California gold-rush society are visible in "The Miners' Ten Commandments," attention to the particular context in which Hutchings began his publishing career illustrates the connections between early California print culture and Anglo efforts to assert power in the state. Hutchings' scrapbook offers several clues about his interest in middle-class institutions.[50] Repeated references to church attendance in his scrapbook and diary link him to the Sabbatarian movement that took shape in 1853 as some Californians challenged the common Sunday practices of gold-rush society.

The prevalence of nonreligious social and economic activities on the Sabbath worried a significant number of Californians, enough to pressure the state legislature to pass laws in 1855: one to suppress gambling and another to "prohibit Barbarous and Noisy Amusements on the Christian Sabbath."[51] In his scrapbook, Hutchings included an article entitled "Movement for a Sabbath" from April 25, 1853, describing a petition signed by the "business men of Placerville" who had agreed to close their stores on Sunday, beginning on the first Sunday in June, and urging fellow entrepreneurs to do likewise. Included in this list were A. P. Brayton & Co. and Charles E. Brayton, with whom Hutchings maintained friendships in 1855, as well as other prominent businessmen in the Placerville community. In the same edition of the Placerville *Herald* as the second notice, a "J. M. Hutchins" together with A. W. Bee and T. W. Stowbridge issued a bid for contractors to build a new Presbyterian church in town.[52]

It was in the context of Placerville's Sabbatarian movement, indeed, on the very deadline for the bids to build the Presbyterian church, that Hutchings produced the initial newspaper version of the "Miners' Ten Commandments" in the Placerville *Herald*. Hutchings' interest in church attendance places him firmly in the ideological world of California's emerging elite. Many of the Placerville business leaders mentioned in the *Herald* and Hutchings' diary would go on to become industrialists and even senators. A. P. Brayton was an emerging industrialist, and his brother I. P. Brayton was a minister and editor of the Christian periodical *The Pacific*. In his diary, Hutchings described hearing the latter Brayton give a "good sermon" on April 8, and on the following day "Took tea with Rev. I. Pierpont, in company with Mr. I. Brayton and A. P. Brayton."[53] Yet, the Sabbatarian movement, like many efforts to create order out of the apparent chaos of gold-rush society, went beyond moral suasion to white miners. It also targeted ethnic groups. In the case of Sabbatarianism, some, including Hutchings, blamed Jews for keeping their business open, theoretically making it economically impossible for other tradesmen to close on Sunday:

thy morals and thy conscience, be none the better for it; but reproach thee, shouldst thou ever return with thy worn-out body to thy mother's fireside; and thou strive to justify thyself, because the trader and the blacksmith, the carpenter and the merchant, the tailors, Jews, and buccaneers, defy God and civilization, by keeping not the Sabbath day, nor wish for a day of rest, such as memory, youth and home, made hallowed.[54]

Hutchings' reference to Jews in this passage connects to broader anti-Semitic sentiments he expressed more forcefully in other newspaper articles at the same time. Shortly after "The Miners' Ten Commandments," Hutchings wrote another article for the *Herald*, entitled "A Saw—One of 'em." In it, Hutchings blamed the Jews "that *sawed us out of Sunday*" [emphasis in original]. "So much for Sunday-closing," he continued, "when Jews and auctioneers are more numerous than white folks. A great country this, . . . but, gentlemen of the town council, and others, couldn't you fence it in? The above would make excellent *rail*-ers."[55] The rant stimulated a response. Immediately below his clipping of "A Saw," in his scrapbook, Hutchings pasted the article, "For the El Dorado Republican." It was a refutation, signed by "Many Israelites," complaining of the "ungentlemanly and unkind epithets" of the previous article, and stating that they could not support "any editor who will allow correspondents to make the columns of his paper the medium of uttering vituperation." The article closed with assurances that "we shall always be found ready to cooperate with our respected fellow-citizens in whatever may tend to the prosperity and well being of this community."[56] Hutchings answered the response of "Many Israelites" in the June 25 issue of the *Herald* with "A Chapter," an extended and even more vituperative rant against Placerville's Jewish community:

Now it came to pass, that when the Gentiles reasoned with the Israelites for undermining and defeating the desires of a large multitude of miners and traders who wish to do right . . . the Israelites were offended and considered themselves ill-spoken of, and quoted one Pindar, a poor old Greek, to prove that they were slandered, and then broke off in the middle of a laugh to attend business and take a sixpence; and with drunken Jack Falstaff, made up their avoirdupois by finishing the laugh when the sixpence was in their pocket. "Laugh and grow fat" would suit their condition and my advice, and when they want to censure one Forty-Nine and one Herald for sawing about Sundays, let them think about civilization, and how far they have rolled it backward by their unhallowed seeking after gold.[57]

This article brought another response from "Many Israelites" in the *Eldorado Republican*, this time involving merchants and business owners from the San Francisco community. While the *Herald*'s editor, W. Wadsworth, gamely defended his paper's (and Hutchings') position—"persecution from you, gentlemen, will never hurt us. 'Let her rip'"—the *Herald* never again in its short run published an anti-Semitic diatribe. Perhaps the economic clout of the San Francisco and Placerville Jewish community carried the day or the idea that Jews were the only ones to blame for an entire society built on "unhallowed seeking after gold" was difficult to sustain. Later in his career, after forming a partnership with the Jewish printer Anton Rosenfield, Hutchings did include an unflattering portrait of "the Jew" in a *Hutchings' California Magazine* article lampooning several California nationalities, including Englishmen.[58] Other than this, he appears to have dropped his overt anti-Semitism after publication of "A Chapter."

Hutchings' anti-Semitism in his highly successful first foray into publishing shares several characteristics with other reform efforts in California. Print culture was only one expression of the efforts of community elites, often businessmen holding several positions of authority, to reorder mining town society away from the perceived chaos of the early gold rush. These efforts included the promotion of schools, temperance unions, parades, literary meetings, and the like, while discouraging gambling, saloons, hurdy-gurdy girls, and prostitution. At times, these cultural efforts took a violent turn, as in the case of vigilante actions or the destruction of a Placerville bear-and-bull fight arena in 1853. The owners of the arena filed a lawsuit and named several of Placerville's most prominent merchants and town leaders as defendants. Nearly all of these men were Hutchings' associates, and one was an editor of the Placerville *Herald*. Bear-and-bull fights were a legacy of California's Hispanic culture, a blood sport form of spectacular entertainment usually performed on Sundays and wildly popular with Californians of all races, nationalities, genders, and ages.[59]

The antagonism toward a rowdy, popular Sunday activity was consistent with the *Herald*'s Sabbatarian values. But, the destruction of property and the Hispanic origin of the sport suggest that ethnic conflict and violence lurked just below the surface of the "respectable" Anglo-American efforts to create an "orderly" California society. Hutchings' first publication, emerging as it did in the midst of attempts to assert the traditional institution of Protestant church attendance, represents one example of the way Anglo-Americans harnessed print in their efforts to organize California society along a middle-class model more familiar to industrializing England and "the States," as the East Coast was often referred to.

By 1853, the initial stage of the California gold rush was over, and efforts to organize labor, society, and the environment stretched well beyond the printed matter of Hutchings and other culture makers. Indeed, the dense context of Hutchings' initial publication illustrates the powerful interconnections between landscape ideology, print culture, and the struggle to assert power in California's volatile and cosmopolitan society. For Hutchings, the success of his letter sheet pointed toward a career that would allow him to adapt the cultural tools from his English upbringing to help bring order out of the violent chaos of the gold rush. In the next phase of his publishing career, Hutchings embarked on a yearlong journey into California's mountains to explore the world of his adopted homeland. During that year, his work depended on a range of artistic talent, print technology, transportation and financial infrastructure, and a keen understanding of his audience.

"Such Is Change in California": Technology, Violence, and Race in Post–Gold Rush California

A fickle California spring drenched the foothills around Placerville in March 1855, where Hutchings spent a few days at home to catch up on his business paperwork. "Rain Rain Rain," he wrote in his diary of that year. "Spending a wet day to the advantage of my business, for I posted my Ledger—and in the evening I received that great comfort—a letter from the loved ones afar."[1] The contrast between the "business" of posting his ledger with the "pleasure" of letters from home belied the close interconnections between the two. By the time he wrote this, Hutchings' business *was* letters, or rather, the stationery upon which they were written, illustrated letter sheets. Although letter sheets were published throughout the United States in the nineteenth century, they were especially popular in California. Publishers sought to capture unique aspects of the gold-rush experience and market the sheets to miners and other emigrants as low-cost ways to communicate with "loved ones afar."

A genre perfectly adapted to the needs of transient miners, the letter sheet offered some sense of the adventure in which Anglo miners were engaged through visual depictions of California and text that was often moralizing. Letter sheets and other ephemera offer examples of California printers' and publishers' efforts to support institutions of social order through images and texts that elaborated the values, assumptions, and beliefs underpinning the hierarchical restructuring of industrial society. In the midst of such technological, social, and cultural shifts, Hutchings decided to make a career out of his lucky strike in the letter sheet business. Hutchings became

Hutchings used "Way-Side Scenes in California," a letter sheet from 1854, to address race in the polyglot society of California's gold rush. (Courtesy Bancroft Library, University of California, Berkeley)

one of California's most prolific publishers of these sheets, producing dozens that covered a wide range of topics.[2]

Having discovered a successful formula with his "Miners' Ten Commandments," Hutchings spent 1854 and 1855 traveling through the central and northern mining districts, gathering information and publishing dozens more letter sheets. From the fall of 1854 to the summer of 1855 and his epic trip into Yosemite, Hutchings kept a detailed diary chronicling his travels and the process of producing and marketing his letter sheets. This diary offers an unparalleled snapshot, not only of the mining communities in which he traveled, but the emerging technologies of print, transportation, and mining that had enormous impact on the shape of California society. The timing of this journey is also remarkable—the invention of hydraulic mining technology in 1853 led to the rapid industrialization of California gold mining. Industrialization in California, as everywhere else in the world, had enormous implications for social organization. Hutchings traveled through the mines just at the moment they began to transform from the small-scale mining societies of the gold rush into industrial operations dependent on capitalization. His diary and letter sheets illustrate some of the ways California culture makers attempted to grapple with the wrenching transformations that continued to plague California's social world in the early 1850s.

It was also during this year of travel that Hutchings caught wind of the Yosemite falls and planned his fateful trip there. In 1851, the Mariposa military battalion had pursued a coalition of mountain tribes into the gorge, and rumors from that foray reached Hutchings during his year of travel. Casting his journey to Yosemite as the culmination of a year-long venture rather than a hasty tourist excursion reveals the powerful cultural forces at work in making Yosemite known "to the public eye." Hutchings went to great lengths and expense to make his way to Yosemite in the summer of 1855, and analysis of his publishing work in the year prior to that trip helps to clarify what he hoped to accomplish as a result of that investment. The military nature of the Anglo encounter with Yosemite and the matrix of Hutchings' cultural efforts illuminate the many ways that Yosemite's original entry into public consciousness was deeply bound up in the often violent racial, cultural and technological processes through which Anglos asserted power and laid the foundations for California's industrial expansion.

The Miners' Own Publisher

In the "Miners' Ten Commandments," Hutchings had struck upon a career path that eventually fused his own literary impulses with his desire to see a more stable California society. Hutchings' diary and scrapbook from 1854 to 1855 reveal an efficient businessman who adopted multiple roles: from photographer to salesman, from author to financier. To negotiate these roles he devised a sophisticated system for creating and selling printed material in a remarkably unstable market. His letter sheets also reveal efforts to appeal to his audiences through various topics—many were variations on his initial success.

Nearly all of them were illustrated, and nearly all of these illustrations depicted California landscapes. While some of them, like the "Commandments" and "Articles in a Miner's Creed," were clearly aimed toward miners, others appealed to different audiences, such as "Commandments to California Wives." Several sheets publicized individual towns with bird's-eye views, and one sheet, "Hutchings' Panoramic Scenes: Northern California and Oregon," combined several town scenes with some mining views to depict a region. Others, such as "California Indians," "Way-Side Scenes in California," and "The Mammoth Trees of California," emphasized the exotic elements of California's society and landscape.[3]

Hutchings began his travels with shorter excursions from Placerville in 1853, writing reports from various locations for the Placerville *Herald*. He visited Ione Valley and the "mammoth trees" near Calaveras, which he wrote about for the *Pacific*, the San Francisco Christian monthly edited by his friend I. P. Brayton.[4] In July he went east to Ragtown. In October he wrote from Volcano and the forks of the Cosumnes River. Many of the articles he wrote under the pseudonym "Jeddo" more or less promoted Placerville. In an article reporting from the Carson Valley, "Jeddo" alerted Placerville readers to the presence of "runners" from competing towns in California. These were men who went to Carson and eastward along the emigrant trails to direct parties toward routes that would take them into favored towns, a job Hutchings may have hoped to create for himself. At any rate these regular trips culminated over the course of the following year into a plan to take a longer, more extended set of excursions into the northern mines near the Oregon border to both market his letter sheets and gather information for new ones.

Traveling by foot, horseback, wagon, and steamship throughout California's Central Valley and the mountain mining regions, Hutchings sought communities where he could sell his wares as well as collect interesting stories and scenery that he could transform into new publications. He took notes from his observations and interviews with local residents, copied and clipped articles from local newspapers, took daguerreotype images, and hired artists to create sketches of scenes and people. In this combination of hired artists, photography, and print media, Hutchings established his lifelong practice of adopting and promoting cutting-edge media techniques to capture and disseminate landscape imagery. Hutchings' travels took him from the metropolitan centers of San Francisco and Sacramento, through secondary cities like Marysville and Nicholas that operated as bulk-break points for transshipment of goods into the mines, and on to the mining towns and camps themselves. Passing through the secondary cities several times allowed Hutchings to leave letter sheets behind with local businesses and pick up the profits on a return trip, as well as securing advertising "puffs" in local newspapers. Thus, Hutchings' work during this year reveals some of the geographical nature of print culture as it was becoming established in California.

Like most California travelers, Hutchings used the Sacramento and San Joaquin river systems as major thoroughfares to move from San Francisco to the interior reaches of the state and back again. In 1854 the emergence of the California Steam Navigation Company monopoly stabilized rates and made such travels smoother than in previous years. In September, Hutchings hired the French artist Edward Jump to sail with him from Sacramento to Marysville and then overland to Nevada City. From there, Hutchings and Jump went into the high mountain communities of Downieville, Goodyear's Bar, Galloways, and Cold Spring. In December, they returned to the Sacramento River to sail to Weaverville and Yreka, after which Jump departed for the cities.

Hutchings spent January and February in the vicinity of the Oregon border, collecting views (probably with his daguerreotype camera) and information in the mining districts of the Trinity Alps and Mt. Shasta. By March, he was in Sacramento, bargaining with engravers Barber and Baker for "six views—Shasta, Yreka, Jacksonville, Scotts Bar, Shasta Butte, and Weaverville." He ultimately published these views in a letter sheet entitled "Hutchings' Panoramic Scenes—Northern California."[5] From March through the end of May, Hutchings traveled through the central region of the California mining towns, continuing his combination of sketching, distributing, and gathering information. By June he was in San Francisco, preparing for his trip to Yosemite and establishing an expanded publishing business.

Hutchings relied upon the talents of the numerous artists, printers, and lithographers who had established themselves in California by 1854. Jump supplied sketches that may have been supplements to Hutchings' camera in the northern mines. In the summer, Thomas Ayres joined him on his explorations to Yosemite.[6] These artists created sketches that Hutchings then delivered to engravers. They copied and carved the artist's design into the grain end of a very hard wood, such as boxwood, and used the resulting image to print multiple copies. Hutchings also used artists/engravers such as Charles Christian Nahl or Harrison Eastman to refine his own daguerreotype images for engraving. By the early 1850s, several artists were based in Sacramento and

San Francisco, and their shops were producing voluminous quantities of woodcut engravings.

Harrison Eastman, who illustrated the "Miners' Ten Commandments" letter sheet, was one of the first artist-engravers to establish a business in California.[7] Hutchings also worked with George Baker of Sacramento, the firm of Kuchel and Dresel of San Francisco, and W. C. Butler of Sacramento and San Francisco, among others, an indication of the range of artistic talent available in California within five years of the U.S. conquest.[8] Hutchings delivered his sketches from the northern counties to Barber and Baker in March 1855 and his proofs were ready two months later. Hutchings then commissioned a printer such as Excelsior Print, or a lithographer such as Britton and Rey, and combined the engraved images with his own text to produce the finished version.

Most of the printers and lithographers Hutchings patronized for his 1854–1855 publications were in San Francisco or Sacramento. He also took advantage of the presence of printers, newspaper offices, and stationery stores in some of the most remote towns in his circuit through the mountains. In September 1854, for example, he had extra copies of the "Miners' Ten Commandments" letter sheet printed in Nevada City before venturing into the nearby mining camps where he hoped to sell them. His ability to have R. H. Stiles print extra copies indicates that Hutchings may have carried stereotype plates or lithograph stones with him.[9] Hutchings befriended newspaper editors in the towns he visited, interviewing them for stories of interest. Such friendships probably account for several of the promotional newspaper "puffs" he clipped and pasted in his scrapbook. Hutchings took advantage of the multiple roles played by small-community newspapers, which usually functioned as merchandising agents and print shops, to distribute his sheets or reprint extra copies.[10]

While we do not have a record of his earnings, Hutchings' travels and business pursuits evidently were satisfactory to his purpose. They enabled him to move to San Francisco, form a partnership with Jewish printer Anton Rosenfield, and at least partially fund the expedition to Yosemite. In so very direct a way, the money earned by the labor of miners tearing up riparian ecosystems in the mines translated into the first expedition to California's first and most famous sacred landscape. "It has been a year of many changes" Hutchings reflected in his diary, "Not being able to pay my board at the end of a week I have hired out at mining at $3.50 per day. A month afterward I cleared $1,000. Such is change in California."[11]

In 1853, the same year that Hutchings published the "Miners' Ten Commandments," Edward Matteson created a new technology that accelerated the changes already occurring in California's land use and dramatically altered the social arrangements built around mining. By connecting a wooden nozzle to a canvas hose to blast earth away from gold deposits with a high-pressure stream of water, Matteson invented the process of hydraulic mining.[12] Hydraulic technology allowed California miners to access ancient gold deposits far from modern river beds by transferring water long distances. The technology required capital investment and wage laborers to construct the flumes and ditches and to extract gold from the resulting slurry. Matteson's invention had profound implications for California's society and environment, accelerating the development of California's industrial base while radically expanding the environmental impact of gold mining.

Just as the earlier technological developments of mining sluices and long toms gave rise to miners' associations; the technology of hydraulic mining demanded a reorganization of the mining labor force that would lead to more stratified, less fluid societies, akin to the factory systems of the Atlantic world. By 1855, more and more miners were taking on wage work for others, undercutting the dream of yeoman independence and making the social mores of the 1853 "Miners' Ten Commandments" obsolete. This restructuring of the industrial workforce appealed to those Californians who were unsettled by the apparently chaotic individualism of the initial gold rush and who saw in the emergence of social hierarchy signs of "order" and "progress." But the power of the yeoman miner ideal lived on, inspiring those miners who sought independence in the gold fields to resist the wage-labor system through strikes and protests and by maintaining independent claims that they worked individually in their free time.

Hutchings may have perceived that mining would not continue to support the majority of Anglo Californians, as throughout the decade real wages declined steadily. Several of Hutchings' publications in this decade speak to the shifting social world of mining during this era. In "Articles in a Miners' Creed," an 1855 letter sheet, Hutchings spoke to the emerging structural changes. The letter sheet was not illustrated and simply listed thirty-five "articles," each beginning with "He Believes. . . ." Like the "Miners' Ten Commandments," "Articles" combined humor with the mock-serious form: "He believes that Gold is found in Quartz, but he would be satisfied to find it in

THE MINERS' TEN COMMANDMENTS.

In this detail from the 1853 letter sheet "Miners' Ten Commandments," Hutchings included images of the hydraulic mining technology that would dramatically alter gold-rush society. (Courtesy California State Library, Sacramento, CA)

pints—or even half-pints." But several "articles" reveal more sobering aspects of mining as the heady days of the gold rush came to a close:

> He believes that labor is not the only capital now required for a good claim.
> He believes in "the good time coming," but thinks it must have started for the mountains on a prospecting trip, and got lost in a snow storm. . .
> He believes that hard work, hard prospects, hard beds and hard living will harden him into premature old age.
> Still
> He believes that after all that three or four dollars a day is better than six bits.[13]

A few years later, Hutchings published an article in his periodical *Hutchings' California Magazine* that provides an even more striking depiction of hydraulic technology's impact on the miner. In the story of "Suspension Flume across Brandy Gulch," water and industrial technology were cast in an allegory of California's early mining. Ostensibly a celebration of the technological insight behind the design and construction of this flume, the article manages to illustrate the many connections between landscape, technology, class, and California identity. The author, identified only as "S—," begins the article by praising the "remarkably ingenious" construction of the 1,500-foot-long flume, "elevated to a height of 206 feet [and] through which from four to five hundred inches of water" passed daily.[14]

The author then continues to discuss the importance of water in California's economy. In a remarkable if disingenuous analogy, "S—" compares California's "gorgeous treasury" to the conquests of Rome, England, and Spain, remarking that "theirs was the genius of war; ours the conquests of peace. The music of our march is the revelry of the gushing stream, and the only chains we forge are those that bind the captive water."

Charles Nahl's illustration accompanying this article, engraved by Anthony Armstrong, depicts a slender flume angling into the distance and surrounded by forest trees. The illustration portrays the flume built on "living trees, at intervals of about a hundred feet . . . the tops of which being cut away, contribute materially to the permanency of the structure." Whether any such structures were actually built, a flume perched on living trees certainly would not be very permanent. While the illustration gives the impression of a structure built in harmony with the surrounding environment, the relationship between technology and its "captive" nature is more ambivalent in the text. The article describes the transformation of water itself from "the sheet of vapor which hangs in dreamy silence above the brow of the 'Sierra'" to "its debasing destiny of labor in the mines. At the day's end, the drop of water surveys itself, how sadly changed. Its face discolored! The luster of its eye is vanished! In disgust it turns away to rest, not on the fair face of the pale flower, which cast it on the pitiless world, but to lose its identity among swarthy companions, in a neighboring pool."

In utilizing the power of water under pressure to blast away mountainsides in search of gold, hydraulic mining did indeed transform clear mountain water into "swarthy" silt-laden streams and pools. As early as 1852 travelers commented on the muddiness of rivers draining the gold fields and by the late 1850s, when this article was published, mining detritus was spreading across the San Francisco harbor.[15] However, the reference to "swarthy companions" evoked both the ethnicity of wage-earning miners who could be black, Mexican, Kanaka (Hawaiian), Chinese, or, increasingly, Irish, as well as Anglo, and the grubbiness of mining labor. Mining required such intense physical labor that, like the imaginary drop of water, miners found themselves "sadly changed" in appearance after a few years in the mines. Back-breaking labor, poor diet, shabby living conditions, and rampant disease aged men quickly. In 1858 the North San Juan *Hydraulic Press* noted, "Nowhere do young men look so old as in California."[16]

The metaphorical relationship between the drop of water and the status of miners as wage laborers is also remarkable in casting the waterworks of flumes and ditches as the transformative agents. By the end of the decade hydraulic mining was fully industrialized, intensely capitalized, and dependent upon wage labor. In 1857 $12 million had been invested in over 4,000 miles of canals, ditches, and flumes to supply water to the mines.[17] The industrialization and capitalization of hydraulic mining had social consequences, organizing the fluid gold-rush society into hierarchical forms resembling the emerging class divisions of older Anglo society. For Hutchings and his contributors, such developments could only benefit miners: "The flume . . . is not only of inestimable value to the miners, and thereby to every other interest, but also promises to be a lucrative investment."[18]

But not everyone agreed about the benefits of wage labor for the working miners, and the industrialization of mining and resultant shift in status of formerly independent yeoman miners to poverty-stricken wage laborers fueled antagonisms between miners and entrepreneurs. As mines closed down or consolidated through the 1850s, the average miner's wage dropped from approximately $20 per day in 1848 to $5 per day in 1853 and $3 per day in the late 1850s. By the late 1850s, miners in Grass Valley and Nevada City were living well below the national poverty rate.[19]

Water companies controlled the price of water and therefore the level of profits miners could earn, often forcing smaller, more independent mining outfits to capitulate to larger conglomerates. Reflecting their hostility toward water companies, miners in the Columbia mining district characterized the Tuolumne County Water Company as the "enemy that would take from you the proceeds of the sweat of your brow, the bread you eat, the clothes you wear, and your last shilling."[20] However, miners' attitudes toward waterworks were shifting and complex. While some resented the works to the point of committing sabotage, others welcomed them to their districts as the only way to continue mining. Even the miners in Tuolumne recognized the need for water-delivery systems; they challenged the Tuolumne County Water Company by erecting their own system. Regardless of the response to the hydraulic mines, the fact remains that such systems were some of the most powerful symbols of the connection between environmental, technological, and social organization in post–gold rush California.

Hutchings' sympathies were clearly with the ditch companies, in which he may have continued to invest during this period. "If at any time a miner should . . . be so disposed to think lightly of water companies, we wish them to visit the upper end of most of our canals, there to witness the expense, labor and energy expended on them."[21] Water was and remains one of the most chaotic and unpredictable features of the California landscape, its availability fluctuating in wide extremes of drought and flood. Together with the practical needs of miners and agriculturalists, the impetus to control water supplies reflected a cultural desire to impose order on a chaotic and threatening territory.

Like many other writers, Hutchings responded to economic crisis by focusing on the water supply as both the culprit and ultimate solution to economic stagnation. In this, he adopted a position common among Anglo boosters when he depicted the landscape in terms that could be controlled by technology and capital and overlooked the possibility that economic instability might be dependent upon other factors, such as the declining gold supply, beyond the scope of human control.[22]

Regardless of whether one thought that the ditch companies were evil monopolies or blessings of progress, it is clear that the industrialization of mining technologies influenced the shape of California mining society. Previously independent miners who remained in the industry most likely became nonunionized, wage-earning laborers in an industrial system. As mines consolidated, they increasingly came under the control of absentee owners, managed by the engineers, accountants, and attorneys who comprised the local elite of mining communities.

Way-Side Scenes of Race and Violence in California

When Hutchings conducted his tour of the mines in 1854–1855, the trajectory of industrialization and its social impact was not entirely clear. While visiting with editors in the northern mining camps, he gathered a story that got him thinking about race in California. The strenuous resistance of "Many Israelites" to his anti-Semitic diatribe in the Placerville *Herald* may have tempered his attitude toward Jews, but he was not finished trying to work out California's multiethnic society in print.

The result was the 1854 letter sheet entitled "Way-Side Scenes in California," which develops several ideas about race and ethnicity in California. Two lengthy captions are sandwiched between their corresponding illustrations on the top and bottom, and framed at the left and right by two more illustrations of California Indians borrowed from a separate publication. The top image depicts several Californians of various backgrounds encountering each other on a mountain road, while the bottom depicts the midst of a Chinese Tong war that occurred in Weaverville in 1853.

Detail from the 1854 letter sheet "Way-Side Scenes in California." Artist Charles Christian Nahl deploys landscape imagery in his visual arrangement of California ethnic groups. (Courtesy Bancroft Library, University of California, Berkeley)

Hutchings hired Charles Nahl, a highly prolific painter and commercial artist, to draw the images based in part on information Hutchings had gathered during his 1854 travels through the mountain mining towns of California. Nahl had great skill in depicting the variety of California's polyglot society and an eye for landscape detail—so that many of the images he produced for Hutchings include carefully rendered landscape backgrounds. In the case of "Way-Side Scenes," for instance, the top and most prominent image frames the characters with mountain peaks in the distance and shrubs and trees in the foreground. Hutchings' text also frames his discussion with a description of the "hills . . . covered with pines and oaks, and shrubs, and flowers of every description and variety." Nahl's illustration depicts California Indians, Chinese, white miners, and wagon train drivers in various stages of travel on a mountain road. Hutchings' text, on the other hand, arranges the various racial and ethnic groups in a clearer pattern:

> The Stranger, as he ascends the mountains towards the mining towns . . . notices the contrast in the scenes around him from anything he ever saw before. . . . Indians are met in groups, and in every stage of filth and pitch, carrying their "papoose" or baskets of "chemuck" (food) upon their backs. . . . Strings of Chiniamen [*sic*] pass and greet you in broken English with "how you do, John?"—we are all Johns to them and they to us—their faces, tails, and dress, their bamboo canes and heavy

loads are strangely singular to us. Next comes a Negro, with polite "good morning, sar," or Chileno, Mexican, or Kanaka, with his bony horse and heavy load; then come horse teams, mule teams, ox teams, or mules laden with provisions, tools and clothing for the mines. Now a stage whirls past, or ladies and gents ride by in buggies or on horseback, to look at whom the miner drops his pick and wipes his brow. Here comes the expressman, he who links the vallies with the mountains, brings gladdening words of love from home, of tidings from the absent ones, of friendly hopes and cheering thoughts; he is always welcome, through rain or snow, or danger, dust and mud, onward he rides, and brings the latest news.[23]

Hutchings' race-based hierarchy divides California society into clearly recognizable groups related to each other in obvious degrees of civilization. Beyond the vision of California were the presumably middle-class writers of letters carried by the express: "Did our friends afar but know how dearly prized their favors are . . . no mail would leave the shores of the Atlantic without a letter to the absent ones in California." It seems as if Hutchings could not resist a plug for the letter writers on whom his letter sheet business depended.

While Hutchings' fantasy was clearly racist by twenty-first-century standards, it was not just another pitch for the supremacy of whites. It was also a way of replacing the social disorder created by the gold-rush demolition of recognizable Anglo class and gender constructs with recognizable categories based on race. Compared to mid-nineteenth-century Anglo Californians' genocidal practices, it was a peaceful vision that belied the violence and antagonism fracturing mining society, frequently (but not always) along lines of race and ethnicity. As the assumption of white racial superiority was implicit in the definition of yeomanry, the idea of organizing California into a race-based hierarchy had special appeal to yeoman miners. And the "ladies and gents" in buggies suggests an emerging elite group who also found comfort in a vision of social hierarchy.

The next caption, describing the internecine battle of Chinese Tongs in "Five Cent Gulch," sensationalizes the exotic weaponry and funeral rites of the Chinese while dismissing the cause of violence as originating in "sectional hatred and clannish differences brought from their native land." Sidebar images of California Indians depicted, on the left, men harvesting grasshoppers for food, and on the right, women naked from the waist up pounding acorns. There were no explanatory captions for these images, which were reproduced from a separate Hutchings publication apparently for the purpose of framing the text on either side. Perhaps the image of naked breasts would make the document more appealing to potential customers. Together, the four illustrations and much of the text appear to be designed to convey the exotic qualities of California's native and émigré population, a common theme in western popular culture from the nineteenth century to the twenty-first.

However, there are additional layers of meaning to this publication. At first glance, the two primary illustrations and captions, one emphasizing the organization of California's mixed social world and the other depicting Chinese violence, seem only tangentially connected to each other. Placed within the context of Hutchings' experience of gold-rush society, though, these two concepts reiterate common themes of social order and violence. The captions' text offered a vision of California society that replaced random, race-based violence with a hierarchical social order also based on race and ethnicity. And though it was racist, this depiction lacked the vituperative quality of Hutchings' earlier anti-Semitic diatribes. The odd juxtaposition of Chinese violence and the peaceful ordering of California society in racial hierarchy, the unexplained addition of California Indian practices, and the careful rendition of landscape as a framing device, all suggest the efforts of an individual attempting to make sense and order from a world in which familiar values and assumptions only partially applied.

Perhaps what Hutchings does *not* say about California violence is more telling than what he does mention in this text. For one thing, his published description of the Chinese Tong war differs in small, but telling, ways from the editor's story that he recorded in his diary. There, he described the confrontation between the "large party" and the "small party," as well as the American involvement:

> large numbers of Americans went to see the battle, and a majority were with the smaller party in sentiment. This party began the fight by one man advancing. . . . Then the remaining 124 rushed in with a bold charge and put the others to flight. And as the Americans interfered when the large body were about to charge, they took safety in flight. . . . An American fired a revolver several times amongst the Chinamen and someone from behind shot him through the head, and that finished him."[24]

The letter sheet text, on the other hand, introduced the story with the line "all endeavors by their leaders or Americans to settle [the conflict] amicably were in vain." In the letter sheet version, Americans acted only as spectators cheering on the efforts of the "small party," while the man with the revolver became "an excited Swede." The changes between the diary and the text de-emphasized the random or sporting quality of Anglo violence. At the same time, this text perpetuated an image of the Americans as arbitrators and spectators, but never agitators, in the internecine conflicts of another race. Thus, in obscuring the violence that Anglos perpetrated against Californians of other races, Hutchings' depictions of California's multiethnic population in "Way-Side Scenes" idealized race relations at the same time that they offered visions of social order.

The family of California indigenes in Nahl's illustration exits the scene of their own free will. In reality, it took widespread violence—both systematic and random—to divest Amerindians of their homeland. California's nonexistent legal infrastructure meant that there was no effective system to handle the displaced, such as reservations or treaty lands. All too frequently, groups were rounded up and forced to march sometimes hundreds of miles and then abandoned or kept captive with no resources to feed or shelter them. One such episode with powerful ramifications for Hutchings' own future offers a stark contrast to his printed efforts at idealized race relations.

Mariposa Battalion

One year after Hutchings arrived in Placerville, events in remote areas of California transpired that would profoundly affect his later career. Gold discoveries along the Merced and Tuolumne rivers south of Placerville drew miners to the southern foothill regions as they did throughout California. The influx of miners put enormous pressures on the large populations of native Miwok and Yokuts people who lived in the region. James Savage was an early emigrant who tried to exploit both the miners and his familiarity with native languages by opening a trading post at the Fresno crossing. Known to both contemporaries and historians as a shady character, he kept several hundred "domestic" Indians in his employ (or as wives, or captives, depending on one's interpretation). In December 1850, a coalition of Yokuts, Miwok, and Mono people attacked Savage's trading post, although it is unclear whether this attack was directed at him personally or as a representative of the whites in the region more generally.

Earlier that year, the newly formed California legislature had authorized the muster of battalions to conduct "expeditions against the Indians," wherein citizens of a county could create their own military battalions and receive state funds in return for service. In April 1850, it had also passed the "Act for the Government and Protection of Indians," which denied Indians the right to vote or testify in court and, under limited conditions, allowed them to be pressed into service or, if minors, be "adopted." Although the language of this law emphasized consent and humane treatment and required contractual agreements for labor, these niceties were often ignored as Indians were rounded up or kidnapped to serve as domestics and farm laborers.[25] In his annual address to the California legislature in January 1851, Governor Burnett articulated both the official and popular sentiment toward California indigenes: "That a war of extermination will continue to be waged between the races, until the Indian race becomes extinct, must be expected. While we cannot anticipate this result but with painful regret, the inevitable destiny of the race is beyond the power or wisdom of man to avert."[26]

In February 1851, Savage commanded a muster of three companies totaling around 200 men to retaliate against the attack on his post. In a series of campaigns from March through May, the famed Mariposa Battalion pursued the Yosemites (Miwok) and Chowchillas (Yokuts) into the mountains and eventually captured several hundred of them in Yosemite Valley in May 1851. These were then removed to a rancheria in the valley outside of Fresno. The members of the battalion were the first Anglos in the written record to set foot into Yosemite Valley.[27]

The removal of Yosemite's Indians is more well known than the hundreds of parallel events because of its association with the famous landscape. This led several participants to publish memoirs of it. Despite its fame, the Mariposa Battalion was one of many such efforts to dispossess California indigenes across the state. As such, it shares several features of that removal with other widespread practices among whites seeking to "control" native California residents. One is that the "trigger" initiating the military response was action on the part of Indians indicating coalitions among tribes, particularly threatening to whites. Another is that the ultimate purpose of the military activity was not to actually gain territory for white control, but to remove Indians from a region where they could remain independent of Anglo authority. Such "removals" took place among mountain tribes (or lowland tribes who had fled into the mountains) across the state and usually involved brutal forced marches that brought the Indians into lowland rancherias, unfunded reservations where they were pressed into service as agricultural laborers and where many suffered from malnutrition, disease, and death.[28]

Such was the case with the Fresno Rancheria where chief Tenaya and his people were moved after the Mariposa Battalion drove them from the mountains. None other than James Savage took it upon himself to manage the ranch; newspaper articles from the summer of 1852 reveal that Savage was raising barley on a Fresno River ranch with the labor of several hundred Indians, presumably those removed from their mountain homes in and around Yosemite.

Amerindian labor was involuntary and uncompensated; however, California lacked the necessary legal and enforcement apparatus to keep native Californians bonded as chattel on the model of African American slavery in the American South. Those who survived the forced marches and who retained their health and presence of mind continually slipped away from the rancherias. The Miwok, Yokuts, and other tribes of the Yosemite high country were no exception, returning to their old Sierra haunts as testified in oral histories.[29] Many of these would eventually adapt to the Yosemite Valley tourist industry, reestablishing a permanent or semi-permanent residence that lasted well into the twentieth century and took the concerted efforts of the National Park Service to remove.[30]

The story of the Mariposa Battalion became a popular narrative as Yosemite's reputation grew, with early versions appearing in *Hutchings' Illustrated California Magazine* and in Hutchings' California tour guide, *Scenes of Wonder and Curiosity*. The most-cited account of the expedition is that of Lafayette Bunnell, the young doctor who accompanied this battalion and later wrote eloquently of his appreciation for the stunning scenery as he entered the valley. At the point where he does this, his narrative seems to depart from a clear explanation of the goals of the battalion. The reader is left to assume that once the sublime wonder of Yosemite was revealed to them, the captors discovered a higher purpose in removing the Ahwahneechees from their home: to set the landscape aside for the enlightenment of future generations of the kinds of Americans who could appreciate the divine presence in the sublime landscape.[31]

Yosemite's expanding fame as a scenic landscape for tourism led most writers to assume that the securing of this landscape for tourist appreciation was the primary benefit resulting from the activities of the Mariposa Battalion, and Lafayette Bunnell's version of events has gone largely unquestioned, either at the time or by historians, although there has been wide disagreement about whether or not the actions were a good thing.[32] In contrast, as the subsequent activities of James Savage suggest, far from revealing the scenic wonders of the Yosemite to generations of admirers, or even retaliating against Indian violence, the immediate effect of the action was to use the excuse of a fracas at his store to secure legal and military authority for a slaving raid.

The story of the initial white "discovery" of Yosemite illustrates two critical points to understanding the idea of Yosemite as it emerged in the context of midcentury California. One is that, in order to perceive Yosemite as a sublime landscape and later a wilderness, it had to be emptied of its original inhabitants, at least conceptually. Despite the continued presence of Yosemite, Miwok, Mono, and Ahwahneechee Indians in Yosemite throughout the nineteenth century, the *story* of the Mariposa Battalion, as published in tourist guides and elsewhere, satisfied tourists that the original inhabitants, who were only using the land temporarily anyway, had been effectively removed. Some even took this to mean that the Indians they encountered in the valley were not "really" the original inhabitants.[33]

The second point has to do with the probable "real" purpose behind their removal, which was not, at least initially, to obtain the land so much as to wrest the people from it to use them as laborers in California's emerging market economy. In the 1850s and later, the issue of labor was an intensely fraught one as many gold-rush miners fiercely opposed the idea of going to work for somebody else. As we have seen, it was the independence promised by California's mining economy, at least during the first years, that drew miners out of the industrializing east in the first place and often what kept them in the state long after their dreams of instant wealth faded. Even so, most miners saw themselves as temporary sojourners in California and had little or no interest in investing in the future of its society. For those who hoped to build California into an industrial, urban empire this situation was problematic on several counts. For one thing, gold-rush society was a volatile and unpredictable mix that could give way to violence at any moment. For another, white miners' independent mentality made their acquiescence in becoming industrial laborers a challenge, at least until the placers gave out and they had no real alternatives. Finally, for multiple reasons, institutionalized race-based slavery on the model of the American South was not a viable option, but it did point toward the usefulness of race as a category for organizing individuals into the labor force necessary to transform California from the sleepy Mexican backwater to an industrialized powerhouse in less than a decade. So the Amerindian rancherias attempted to put their captives to work raising grain and other agricultural products to feed the miners.

Like many men of his age, Hutchings exhibited powerfully conflicting attitudes toward native Californians throughout his lifetime. It was George Catlin's Birmingham exhibit of the paintings and artifacts of Plains and Mandan Indians that inspired Hutchings to travel to America in the first place. He described being fascinated by them in his overland diary. At one point, he left his party to explore some funereal bowers of Plains tribes, and climbed into one of them, handling several artifacts. Though "curiosity might have led me to stealing. . . my respect for the creed of the Indian bade 'hands off.'"[34] In California, Hutchings frequently went out of his way to observe and record native practices, rituals, and political treaty negotiations and to visit and comment on rancherias. He did not condone the violence perpetrated against California tribes, but he did not denounce it, either. Rather, he tended to adopt the "vanishing race" view of many of his contemporaries: that it was a sad but unavoidable "fact" that native Californians were destined to make way for the "progress" of the more "advanced" civilization represented by Anglo culture. His attitude must have changed in later years, for in 1884, he adopted his long-time Mono employee, Tom, and dedicated his culminating life's publication, *In the Heart of the Sierras*, to Tom Hutchings.

Hutchings' scrapbook, diary, and publications prior to 1855 illustrate some of the ways that the California gold rush was the crucible test and transformed Anglo ideologies about social norms, values, and identity. In the process of consolidating economic and political power and cultural authority, Anglo culture makers like Hutchings adapted Atlantic institutions built around class anxiety to the unique qualities of the California context. Radically different features of midcentury California—including the unpredictable environment, multiethnic population, nonexistent legal and technological infrastructure, and regular outbursts of spontaneous violence—posed enormous challenges to those who would build a future there. And, in the midst of his struggles to do just that, Hutchings fixated upon a passing rumor from a member of the Mariposa Battalion. Somewhere in the central Sierra Nevada was a waterfall 1,000 feet high. "A *thousand feet!*" thought Hutchings. "Why Niagara is only 164 feet high." Niagara had become the paramount symbol of all things sublime in America. Could California have its own version? And so, at a crucial crossroads, as California was making the wrenching transition from gold rush to industrial powerhouse of the Pacific Rim, and as Hutchings prepared to launch himself into his career as a prolific publisher of landscapes and California society, he organized a trip into the California mountains in search of an icon.[35]

"Yo Hamite Falls," by Thomas Ayres, James Mason Hutchings lithographic print, 1855. The first visual image of Yosemite clearly communicates the sublime qualities of the Sierra landscape. (Courtesy Bancroft Library, University of California, Berkeley)

Part II
The Church of California:
Yosemite and the Regional Sublime,
1855–1860

In the summer of 1855 Hutchings took his first trip to Yosemite and moved from Placerville to San Francisco. There he would consolidate and expand his publishing business to its fullest potential, dedicating the next decade of his career to the promotion of California's "beautiful scenery and curiosities," including Yosemite. Hutchings' work to "open the sealed book" of Yosemite to "the public eye" largely took place in San Francisco, the emergent international metropolis perched on the edge between the American West's vast hinterlands and the trade networks of the Pacific. This is true to the extent that the story of Yosemite in that first decade is largely a story of San Francisco. It was San Francisco's cultural elites whom Hutchings pressed into service to help spread the news and San Francisco's emerging bourgeois classes who purchased the lithographs and took the first vacations there. San Francisco's industrial base provided the technologies of print and photography to convey the message, and San Francisco's hinterland transportation networks carried the first artists and tourists into the valley. Without the metropolis to provide the audience, technology, and transportation networks, Yosemite might have remained a half-baked rumor on the lips of old battalion soldiers, a relatively undisturbed haven for weary California indigenes.

By the same token, Yosemite provided value to San Francisco: an image of divine order and sublime beauty that betokened something grander than grubbing after gold or ongoing speculation in the city's dusty streets. For people like Hutchings, Yosemite offered an antidote to the chaos and violence of the gold rush, a secular sermon that might reach those for whom "the gospel is nothing but a reproach." As a tourist destination, Yosemite, along with other exotic and interesting places, gave new residents a reason to want to settle in California, to make this strange place home, and in so doing create an orderly bourgeois Anglo society in the foreign landscape. This became the full expression of Hutchings' vision of order that he had been working out in his earlier publications.

For San Francisco 1855 was also a momentous year. Several fires and financial collapses, as well as competition from other ports, threatened the city's dominance of California's economy. But in a classic expression of capitalist "creative destruction," San Francisco emerged from the chaos with a renewed sense of purpose and future direction. To the extent that the vision of Yosemite helped to consolidate the middle and upper classes around a shared investment in California, its early iconography was instrumental in this urban renewal. Just as the icon Yosemite was born of the social, economic, and technological frameworks of the gold rush, its early development simultaneously fed and was dependent upon the rising international metropolis, San Francisco.

The initial production of Yosemite landscape imagery took place within the multiple contexts in which Hutchings and others worked. These contexts were cultural: the aesthetic and ideological values that made people like Hutchings see worth and beauty in certain kinds of scenes. They were technological: the rapidly evolving transformation of midcentury media that made the proliferation of images and texts possible. Midcentury economic sensibilities also defined the scope of what was and was not possible or desirable for entrepreneurs like Hutchings. And, finally, these various contexts combined underscored a reality that flies in the face of many of our contemporary mythologies about landscapes like Yosemite: the values, economics, and technologies that underpinned and drove the first phase of Yosemite's creation as an icon were fundamentally and intensely urban and industrial.

So the story of Yosemite as a symbol of California is a story that weaves together the urban and the rural, the industrial and the artistic, social unrest and cultural efforts to contain it. It is a story that brings these multifarious complexities together in a crucible of modernity—where image and artifact become signifiers of social import, and where various strands of Anglo-

American thinking about landscape and society come together in a powerful cultural amalgam. Analysis of Yosemite's original iconography within the broader context of Hutchings' own publishing oeuvre and the role of print itself in the rapid consolidation of urban control over hinterland areas reveal the multiple connections between the creation of Yosemite landscapes and the modernization of the American West.

"Opening the Sealed Book": Making Yosemite Known to All

In all his peripatetic lifetime, Hutchings' most celebrated journey took place in the summer of 1855, the culmination of his year of touring the California mining districts. Following the clues dropped during his innumerable conversations that year, Hutchings gathered together a party of fellow Englishmen and headed south to Savage's old trading post on the Fresno. Asking around for Mariposa Battalion veterans, he finally located two Miwok men, Kos-sum and So-pin, who agreed to guide the party that included Hutchings' cabinmate from the Gertrude, Walter Millard, together with Alexander Stair and the artist Thomas Ayres. The group then headed into the mysterious valley home of the "thousand-foot waterfall." The journey took several days over the ancient Mono trail that enters the valley from the southwest. Encountering the first view of the valley from near modern-day Inspiration Point, Hutchings wrote that the scene "took away the power of thinking, much less of clothing thoughts with suitable language."[1] And indeed, for once in his very voluble lifetime, James Mason Hutchings literally fell silent, recording almost nothing in his diary during the five days that he and his party toured the valley floor.[2]

The spell did not last. Upon leaving the valley, Hutchings stopped by the office of the nearby Mariposa *Gazette* to write the first published account of Yosemite. Returning to San Francisco, Hutchings turned Ayres' sandpaper sketches into two large-scale lithographs: one the image of "Yo-Hamite Falls" and the other the view of the valley from near modern-day Inspiration Point entitled, "General View of the Great Yo-Semite [Yosemite] Valley, Mariposa County, California." Reminiscing many years later, Hutchings wrote that "the Yo Semite Valley, at that time, was *as a sealed book to the general public,* . . . it was our good fortune to be instrumental in opening its sublime pages to the public eye, that it might be "known and read of all men."[3]

It was upon returning from his first visit to Yosemite Valley that Hutchings wrote in his diary, "Took me an office in Armory Hall and furnished it. I like it."[4] This simple comment signaled Hutchings' move from Placerville to San Francisco and the beginning of his six-year publishing partnership with Anton Rosenfield, the peak of his publishing career. Armory Hall may have been the situation at 201 Clay Street where Hutchings and Rosenfield published for a short period in 1855. The majority of their publications and advertisements, as well as the San Francisco city directory, identify their office and shop as 146 Montgomery Street, "second door north of Clay."[5]

From this location, Hutchings and Rosenfield became among the most prolific midcentury publishers of California ephemera. While they continued to produce the letter sheets that Hutchings had researched and designed during his travels in Northern California, the firm expanded on this initial body of material to produce a wide range of publications: maps and promotional tracts, children's literature and almanacs, steamer papers (marketed to steamship passengers), and, most famously, the periodical *Hutchings' Illustrated California Magazine.*[6] The office at 146 Montgomery was also a shop carrying "books, letter paper, writing materials of any kind, magazines, steamer papers, views of California scenery, musical instruments, pocket knives, paper cutters . . . or anything generally kept in a book and stationery store."[7] By locating their shop in downtown San Francisco, Hutchings & Rosenfield placed themselves at the geographical center of printing in California, indeed the entire Pacific Slope. San Francisco's print culture was a critical factor in that city's dynamic growth as a regional and international imperial metropolis.

Just what *was* it that Hutchings and his companions saw in Yosemite during that week-long excursion in the summer of 1855? The physical features of Yosemite Valley are well-known: a flat valley of open meadows threaded by the meandering Merced River surrounded by perpendicular granite walls and plunging waterfalls. The granite walls take on various shapes including domes, spires, sheer cliffs, cliffs broken by rock falls, and forested slopes that surround the valley. And, in Hutchings' day, at the far eastern end of the Merced River, a still pond provided a perfect reflection of the Tis-sa-ack, the mountain known as Half Dome.

What Hutchings' Miwok guides saw in the scene before them is lost to history. Was it their homeland? A space to travel through on the way to somewhere else? The site of neighbor or rival villages? All they left for the historic record was the name Hutchings adopted and attached to his first lithographs, "Yo-Hamite." Hutchings later changed it to Yo Semite and kept the separated spelling his entire life, even as popular nomenclature shifted to the modern version.

For Hutchings and his Anglo companions the cascades, valleys, and mountain peaks were the very embodiment of Romantic landscape tropes. As discussed in chapter 1, Romantics viewed wild nature as the true seat of the divine and thought that if moderns wished to encounter God, they should eschew physical churches and seek out places in nature where they could encounter the sublime. The sublime was found in those places where individuals lost their own sense of self in the face of the raw power of nature; thunderstorms and storms at sea were good examples of the sublime, but so too were cataracts, cliffs, tumbling waterways, and mountain peaks. All of these the Yosemite Valley had in abundance. As Richard Grusin notes, Yosemite was a compilation of physical features charged with the most potent landscape symbolism that nineteenth-century Anglos had dreamed up in the fifty years prior. "The union of the deepest sublimity with the deepest beauty of nature, not in one feature or another, not in one part or scene or another, not in any landscape that can be framed by itself, but all around and wherever the visitor goes, constitutes the Yo Semite the greatest glory of nature," wrote Frederick Law Olmsted ten years later. More specifically, Yosemite strongly resembled the "lush, loving description of Eden" in John Milton's *Paradise Lost*, a text so familiar to nineteenth-century reformed Protestants that many could quote long passages of it from memory. It was as if Hutchings, Millard, Stair, and Ayres had stumbled into a living painting, with all the sacred import of a half-century of Romantic and religious culture conveying meaning to their eyes.[8]

For a man who had already set about deploying California landscape imagery and description to reshape California social mores, the symbolic treasure represented by Yosemite was more significant to Hutchings than the piles of gold haunting the dreams of so many of his compatriots. With Ayres' sketches in hand, Hutchings returned to San Francisco to inaugurate the next phase of his career, a publishing firm dedicated to interpreting California culture and landscapes in print. For the next six years, Hutchings continuously produced and reproduced stories, images, and guided trips of and to Yosemite as a central motif in his publications. The narratives and images of Yosemite that graced these texts were part of Hutchings' broader efforts to "portray [California's] beautiful scenery and curiosities; to speak of its mineral and agricultural products; to tell of its wonderful resources and commercial advantages; and to give utterance to the inner life and experience of its people . . . the lights and shadows of daily life."[9]

In his enthusiastic promotion of California's positive attributes, including industrialization, agriculture, urban growth, and natural scenery, Hutchings shared a booster identity with many other western writers and promoters of the nineteenth century. These boosters sought to portray "their western places as promised lands because they desperately wanted their own dreams to be realized."[10] However, the themes and content of Hutchings' publications are not completely explained only by a desire to promote the uncontrolled expansion of California's economy. In his miscellany collections of fiction, poetry, history, and many-faceted descriptive essays, Hutchings appears primarily motivated, as he said, to "give utterance to the . . . life and experience of its people," by whom he means, not the indigenous inhabitants who had occupied California for millennia, nor the Californios of the Mexican-Spanish period, but the newly arrived Anglo tribes. In the contents of Hutchings & Rosenfield's midcentury publications, we can see that Hutchings drew upon his English past in promoting science, education, general Protestant sensibility, sentimental fiction and poetry, and scenic landscapes—all key components of Anglo bourgeois culture.

It would seem natural enough that a man of Hutchings' taste and ambition would seek to promote his favored interests in his own publications. But placed within the context of California's midcentury growth as a node in the expansion of Anglo global power, Hutchings' publications illustrated the cultural dimension of efforts to bring the resources of the Pacific Rim into the expanding industrial empires of Europe and America. By reconfiguring California landscapes and inhabitants from the exotic and fantastic into the familiar if sometimes "wonderful" and "curious," Hutchings worked to transform Anglo visitors into settlers and residents. These residents, stable middle-class families preferably, were to replace the chaos of the gold rush with institutions of social order like schools and churches, the polyglot world with an orderly English-speaking social hierarchy organized according to race, ethnicity, and class.

Hutchings expressed his belief in the power of bourgeois aesthetics and institutions to solidify California society in multiple ways: from the very formats he chose to convey his ideas, like lithographic prints, monthly magazines, and almanacs, to his constant celebration of such aesthetics and institutions. It is within this particular social agenda that one understands the initial creation of Yosemite not as the prophetic vision of proto-environmentalists, but as a

symbol of divine order to help transform the chaotic fluidity of gold-rush society into an orderly world of middle-class Anglo institutions. But even beyond Hutchings' individual effort is the relationship between landscape and
imperialism posited by W. J. T. Mitchell, who raised "the possibility that the
representation of landscape is not only a matter of internal politics and national or class ideology," as it would be for Hutchings, "but also an international, global phenomenon, intimately bound up with the discourses of imperialism."[11] From this perspective, the timing of Yosemite's inauguration
as an icon at just the moment that San Francisco began to consolidate its economic power over hinterland resources and Pacific Rim markets is no mere
coincidence. The relationships between these phenomena are explored in
more detail in chapter 4.

The Mountain, the Metropolis, and the "Law of the Few"

On his way back from visiting Yosemite, Hutchings quickly wrote an
article for the Mariposa *Gazette*—a snippet of long-lost ephemera that turned
up in the mid-1990s in the scrapbook acquired by the Yosemite Library. The
raggedy column was prized by collectors because it was the first printed account of Yosemite. However, Hutchings did something else upon his return
that was almost as important to building the iconography of Yosemite yet has
been largely ignored by historians and collectors alike. He visited his friend,
the Reverend William A. Scott, and "the subject of the scenery of the Yo Semite was discussed, and sketches shown." Scott and Hutchings arranged for a
trip to the valley, and upon his return Dr. Scott "gave several eloquent discourses and published some tersely written articles upon it."[12]

These days, Reverend William A. Scott is not a name often associated with
Yosemite history or much else for that matter, but in his time and place he
was an influential individual. He had come to San Francisco as a Presbyterian
minister from New Orleans and led the congregation of Calvary Church, spiritual home of many of the city's business and cultural elites. That Hutchings
sought to bring the word and image of Yosemite to a clergyman as part of
his early publicity campaign illustrates one important dimension of the San
Francisco–Yosemite story.[13]

William Anderson Scott was a leading figure in a community strenuously
seeking to establish a sense of middle-class stability rooted in Protestant the-
ology. In turning first of all to Scott, Hutchings was sharing his new find with
a kindred spirit, a man who, according to his writings, found deep parallels
between Protestant Christianity and science, particularly the science of geol-

ogy. Although I have not been able to find Scott's "tersely written articles" specifically about Yosemite, he discoursed more generally on the connections between landscape/geology and social morality and order in tracts and articles published by Hutchings & Rosenfield.[14] We can assume that such connections formed common themes in his Sunday sermons to the midcentury San Francisco bourgeoisie. By late summer, when Hutchings returned from Yosemite, he was only just getting his own publishing business off the ground and very likely did not have the widespread recognition that Scott did, so Scott's enthusiastic reception of Hutchings' Yosemite message was important in generating early interest among San Francisco residents. Scott's status in the community gave his enthusiasm for Yosemite special weight; and his writing, lecturing, and sermonizing on the subject was an important early step in the creation of Yosemite as an icon even though his name has long vanished from the chronicles of the area.

If Hutchings continued to keep a daily record of his doings after the diary of 1854–1855, it has been lost to historians. But assuming that the social patterns that Hutchings engaged in during that year continued through his lifetime, we can infer that he was a gregarious, outgoing person who cultivated many friendships, especially with influential and intellectually engaging individuals. Hutchings' diary offers a rare glimpse into the importance of his sociability to the creation of Yosemite as an icon. "Went home with Rev'd I. P. Brayton, Ed[itor] of Pacific—. . . Spent the evening in pleasant conversation with Mr. Ayres on pictures, artists and drawings—He has some beautiful views I ordered one view of his sketching of the Golden Gate (entrance to San Francisco Bay) for whc' I am to pay $75—and have the right to publish it."[15]

A couple of days later, Ayres and Hutchings continued to develop their relationship with a daylong walk to the coast and Fort Point, and a month later the two were touring the Yosemite Valley. Hutchings had met I. P. Brayton the year before in Placerville, and so by continuing the social practice of afternoon teas and evening visits, Hutchings reinforced old ties and developed new ones, deeply instrumental to his professional work. Even without the diary, Hutchings & Rosenfield's publications contain ample evidence that Hutchings' social network contributed significantly to the creation of California identity in this venue. Granville Sproat, his boardinghouse landlord, wrote poetry and children's stories for *Hutchings' California Magazine*, as did Albert Kellogg, botanist and founder of the California Academy of Science. Kellogg and Hutchings remained lifelong friends, frequently venturing into the Sierra to explore new mountain reaches and discover new species. Several other influential San Francisco leaders wrote regularly for Hutchings during this time, including W. A. Scott.

Hutchings' diary and publications point to the importance of his individual personality and social networking skills in building the California audience for Yosemite iconography. Malcolm Gladwell points to the critical roles played by "salesmen," "connectors," and "mavens" in launching a tipping point. Hutchings, a consummate salesman and connector, instinctively recognized W. A. Scott as a San Francisco emerging maven: "There are people specialists, and there are information specialists. Sometimes, of course, these two specialties are one and the same."[16] If, as Gladwell argues, the personality traits of individuals are more important to furthering the spread of an idea even with all our high-speed communications technology, how much more true was this in mid-nineteenth-century California with its fledgling mail system and still many years away from telegraph or effective transportation? Clearly, Hutchings' face-to-face networking was simply the primary method of communication in that world, so he was not unique in this regard. But it was the compound chemistry of Hutchings' own skills and social ties, his passion for the California mountains, and the particular contexts of Anglos settling into and building California that helped make the idea of Yosemite as an icon first tip and "spread like wildfire."

The Cultural Work of Hutchings' California Magazine

One place where it is possible to reconstruct some of the strands binding together Hutchings' network of associates is in the pages of his periodical, *Hutchings' California Magazine*. This monthly, published between 1856 and 1861, became the central and most famous of Hutchings' publishing ventures. Many of Hutchings & Rosenfield's other publications, such as the travel guide *Scenes of Wonder and Curiosity*, were simply reprints of material reworked from this original context. Of all Hutchings' publications in this period, *Hutchings' California Magazine* is the most familiar, at least to historians. Devoted to portraying "the lights and shadows of daily [California] life," each issue contained "Forty-Eight pages of interesting Reading Matter, in double columns, with several Illustrations of the Scenery, Incidents, Curiosities and Resources of [California]."[17]

The illustrations were among the magazine's greatest selling points. Averaging seven per issue, the engravings, some original to the magazine, many reprinted from letter sheets, highlighted articles on California tourist destinations, essays on flora and fauna, and an occasional biographical portrait.

Hutchings' California Magazine, *cover illustration, May 1857. Hutchings'*
magazine was an important forum for California's emerging middle classes
from 1856 to 1861. (Private collection)

Although there were other illustrated California periodicals in the 1850s, such as the *Wide West*, none boasted the number and quality of illustrations of *Hutchings' California Magazine*. Indeed, *Hutchings' California Magazine* was in many ways a pioneer publication.[18] San Francisco had hosted two literary periodicals, the *Golden Era* and the *Pioneer*, but neither was illustrated and both were short-lived. In its range of material, if not the quality of writing, *Hutchings' California Magazine* anticipated Bret Harte's *Overland Monthly*, which continued in various formats from the 1860s until the end of the century. With its range of topics, from scientific essays to sentimental poetry, it has served as a repository of information for several generations of California historians. In this way, Hutchings' vision continued to inform the creation of California identity for decades even after his publications ceased.

Hutchings relied on unpaid contributors, an economical strategy, but also an effort to promote literary talent in California. Many of these authors remained anonymous or signed with initials; women and men are represented almost equally in published contributions that were signed, and some children's writings were published as well. It is also impossible to ascertain the percentage of articles outside of his regular columns that Hutchings wrote himself. His "Monthly Chat with Correspondents" column indicates that readers from all over the northern portion of the state submitted work. These included "G. H. R., Secret Diggings"; "C. D., Springfield"; "Exeter, Upper Placerville"; "A., Downieville"; "Jessica, Sonora"; and "A., Oroville."[19] Far fewer notices were directed to anyone south of Monterey. The geographical locales identified in Hutchings' correspondence to contributors suggest that the *California Magazine*'s distribution range paralleled his 1854–1855 travels through the central and northern reaches of the state. It is likely that the personal connections he made during that year of travel were the basis for these contributions.

His reliance on friends to supply written material for publication highlights how Hutchings used his work to continuously develop and reinforce his relationships with those who were or aspired to be California's cultural elite. Signed pieces demonstrate Hutchings' reliance on his social circle for contributions: Albert Kellogg, William Anderson Scott, Anna Bates, and Granville T. Sproat were regularly featured authors. Dr. Albert Kellogg was cofounder of the California Academy of Science and an amateur botanist, and Scott, as discussed, was the popular minister of San Francisco's Presbyterian Calvary Church.

When he moved to San Francisco, Hutchings resided at the new boardinghouse owned and operated by Granville and Florantha Sproat with whom he developed a lifelong relationship. Florantha Thompson was the daughter of Cephas Thompson, a portraitist in Middleborough, Massachusetts. She married Granville Temple Sproat in 1838, and together they moved to La Pointe, Wisconsin, where they both taught in the Ojibway Indian Mission. Florantha and Granville's two daughters were born in Wisconsin before they moved back to Middleborough, then to San Francisco in 1854, where Florantha ran the boardinghouse. Granville wrote poetry and children's literature and contributed children's stories to *Hutchings' California Magazine*, which were later collected and published by Hutchings & Rosenfield as *Uncle John's Stories for Good California Children*.[20] In 1860 Hutchings married Elvira, the Sproats' seventeen-year-old daughter; later, Granville drifted away from his family, eventually joining a New York Shaker colony.

Following the popular nineteenth-century format of a miscellany, *Hutchings' California Magazine* published a broad variety of content: humor, poetry, scientific analyses, and social commentary. Hutchings kept the price of the magazine low at 25 cents per issue and frequently published stories romanticizing yeoman miners, indicating that he continued to see the hinterland miners as an important audience for his work. But the magazine took on a stronger bourgeois flavor than the letter sheets had, suggesting that Hutchings hoped to cultivate a more middle-class audience as well.

It is important to note that at this point in history the fluid social matrix of midcentury California complicates the notion of class beyond its already fraught definitions. Economic "class" in terms of wealth or poverty was often very different from one's cultural sensibilities, as impoverished miners had often been raised in well-to-do homes back East while illiterate "nabobs" could rise to sudden and extravagant wealth. Perhaps Hutchings was looking not so much to address the middle-class audience as to actually *create* it, to bring it forth through his various efforts in promoting bourgeois institutions and values. In this, Hutchings was not unique among midcentury publishers throughout the Anglo world. What made his work different was the consistent and ongoing emphasis on California landscapes as the vehicle for cultivating this bourgeois sensibility.

The Power of Context: Economy, Technology, and Society

Although Hutchings seems to have continued marketing his wares to miners, as California's economy industrialized, his publications increasingly expressed paternalistic assumptions about industrial capitalism in which potentially "unruly" working-class sorts benefited from the "discipline" of industrial work. For example, in *The Pavilion Palace of Industry*, a pamphlet commemorating the first exhibition of the San Francisco Mechanics' Institute, Hutchings and his friend William A. Scott celebrated industrial growth while seeking to maintain orderly social relations.[21] The text was the print version of Scott's "discourse delivered in Calvary Church," entitled "The Mechanics' Industrial Exhibition, or the Useful Arts: Exponents of the Nature, Progress, and Hope of Christian Civilization."[22] The cover displayed a W. C. Butler engraving of two men clasping hands in front of a beehive set on a pedestal. The man on the left wore a leather apron and carried a hammer in his right hand, while the man on the right wore a suit and vest and held a scroll of paper and compass in his left hand. The iconography of this image was fairly straightforward. It symbolized the union of the workingman and the thinking man for the good of the whole.[23] With the increasing industrialization of California and the prospect of factory toil from which migrants from the East had intended to escape, men such as Hutchings and Scott may have recognized in the advent of industry the potential for worker discontent as much as for "progress on the Pacific coast." Like the iconography of the cover, Scott's address also imagined the unity of workingmen with thinking men, but it did so to ultimately configure the thinking men as superior to, and "naturally" in charge of, the workers.[24]

This symbolism expresses the philosophy underlying mechanics' institutes in general—as fraternal organizations for workingmen, supported if not initiated by men in managerial positions, they were meant to replace radical unionization with a form of organized self-improvement. The Mechanics' Institute of San Francisco was one of the longest-lived of such institutions in the United States. One noteworthy feature of the *Pavilion Palace* was Scott's invocation of nature, particularly geology, as a model for understanding and organizing industrial social relations, echoing the Victorian preoccupations of Hutchings' native England. Hutchings and Scott clearly agreed on the interconnectedness of religion and science and the utility of both in organizing an orderly society. As visitation to Yosemite increased over the decades, the rhetoric of both science and religious sublimity continued to be central to the proliferating discourse over Yosemite's iconographic landscapes.

As the initial context for that discourse, the publications of Hutchings & Rosenfield reveal the central role of California's culture makers, and their ideas about the society in which they worked, in shaping the meaning of Yosemite. Hutchings' social circle of ministers and scientists, educators, writers, and artists gave voice to the Anglo value of linking landscape imagery and description to social order, constituting the power of the few to express the emerging new idea—or, more accurately, to adapt the old ideas into a new context. The intended audiences for these publications, who were literate, English-speaking fellow bourgeoisie, yeoman miners, women, children, and working-class folk—also suggest the importance of the social context giving rise to Yosemite's iconographic status.

Some of those audience did, indeed, respond to Hutchings' vision, comprising the early trickle of consumer tourists into the valley, purchasing and displaying Hutchings' lithographs, or simply reading their way as "armchair tourists" into California's landscapes. Others of the intended audience may very well have rejected Hutchings' exhortations toward moral value and self-improvement or may have been among the rural entrepreneurs who took their summer livelihood into the mountains to capitalize on the nascent tourist trade. And beyond the circle of writers and intended audience were all the other citizens of California—the multiethnic, non-English-speaking people who also worked to build (or rebuild) their homes in this chaotic place, but who were deliberately excluded from the Anglo vision of divine, orderly "progress" embodied in the sublime features of Yosemite.

The Yo-Hamite Falls

The first public visual image of Yosemite is an artifact that embodies the diverse strands of culture, technology, ideology, and economy informing the regional stage of Yosemite iconography, and its significance stretches forward through the centuries of Yosemite image making. Born of Hutchings' first trip into the valley, the initial image was sketched onto sandpaper by Thomas Ayres in the summer of 1855. Upon his return to San Francisco in August, Hutchings commissioned lithographers Kuchel and Dresel to commit the image to stone. Britton and Rey printed it, and Hutchings sold the prints for $2.50 each. Entitled "Yo-Hamite Falls" (after the place-name provided by the party's Miwok guides), the lithograph portrays towering cliffs surrounding the graceful cataract. Depicting the falls from a slightly elevated position, the image places the vertical lines of the falls and mountains in balance with the horizontal lines dividing upper falls from the lower, and the bottom of the cliffs from the meadow foreground. In the bottom third of the image, park-like grasslands studded with oak and pine stretch toward the viewer, bisected by the meandering Merced. In the near foreground, horses graze in the meadows while a group of travelers surrounds a campfire. Below the image, Hutchings printed the title, "The Yo-Hamite Falls" and the caption: "This magnificent scene is situated in the Yo-Hamite Valley near the source of the middle fork of the river Merced, Mariposa County California.

It is the highest waterfall in the world—rushing over the precipice, at one bold leap it falls 1,300 feet—the whole hight [*sic*] from the Valley is 2,300 feet" (see "The Yo-Hamite Falls" by Thomas A. Ayres).

In producing this piece, Hutchings drew on San Francisco's substantial technical resources, his own professional and social networks, and the cultural resources built over decades of Euro-American landscape interpretation keying the sublime to such features as waterfalls, cliffs, and gentle meadows. His intended audience would have been solidly middle class—at $2.50, it was beyond the reach of most miners. At the same time, it is noteworthy that Hutchings' effort to capture the image translated to a commercial publication rather than, say, an oil painting. The painting would have been a one-time representation, something to own and display, while the lithograph would appeal to a broader audience. The choice was clearly an entrepreneurial one for Hutchings—he did intend to make money by his efforts. But that fact does not negate the other fact, which is that Hutchings also wanted to make Yosemite "known to all," its symbolic significance accessible to a wide audience. In this, he was simultaneously entrepreneurial and democratic—interested in disseminating the beauty and cultural value of a place to a broad audience as well as in the profit it might bring him.

In the "Yo-Hamite Falls" image, Ayres dutifully frames and arranges the physical features into the conventions of European landscape art: alternating bands of light and dark dividing the near, middle, and distant planes; the miniscule figures in the foreground standing in for us, the viewers; and the emphasis on the falls themselves as familiar symbols of the sublime in nature. The conventionality of Ayres' depiction would make it quite boring if it were not for its unique quality in the range of landscape depictions at play in Anglo California at the time. Prior to 1855, for the vast majority of non-Indian Californians, the most important purpose of landscape depiction was to locate resources (gold, of course, but also water, timber, and foodstuffs) and to make the path to those resources clear—that is, through maps. Like the maps, representations of urban scenes and settlements through the elevated "bird's-eye view" format served the commercial purpose of orienting visitors, "boosting" a location with the image of permanence, and providing an advertising vehicle for sponsors.

Hutchings' lithograph also signaled a transformation in the cultural meaning of the Sierra Nevada themselves. For thousands of years, California and Nevada Amerindians called the Sierra their summer hunting grounds, and several high-country plateaus served as annual gathering sites for tribes on both sides of the range to trade and conduct festivals. When the 1846 Donner Party became stranded by early snows, many of its members starved to death or resorted to cannibalism. This disaster, repeated in the sensationalist press, established the Sierra as a fatal danger zone—the final barrier in a bitter overland struggle that would test the mettle of would-be settlers and miners. The Sierra as a threat to progress and individuals was repeated in countless illustrations and stories throughout the gold rush and early 1850s—including the imaginary scenario of Yosemite itself as a "fortress" where previously competitive bands of Indians could convene in a war council and descend upon the foothill communities— that launched the Mariposa Battalion in 1851. Although Hutchings was attracted to the mountains from his first encounter with the Carson Pass, many more Californians in the early 1850s preferred to settle in areas where transportation was easier and climate more conducive to farming.

A travel narrative entitled "A Trip to Walker's River and Carson Valley" expresses some of this perception of the Sierra as a danger zone. Published in the April 1858 issue of *Hutchings' California Magazine*, the story described a journey from the previous September, when a party of four men left the charred remains of the town of Columbia to embark on "a journey of adventure and, mayhap, discovery, to the little known . . . Walker's River." Twenty-seven days later, the party returned "where our friends met us with some doubts as to our identity, so disguised were we under our sunburnt skins and tattered habiliments."[25] The adventure took the anonymous party on a 450-mile loop over the Sierra, into Carson Valley, then back over the Sierra on the Hope Valley trail down into the Big Trees grove. Traveling by horseback with pack mules, they took with them "tools for prospecting, guns for hunting, fishing-tackle for fishing," and two dogs.[26]

In writing his narrative of the journey, the author, identified only as *.*.*., cast the journey to Nevada as a difficult, even harrowing one that continually contrasted the "civilization" of California with the "wilderness" of Nevada.[27] As the party ascended to Strawberry Flat, the author noted the presence of Tuolumne County water company ditches, and the party even took a detour to visit the reservoir at Strawberry Flat (warranting an illustration). These signs of progress and civilization gave way to the wrecked wagons and skeletal remains of livestock littering the "old" emigrant road of 1852 (a whole five years old at the time of this journey, and probably still in use).[28] Evoking the mountain passes as sites of death and danger, "*.*.*." recalled the dismal fate of the 1852 Clark-Skidmore party that ventured over Sonora Pass before the road was really constructed for wagon travel. The party lost several cattle in their efforts but were eventually rescued by relief parties from Columbia. "In many places where all signs of the trail were obliterated, we took our course by the whitened bones alone." The approach to the summit evoked ever-more foreboding descriptions: "We were now in a truly wild spot," "barren and dreary," "we threaded our way in gloomy silence": "Nothing of any description appeared to claim residence here but the little chipping squirrel, and he seemed to gain but a meager subsistence, judging from his puny appearance— not even a raven hovered about to breathe the gloomy silence with his ominous croak—all was dreary and cheerless, and we hastened our steps onward to find a more congenial scene."[29] The author described the route into Nevada as one of desolation and destruction, physically and conceptually distant from the civilization and warm climate of California. Passing over the "dreary and cheerless" pass, the party then descended into the eastern slopes of the Sierra and basin and range regions of western Nevada.

Although the journey from Strawberry Flat to Genoa (at the base of the eastern Sierra) occupied thirty-two columns of text, the story of the path back over the Sierra via Carson Pass only took two-and-a-half columns. Here, rather than dwelling on the mountain scenery, the author chose to emphasize the excellence of the road, in "strange contrast with that over which we passed in our outward journey." Shortly after crossing back over the summit, the party looked west over "the broad view of the receding hills, even to the valley of the San Joaquin before us" and felt "a thrill of devotion" to God upon realizing it was the Sabbath. It should be noted that *.*.*. took many, many liberties with the actual situation he traveled through, including the fact that the Sonora Pass saw several thousand parties and mule trains crossing safely every year after 1852. Despite the changing realities of trans-Sierra travel, the author of "A Trip" reinforces the older narrative of the Sierra as a danger zone.

By the time Hutchings published the "Yo-Hamite Falls" print, the Sierra was becoming more familiar and accessible to most Californians. Aggressive road-building efforts by local municipalities, ongoing Indian removals, and the construction of military forts had secured several trans-Sierra routes. These then enabled more frequent travel and the shipment of goods across the mountain chain, linking emergent Nevada communities and resources with San Francisco and other hinterland towns. Sierra forests were already becoming sources of lumber for town building and mines, while valley farmers on both sides of the range were beginning to summer their stock in the mountain meadows. "Yo-Hamite Falls" and Hutchings' subsequent *California Magazine* articles marked the shift in the cultural interpretation of the Sierra from a zone of disaster and danger into sites of renewal and redemption, just as Californians were "taming" the mountains into yet another dimension of San Francisco's economic hinterlands.

So, on one hand, "The Yo-Hamite Falls" was connected to strands of culture through its representation of European landscape art, and on the other to society through its audience of middle-class viewers (or those aspiring to middle-class status). In another aspect, it connects to economics on several levels. One is the economic diversification and stratification that gave rise to bourgeois values and sensibilities, thus making a market for this image viable. The second is the very fact that Hutchings deliberately set out to commodify Yosemite, even before he saw it, evidenced by the care he took to hire Ayres to join the traveling party. Hutchings intended to move his middle-class audience with the image alone, but for others who would be more impressed by statistics, he included the data about the height of the waterfall (as well as directions to get there) in the caption.

Hutchings introduced Yosemite as a potent symbol to link California with other sublime landscapes. But by doing so through a saleable commodity, he also recognized (and helped to create) Yosemite's economic value. Here is a controversial point because it exposes the mythic assumptions that Americans have created about Yosemite—that it is a "sacred" space, separated from if not antithetical to the workings of market capitalism. But this myth is itself part of the cultural work of landscape itself, as Mitchell points out: "At the same time that it commands a specific price, landscape represents itself as 'beyond price,' a source of pure, inexhaustible spiritual value,"[30] again, an insight that captures precisely what devout Protestants like Hutchings, the Reverend Scott, and Yosemite's more famous Christian spokesman, Thomas Starr King, saw in the place.

The "specific price" of the "Yo-Hamite Falls" print—$2.50—alludes to the economic network that supported and mediated the production of this symbol. Hutchings' plan to sell a couple hundred prints at $2.50 would allow him to recoup the costs of production (including the cost of the trip itself, allegedly financed by Rosenfield) and make a profit of about $1.00 per print. But the economic value of this print to Hutchings stretched beyond the specific object itself: it enabled Hutchings to position himself as the primary interpreter of and tour guide to Yosemite Valley. Along the way, through the pages of his *California Magazine*, the Almanac, more letter sheets, pamphlets, and other publications, Hutchings built up Yosemite's cultural capital along with that of other California landscapes, created a local tourism industry, and encouraged California residents to develop a sense of place rooted in the cultural appreciation of California's unique scenery.

In fostering this sensibility, Hutchings instigated a shift in the relationship between Anglos and California landscapes. Gold miners, farmers, and lumberjacks primarily worked the land, their relationship to the environment mediated by the tools of their trade. For them, the environment could be a source of wealth and it could also be a threatening, unpredictable force. Hutchings shifted this mediation into the realm of consumer culture—Californians could now purchase images of California places and absorb their meanings through print culture and photography. Many, no doubt, were content to remain armchair travelers, experiencing Hutchings' day trips vicariously through print. Others became inspired to see the places themselves; but even as they did so, their experience would have been mediated, defined, and to some degree predetermined by the images, text, and speeches that convinced them to go in the first place.

Again, this shift to consumer-based landscape appreciation mirrored the patterns that had already taken place in the eastern United States, England, and Europe. Consumer tourism had overrun Niagara Falls decades before, likewise with the great sublime destinations of the Lake District in England, the Alps in Europe. Hutchings and others were simply adapting the tried-and-true formula of Romantic tourism to the California context. In retrospect it seems to be a pretty unremarkable act. However, it is noteworthy that the "Yo-Hamite Falls" print and *Hutchings' Illustrated California Magazine* made their way into California's market and consciousness at precisely the moment that San Francisco began to consolidate its identity as a regional metropolis— that is, at the moment that San Francisco launched its imperial trajectory. How the remote mountain gorge became a powerful symbol in the context of San Francisco's expanding imperial and industrial engine is the subject of the next chapter.

Hutchings and Rosenfield in
the Print Metropolis

Although he would soon move there, Hutchings was unimpressed with the City by the Bay in the spring of 1855.[1] "People may say what they please in praise of San Francisco," he wrote, "but I do not ask to live where . . . you no sooner get fairly to going in the morning than you begin to perspire freely. If you are out by noon up comes a cloud of dust and sand that fills your eyes, ears, mouth and pockets, makes a store-house of your hat, and your coat! Who can tell the color of that? With the exudencies, your face is stuccoed."[2] Famously built on shifting sand dunes, San Francisco in 1855 was indeed a dusty, windy place with few indications of its future cosmopolitan greatness. Stone and brick buildings were beginning to replace the flimsy tents, clapboard structures, and reconstituted sailing ships that had posed enormous fire hazards in the early years. And, despite his June complaints, Hutchings apparently found enough in the "instant city's" potential to permanently relocate there by the end of the summer. In doing so, Hutchings paralleled the flow of material resources (such as profit from mining), which initially gathered in the mountain and foothill mining towns like Placerville, before ultimately collecting in San Francisco.

Prior to 1855, San Francisco had experienced seven years of turmoil, with a series of devastating fires, banking collapses, and Vigilance Committees attempting to establish law and order through ad hoc and completely unconstitutional lynch "trials." Cities like Benecia and Vallejo jostled with San Francisco to become the port of entry to California's river system. In 1854, the year Hutchings traveled through the northern mining towns, the inflated prices and expectations of the gold rush finally collapsed, bringing down several banking houses.[3] Seventy-seven bankruptcies were declared that year in San Francisco alone. In February 1855, the city faced a financial panic, "the most terrible financial storm that has ever devastated any community," according to William Tecumseh Sherman, whose own bank barely survived the series of runs. In 1855, over 200 firms declared bankruptcy.[4] Hutchings himself found out about the crisis on February 26 while sojourning in Yreka, near the Oregon border: "Was staggered upon going downstairs to find that Adams & Co. had suspended payment in their express offices. A messenger, in haste, arrived last night . . . Men rushed to draw out their deposits and every paper which was presented, having the signature of Cram & Rogers was paid, as though it hadn't happened to Adams & Co."[5] But, like the fires that cleared out makeshift buildings to make space for the new brick and stone structures, San Francisco's financial crises were the prelude to a rapid expansion and consolidation of economic power. In the decades after 1855 San Francisco rose to prominence as an imperial metropolis that controlled a vast hinterland territory and channeled goods and people throughout the Pacific Rim.

That Hutchings made his move at the same time that he published "The Yo-Hamite Falls" is a telling link between the city and the mountain valley. Hutchings was not the first white man to visit Yosemite: historians believe that explorer Joseph Walker's party was the first to witness and write about the place in 1835. The Mariposa Battalion had also, famously, chased the Miwok and Yokuts coalitions into and through the valley in 1851. There were probably several mountain men and other anonymous travelers who never reported or wrote down what they saw. Hutchings was different because he was the first person to see Yosemite *as landscape*. Indeed, Hutchings went to the valley fully prepared to see it that way, based on his journal entry from the year before: "A waterfall of a thousand feet—why Niagara is only 164 feet!" For Hutchings, as for every visitor since, Yosemite was "already artifice in the moment of its beholding, long before it became the subject of pictorial representation."[6]

Even without Hutchings, somebody would have "discovered" and packaged Yosemite as sublime landscape, because the moment was ripe in California's and especially San Francisco's trajectory. To help pull itself together, San Francisco needed the cultural power of an icon like Yosemite. Yosemite on the lips of W. A. Scott (and soon Thomas Starr King) gave San Francisco elites the vision of a greater purpose, a divine sanction, a symbol of urban greatness with the moral authority to dominate the hinterland regions and Pacific resources. Yosemite, as an icon, provided potent symbolic power to

Charles Christian Nahl, sketch of Sacramento Street, San Francisco 1854. Midcentury San Francisco was a dusty place with few indications of its future cosmopolitan greatness. (Courtesy Bancroft Library, University of California, Berkeley)

San Francisco elites, and San Francisco provided the technological, material, and cultural resources to develop that icon and make it "known to all men."

Imperial San Francisco

San Francisco's rapid growth mirrored, and was supported by, the astonishing pace of midcentury California's industrialization and economic diversification. By 1850, California's industrial output had skyrocketed from almost nothing at all during the Spanish and Mexican period to rank sixteenth among the thirty-six states and territories. In the decade after the gold rush, California's industrial sector grew fivefold.[7] Mining itself rapidly industrialized throughout the 1850s, as hydraulic technology spread through the state. Most of the initial industries were developed to support mining but quickly spread to other sectors, such as clothing, food, transportation, and printing. Along with expanding agriculture, such industrialization reflected the diversification and independence of California's economy from the small-scale mining of the early gold-rush era. Economic changes led to the concentration of power in the hands of Anglo elites, and in the rising importance of San Francisco as the regional metropolis.

Nineteenth-century San Francisco has been the subject of wonder, admiration, and critique from numerous historians and geographers; including Earl Pomeroy, Gunther Barth (who coined the term "Instant City"), Eugene Moehring, and Gray Brechin. The city was the first in the United States to establish its economic base in the mining of precious metals. From this base, nineteenth-century capitalists in the city's stock market exchange financed the expansion of mining into Nevada and ultimately to the far-flung districts in Arizona and Idaho. At the same time, the city encouraged and benefited from California's ongoing economic diversification into cash-crop agriculture, industrial manufacturing, and other extractive industries such as lumbering and construction. The rapid expansion of economic activity created a remarkable city in a few short years. A decade after California's statehood, San Francisco had a population of nearly 57,000, multiple churches, theatres, professional associations, festivals, schools, and urban and interurban rail lines and was connected with the Atlantic coast via telegraph and overland mail. Among the many features of this urban world that appealed to Hutchings were his proximity to a growing network of friends and cultural events like the Shakespearean theatre where he spent several evenings.

But the city rose on the environmental damage wreaked in its hinterlands. Unsurprisingly, mining was the first, and for many years, the primary culprit. Even before the advent of hydraulic mining in 1853, miners dug out and rechanneled rivers to access gold nuggets that turned out to be eroding from fossil "tertiary" riverbeds buried hundreds of feet beneath the western foothills of the Sierra. The invention of hydraulic mining with monitors and explosives rapidly accelerated both the ability of miners to access these ancient riverbeds, and the environmental impact of mining. As high-powered blasts of water sheared away walls of earth, the slurry of mud and rocks poured into wooden sluices, where miners rocked away the stone and mud to reveal gold dust and nuggets in the riffles. By 1858, mining companies had built 5,726 miles of flumes, dams, and ditches across the Sierra watersheds to gather enough water for the pressure needed to blast away earth and rocks.[8]

The velocity of the water makes bowlders [*sic*] two feet in diameter jump twenty feet in the air when it hits them . . . Trunks of trees lying in the mine can be made to spin like straws or be hurled away many feet distant. [Yet] the real hydraulic mine presents a wild and desolate appearance . . . The force of the stream directed against the cliffs seems so enormous, and its visible results are so appalling, that ordinary drift . . . and quartz mining seem insignificant by comparison.[9]

Lawrence & Houseworth photograph, "Hydraulic Mine Near Smartsville, California," ca. 1860s. Hydraulic mining devastated the hinterland environment and fueled the growth of San Francisco's industrial engine. (Courtesy University of Nevada, Reno, Special Collections)

As hydraulic mining companies stripped forested hillsides to bedrock that remains barren to this day, the detritus of their efforts flowed into major rivers and spread out in the Great Central Valley below. As early as 1855, the Yuba, Feather, and American River canyons disgorged tons of mud and gravel (called "slickens") to bury valley farms in regular flood cycles greatly exacerbated by the effects of mining. During the thirty years before hydraulic mining was declared illegal by the courts in 1885, 40,000 acres of farmland and orchards were ruined and another 270,000 acres severely damaged. "The top branches of mature oaks poked out of streams braided across cobbled flood plains. In some narrow mountain canyons, rivers flowed over 150 feet of unstable debris washed down from the mines and poised to descend into the valley. It did not take an old-timer to remember deep, clear streams swarming with fish, or the meadows beside them now buried in mining waste." By the end of the nineteenth century, hydraulic mines had poured the equivalent of the earth dug from the Panama Canal as waste into San Francisco Bay.[10]

Industrial mining required, among other things, enormous quantities of wood—and lumbering extended the industry's environmental impact. In 1859, at the same time that hydraulic mining was establishing itself on the Sierra's western slope, silver strikes in Nevada's Washoe Mountains to the east launched another metropolis—Virginia City—around the Comstock Lode. Although Virginia City at its height was second only to San Francisco on the Pacific slope with 20,000 citizens, politically and economically it remained subservient to San Francisco's capitalists. The Comstock Lode supported a series of quartz mines characterized by deep underground tunneling. These tunnels—sometimes as many as 3,000 feet deep—were supported by the interlocking "square set" timbers invented by Philip Deidesheimer. These, together with the need for wood fuel to power Cornish water pumps and stamp mills, caused the Virginia City mines to consume 600,000,000 feet of lumber and 2,000,000 cords of firewood by 1880. The forests around Lake Tahoe and along the watershed of the Truckee and Carson rivers were completely denuded within a few decades, as forests on the western slope likewise were harvested to build the flumes of the hydraulic mines.

During the nineteenth century, farmers in the Central Valley sought to transform California's historic landscape of intermittent lakes into a controlled realm of immense agricultural production. Hydraulic mining's slickens greatly exacerbated California's natural cycles of drought and flood. Central Valley farming communities sought to protect themselves by building levees and drainage ditches, but these were only partially effective until the large-scale engineering projects of the New Deal in the 1930s. Even so, bonanza wheat, rice, and orchard crops replaced the wildlife-filled tule marshes, and roads replaced rivers as transportation arteries when mining's shoals blocked steamboat access to former transshipment centers. By the end of the 1850s, Hutchings would not have been able to repeat his steamship travels of five years prior, so clogged was the Sacramento River system by then.

Travelers to California frequently commented with dismay on the visible impact of mining and lumbering—especially after 1869, when the completion of the transcontinental railroad made such travel far easier than it had been. One famous section of the road, the turn called "Cape Horn," curved over the hydraulic mines at Dutch Flat, providing a panoramic view of the devastation. Mrs. Frank Leslie, of the New York periodical *Leslie's Illustrated Magazine,* wrote:

> A verdant and picturesque hill subjected to a course of this kind of hydropathy assumes, in a few days, the look of those sorts of landscapes Doré loves to depict in his Inferno: every particle of soil, trees, grasses, even the lighter rocks, are washed away, and lie in disordered masses at the foot, while the grim skeleton of the crag . . . remains ghastly, naked, desolate, a monument of man's unmistakable greed of gain and reckless sacrifice of everything that stands between it and himself.[11]

While she decried the destruction, she echoed a refrain common among nineteenth-century witnesses when she remarked that "it is to be devoutly hoped that the gold thus won is used somewhere and somehow to beautify the earth and its inhabitants, for surely the getting of it is defacing to both one and the other."

For Leslie, this hope turned out to be a prophecy—as several days later, she would find herself a guest of honor at the Belmont estate of William Ralston, founder of the Bank of California, who had made millions from the Comstock and California's mines. Quite literally, the devastation of the mines had indeed gone to beautify another part of the earth—at least, according to the nineteenth-century architectural and formal landscape aesthetic. In a parallel, though different sense, Yosemite's iconography was also part of this process. The cultural and financial industries born of mining and developed in the 1850s made the development of Yosemite as an icon of sublimity possible.

Deterritorial Enterprises: California Pictorial Almanac

What environmentalists today would call destruction, most nineteenth-century Anglos called "progress"—even those who disliked the devastation, say, of hydraulic mining, saw it as a "necessary evil" to the forward trajectory of Anglo civilization. If it took something as drastic as hydraulic mining to build a city like San Francisco out of the dusty, untamed wilderness that existed before, well, that was a trade-off that balanced out for the vast majority— just as it did for Miriam Leslie. The notion that a "sacrificial" landscape could be offset with a "sacred" or "beautified" one elsewhere is a powerful construct that underpins modern landscape ideology and becomes a crucial dynamic in the cultural creation of Yosemite as the original sacred landscape of the west.

Scholars of colonialism have coined the phrase "deterritorialization" to describe the process of transforming native environments into familiar landscapes that produce wealth within an imperial framework. Deterritorialization was both a conscious and unconscious process. Consciously, colonizers removed indigenous inhabitants through legal machinations and violence, introduced nonnative species like bees and wheat into the ecosystem, and harvested or extracted resources such as gold and lumber. Settlers unconsciously introduced exotic species to compete with natives through weed seeds attached to materials, or epidemics to which indigenes had no resistance. While the colonialization process in the Pacific slope has been well documented, few analysts have explored the cultural dimension of it, particularly the central role of Anglo print culture in accelerating and intensifying the process. Because California was first settled by Spanish, then Russian and Mexican colonists before the English speakers of the Atlantic and middle states arrived, it offers an excellent case study into the particular role of Anglo print culture in the process of colonization and empire building.[12]

Long before James Marshall discovered gold at Sutter's Mill in 1848, California hosted a diverse population of Spanish, Russian, Aleut, and more than a hundred Native American language groups. After the gold strike immigrants flocked to the West Coast, coming not only from the eastern seaboard of the United States, but also from such distant places as France, Chile, the Canton and Fukien provinces of China, Europe, Australia, and Hawai'i. Despite the cosmopolitan, polyglot population in midcentury California, after 1848 the state was very quickly dominated by English-language institutions. The ubiquitous role of the printing press in Anglo settlement patterns could explain why the Anglos rose to dominance so rapidly, even over the Californio families who had lived there for generations.

In the process of asserting military authority during the Mexican-American War in 1846, the U.S. Navy deployed the only printing press in California, an elderly Ramage locked away in a Monterey storage cabinet, to establish California's first newspaper. Newspaper historian Edward C. Kemble likened the

American adoption of the Ramage press to a liberation, imagining the "wonder and delight with which the hidden and dusty old type . . . broke the thralldom of their fettered speech" (i.e., Spanish) to perform "honest service in the King's English."[13] Within a decade this solitary newspaper had multiplied to more than 500; during the previous century of Spanish and Mexican rule, the northern frontiers had produced fewer than six. Kemble's chauvinistic rhetoric notwithstanding, this contrast does not prove that the United States was more literate than Mexico. Mexico had, in fact, established a thriving book trade centered in Mexico City. Instead the contrast reveals the importance of print to the relatively decentralized process of Anglo colonization. Where the Californios were content to receive their printed matter from distant capitals, Anglo Americans ensured that printing presses dispersed across the territory.

Newspaper and job printing offices supplied local communities with any number of essential tools and services. In addition to publishing newspapers that carried information about mining strikes, legal cases, and skirmishes with Indians, these offices also produced the slips of paper that ensured title to a piece of land, the right to mine it, receipts of deposits made, payments for labor. Additionally, the offices frequently carried books, blank books, maps, map-making and surveyor tools, and the legal forms necessary for land rights, water rights, and mineral-claims procedures. These tools facilitated the ability of ambitious miners, farmers, and lumberjacks to perform the process of deterritorialization, and in the early years of the gold rush printing presses were so valuable to communities that rivals sometimes stole or destroyed them in an effort to undercut the central power point of the settlement.[14]

Print culture in the American West was not only a feature of the institutions spread by settlers, but also an essential vehicle for their efforts to assert power over a cultural and physical landscape marked by diversity. Perhaps nothing demonstrates the role of print in the colonial process of deterritorialization better than the ubiquitous almanac: the ephemeral, cheap booklets and sheets that chronicled phases of the moon and tides and were among the most popular and widespread forms of print in Europe and America from the seventeenth to the nineteenth century. This became true in California at mid-century as elsewhere, and Hutchings & Rosenfield contributed six volumes of the *California Pictorial Almanac* from 1856 to 1861.

Like most almanacs, Hutchings & Rosenfield's *Pictorial* contained astronomical tables and charts for planting and harvesting, climatic predictions, and tide tables. True to its title, the *California Pictorial Almanac* also included numerous engraved illustrations, many accompanied by explanatory text.

These illustrations, several of which were also published in *Hutchings' California Magazine*, offered diverse images of California landscape and society. The almanac for 1861 contained no fewer than twenty illustrations, including "California wild flowers," "Taking out quartz and rock from the mines," "Residence of col. Fremont, Bear Valley, Mariposa County," and "The California Coyote."[15] The use of wood engravings to decorate almanacs had begun at the end of the eighteenth century in England and was soon followed by similar artistic efforts in America.[16] But among California almanacs in the late 1850s, Hutchings & Rosenfield's *Pictorial* contained far more engravings of a far higher quality than any other surviving publication. The multiple illustrations, and the high quality of printing and paper, suggested a finer product than many of the flimsier almanacs published at the same time. The images were also designed to appeal beyond the pragmatic applications of climatic predictions for farmers in the field or fishermen at sea. Almost exclusively images of California, they emphasized the curious and unique aspects of California's wildlife, landscapes, and history, as well as elements of California's developing infrastructure such as the postal service and the federal mint. Additionally, the *Pictorial* published two to four pages of advertisements, most of which were for San Francisco businesses and several of Hutchings & Rosenfield's other publications.

In addition to the engraved illustrations, the *California Pictorial Almanac* included brief articles, tables of distances, poetry, and humorous aphorisms. In the daily tables recording the tides, sunrise, sunset, and phases of the moon, Hutchings included English, American, and Californian historical facts. For example, in the month of January 1860, the almanac recorded:

Jan 6   Heavy fall of rain, 1850
Jan 7   California Star, first paper published in San Francisco by Sm'l Brannan, in 1847
Jan 8   Sacramento City destroyed by a flood, Jan 7–15, 1850
Jan 9   Severe Earthquake at San Francisco, 1854
Jan 10   Stamp Act passed the British Parliament 1765[17]

By giving California history a prominent role (around 60 percent of all the historical briefs), Hutchings clearly hoped to give his adopted state a historical, as well as visual identity.

When they published their first almanac in 1856, Hutchings & Rosenfield joined a burgeoning field among California's printers and publishers. Although the *California Star* had printed the first California almanac in 1848, and other newspapers such as the *Alta California* had continued to do so during the gold rush, almanacs proliferated significantly after 1854. In 1856, California presses produced at least eight different almanacs, more than were published altogether in the six years from 1848–1853.[18] From this year until the end of the nineteenth century, publishers all over the state, but especially in San Francisco, produced almanacs ranging from extremely flimsy pamphlets to elaborate volumes complete with colored-ink pages. Californians published almanacs in English, French, German, and Spanish and for specialized markets such as Catholics and merchants.

It is not surprising that almanacs should appear so quickly on the California publishing scene. Almanacs have a long tradition in western civilization, frequently claiming the status of "first printed" in contexts from Gutenberg's press to the British frontiers of North America and Australia. In America and England, printers found a ready market for almanacs from the sixteenth to the nineteenth century.[19] Printers hoping to secure steady income would rely on a genre with such an established history. James Mason Hutchings was well acquainted with English almanacs: he jotted down notes during his journey from England to America in the *Gentleman's Pocket Almanack*, published in 1841 by Denny & Son of London.[20] Almanacs performed numerous functions, most significantly as calendars to mark time and to identify moveable feast days in the Christian calendar. Through their astronomical and astrological calculations, almanacs predicted weather patterns and gave advice on the best times to plant, harvest, and perform medical operations.[21] Thus, almanacs both shaped and expressed the connections between humans and their environment in very concrete ways. Almanacs guided farmers in their planting cycles, sailors and fisherfolk in their seafaring, and families and midwives in the practice of medicine before the advent of professional doctors. In agricultural societies, such as England up to the end of the eighteenth century and America through the antebellum period, the popularity of almanacs indicates their usefulness to daily life. Maureen Perkins estimates that in England and Wales in 1800, "at the very least one in seven people bought a copy, and since almanacs were often used as family references, most people would have had access to a copy even if they had not bought one."[22]

Almanacs also functioned in Anglo colonial contexts around the world to acculturate settlers to environments that may have seemed disorienting or strange. They organized environmental information into tables, chronologically arranged around annual cycles of planting and harvesting. Phases of the moon, tidal action, the rising and setting of the sun, and other physical characteristics of earthly activity were presented in a form designed to assist farmers in planning their own annual activities. In a sense, almanacs translated landscape from a spatial form into a temporal one. Because the almanac was so familiar to European and American immigrants, it cast an otherwise foreign environment into familiar terms. In this way, almanacs performed a cultural function central to the colonizing process.[23]

There are other reasons why almanacs would have been a popular publication genre in the mid-1850s. By including illustrations and text, Hutchings & Rosenfield's *California Pictorial Almanac* extended the almanac's mediating role between the reader and the environment. Additionally, with the daily notices of California historical events, Hutchings constructed California as a place with a history as complex as, and interconnected with, the places from which Anglos had migrated. In doing so, he implicitly wove California's identity into that of the nation while simultaneously emphasizing its unique qualities. Furthermore, the *California Pictorial Almanac* subtly conveyed the notion that the Anglo presence in California was a natural occurrence, rather than the outcome of a bloody war with Mexico and continued violence against California Indians.

In their emphasis on the cycles of planting and harvesting, almanacs reinforced age-old assumptions about the relationships between humans and landscape as mediated through agriculture. Leo Marx described the Euro-American values associated with agricultural landscapes in art and literature as the "image of an undefiled, green republic, a quiet land of forests, villages, and farms dedicated to the pursuit of happiness."[24] Throughout the 1850s, visitors to and residents of California repeatedly exalted its potential for agriculture in positive contrast to the chaos and greed associated with mining, while ignoring the critical economic ties between mining and agriculture. As early as 1851, Robert H. Taylor wrote that "a spirit is now awakened, which we believe will not cease . . . til the whole valley of Sacramento be dotted with the smiling farmhouses and blooming fields of agriculturists, content to *dig the earth* where she will give up what will render the state of California richer and more permanently prosperous than all the products of the gold mines could make her."[25]

In casting agriculture as a positive alternative to mining, Taylor and other bourgeois moralists performed a similar act to Leslie's hopeful reimagining of the ultimate effects of mining—to beautify some other landscape elsewhere. Drawing on the Euro-American pastoral aesthetic stretching back to Thomas Jefferson, they tapped deep cultural roots to obscure the reality of 1850s California—far from being an antidote to mining, agriculture in the first decades was inextricably linked to it. While barley had been the principal grain grown by California farmers prior to 1848, the miners' demands caused wheat to become the major grain by 1860, when nearly six million bushels were grown. Similarly, miners' demands for mutton and wool encouraged the California sheep population to grow from 20,000 in 1849 to a million by 1860. Likewise, the products of viticulture and orchards flowed to mining communities. Farms large and small were financed with mining's proceeds, the products geared toward mining markets, and, like mining, the profits of agriculture increasingly gathered into the hands of San Francisco capitalists.[26]

The Print Metropolis

Almanacs were one of the most obvious artifacts of print culture linking the business, technology, and ideology of print to the multifarious process of deterritorialization and colonization of California landscapes into the Anglo cultural empire. While San Francisco in the 1850s and 60s was connected to the Atlantic economically and politically, its connections to the Pacific Rim created a unique imperial dynamic far different from the traditional understanding of the "frontier outpost." But the almanac was only one genre among a dizzying variety of publications produced in the center of San Francisco—the print district that occupied the same physical space in the city as the engines of finance and capital that greased the wheels of hinterland development. San Francisco's metropolitan growth was attended by a tremendously rich print culture—printers and booksellers, lithographers and newspaper offices—all centered in the same area of the city that controlled the flow of capital and finances throughout the Anglo Pacific slope. Hutchings' expanded publishing activities reveal consistent efforts to utilize the dramatic technological developments in California's print culture to exploit changes in the region's population and economy. Their imprints reveal that Hutchings & Rosenfield patronized a variety of printers, including Sun Print; Excelsior Print; Whitton, Towne, & Co.; and Charles F. Robbins.

This was easy to do, for the location of their office and shop placed Hutchings & Rosenfield in the center of the San Francisco printing district.[27] An area three blocks long and two blocks wide, the district contained around thirty businesses dealing in some aspect of print culture—booksellers, stationers, job printers, paper suppliers, lithographers, and engravers. Hutchings apparently invested in his own plates early on, for despite the diversity of Hutchings & Rosenfield's publications, they repeat many of the same illustrations and text. Although Hutchings was never at a loss for words, visual imagery was a far more eloquent medium to express the "wonder and curiosity" of

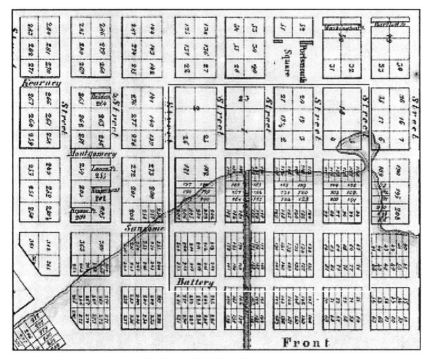

San Francisco Print District Key

San Francisco Print District and Key, 1850s. At the corner of Clay and Montgomery, Hutchings and Rosenfield were at the center of the San Francisco print district, an area three blocks long and two blocks wide containing around thirty businesses dealing in some aspect of print culture. (Reprinted from Proceedings of the American Antiquarian Society *14, pt. 1 [2004])*

Yosemite and other California landscapes, so the availability of artists, lithographers, and printers was crucial to the proliferation of landscape imagery and the early iconography of Yosemite. It is possible that the close proximity of so many print-related businesses helped to shape Hutchings' decision to remain in California and publish. The ready availability of printers and lithographers, as well as California's market for printed goods, may have convinced him that staying was a more feasible option than returning to England, a frequent theme of his earlier journals. Hutchings branched out from the letter sheet business at the same time that California's print culture was becoming remarkably more diverse. Lithographic prints, illustrated newspapers such as the *Wide West*, books, sheet music, broadsides, and other ephemera became more widely available in the mid-1850s. Additionally, imported wares, including books, expanded dramatically after 1855. California presented a seemingly insatiable market for printed materials, and importers as well as local publishers were ready to supply them.[28]

Print technology also illustrates another link between Yosemite's development and San Francisco's metropolitan expansion. By locating their shop in downtown San Francisco, Hutchings & Rosenfield placed themselves at the geographical center of printing in California, indeed the entire Pacific Slope. San Francisco's central importance in the print trades accompanied its growth as a regional metropolis in every sense of the word. The San Francisco printing district where Hutchings & Rosenfield located their business also housed the banks, attorneys, and real estate agents that fueled San Francisco's growing command of its hinterland resources.[29] The spatial proximity between print and the city's financial and legal institutions mirrors print culture's central role in consolidating the city's regional authority and bourgeois institutions, illustrating the links between print culture and power on the Pacific Slope. Printers and publishers were essential to the process of developing capital for the new mining technologies. Not only did they produce promotional material to attract investment; they also printed the maps that directed people and materials to the mines, the bills of remuneration for those materials, the account books for merchants and miners, and the stock certificates that symbolized the flow of capital. Many of these printing jobs were filled in San Francisco: the printing firm of Towne & Bacon had clients throughout the state, as well as in Oregon, Idaho, and Nevada.[30]

To fuel this growing trade, local entrepreneurs developed regional sources of essentials such as paper, type, and book-binding materials. From the mid-1850s, San Francisco printers, engravers, and lithographers commanded increasingly sophisticated technology. In 1856 the Commercial Steam Book and

Job Printing company claimed to possess "one of the largest Mammoth Presses," with which it was "prepared to execute Poster & Show-Bill Printing."[31] In 1859 printer Charles F. Robbins advertised himself as "agent for the sale of Ruggles' Celebrated Job Printing presses."[32] San Francisco had its first type foundry in 1853; J. M. Burke & Co. of San Francisco had established the first regional stereotype foundry by 1855, and in 1856, the Taylorville paper mill north of San Francisco gave publishers access to a local source of paper.[33] With such resources at their disposal, the Clay Street publishers and booksellers purveyed an expanding range of printed materials: from imported books to locally produced lithographic prints, from cheap almanacs to antique European volumes. Several of these dealers advertised their wares in numerous languages: French, German, Spanish, Swedish, and Chinese. In 1854, twenty-two of California's fifty-seven newspapers were printed in San Francisco.[34] Not until the 1880s would Portland, Oregon, then developing as a center of paper production, be able to compete with San Francisco even for local business. San Francisco's command of print resources underwrote its economic dominance of the entire Pacific Slope region until the end of the century.

Photography and the "Seeing Eye for Beauty"

Many publishers, like Hutchings, used daguerreotype photography as the basis for engravings and lithographic prints, stimulating the growth of photographic technology in San Francisco concurrent with the rise of the print district. Boston-born daguerreotypist R. H. Vance, one of San Francisco's most prominent commercial photographers, arrived in the city from Valparaiso, Chile, in December 1850. By 1851, Vance had established a gallery and began taking numerous photographs of California scenes, including mining operations, Indian communities, and satellite towns.[35] Photographic technology advanced quickly in California—by the late 1850s, the collodion process made it possible to reproduce prints from a single image. With the ready availability of silver nitrate from the nearby Comstock Lode, photography flourished. Over the nineteenth century, some of the great American photographers made California their home, including James Weed, Carleton Watkins (who started out working for Vance), and Eadweard Muybridge.

Photographers, like printers, spread out over the mining camps to take portraits of Argonauts and to document the mining process and various other aspects of Anglo California. Although Vance experimented with gallery displays of daguerreotype images, most such images were either produced for individual consumption (as with portraits), or used as the basis for reproducible

NEAR VIEW OF THE YO-SEMITE FALLS.—2,550 FEET IN HEIGHT.
From a Photograph by C. L. Weed.

"*Near View of the Yo-Semite Falls . . . from a Photograph by C. L. Weed,*"
James Mason Hutchings, Scenes of Wonder and Curiosity in California,
originally published in Hutchings' California Magazine, *1859.*

prints such as engravings and lithographs. Hutchings frequently carried a daguerreotype apparatus on his tours through the mining districts, but he also hired artists such as Ayres and Jump to capture the scenes. He may have found the daguerreotype too delicate or unpredictable for his purposes then, but he continued to experiment with the technology throughout his life. He brought the first photographer, Charles Leander Weed, into Yosemite Valley in 1859 and throughout his life continued to experiment with the medium. Weed's photographs became the core images for Hutchings' series of articles on Yosemite in the 1859–1860 issues of *Hutchings' California Magazine*.

Tourism and Travel

Regional travel played a starring role in the pages of *Hutchings' California Illustrated Magazine*, as Hutchings worked to develop a nascent tourism industry in and around California. Constituting an average of fifteen articles per volume, travel narratives were the most consistently and heavily illustrated topic in the magazine. Hutchings published his own and contributed articles and often overlapped travel stories with other themes such as promotion of local technological development. Yosemite was a prominent theme but not the only one, and placing Hutchings' promotion of Yosemite tourism within the context of other places illuminates once again the many strands binding Yosemite into the cultural and economic matrix of San Francisco's imperial development. For Hutchings as editor, tourism was the topic that really defined regional landscapes and made them accessible, literally and conceptually, to the California residents who formed his audience. In his tourist literature as elsewhere, Hutchings wove together several strands of antebellum culture, most prominently science and religion. In discussing California's landscapes in such powerful terms, Hutchings portrayed them as sites where California residents could create their own social identity. Doing so translated identity from a matter of income and status to one's relationship with the landscape. This could be true even for readers who could not afford the expense or leisure time to take their own journeys. Hutchings' narrative style, combined with the magazine's generous illustrations, invited readers to imagine themselves on the journey and in the landscape.

Travel narratives ranged from the elaborate journey required to reach Yosemite or the Carson Valley, to relatively simple day-trips out of San Francisco such as the trip to the Farallone Islands, or a chowder party on the coast.[36] The articles emphasized picturesque scenery, the practical elements of traveling such as transportation times and distances, some natural science, and perhaps a brief history. Hutchings subordinated scientific discourse, however, to the romantic, wild, sublime, and inspirational qualities of a given landscape. In his very first published account of the trip to Yosemite, Hutchings evoked the romantic sublime, casting his reaction to the first view of the valley in apocalyptic terms: "Can this be the opening of the Seventh Seal?"[37]

Once again, Hutchings was building off trends already established in the Atlantic world. While landscape tourism was well established in England by the end of the eighteenth century, in America it became a cultural force during the antebellum period. A combination of factors came together in the early decades of the nineteenth century to make recreational travel a cultural ideal for many Americans. Transportation networks became more efficient, comfortable, and reliable as railroads, canals, and steamships were developed. Such networks may have been originally designed to enhance commercial trade, but they also made destinations such as Niagara Falls or Mount Vernon accessible to increasing numbers of people. That tourism frequently ran along the same transportation networks of industrializing urban centers is one of the many dimensions linking the "sacred" landscapes of tourist destinations to the process of modernization.[38] As Americans with disposable income and leisure time began traveling to such destinations in the East, they created meanings and interpretations that contributed to nascent nationalist identities. Like their eastern counterparts, Hutchings' California tourists were more inclined to travel within the region—until 1869, the lack of a transcontinental railway made the prospect of travel to California purely for pleasure impractical for all but a few. Hutchings' images of California landscapes as packaged for tourists were designed to promote a regional understanding of place and to further strengthen a cultural identity linked to those landscapes.

In addition to pleasure trips, several of the travel narratives in *Hutchings' California Magazine* were geared more explicitly to San Francisco's emerging imperial identity. In "Notes and Sketches of the Washoe Country," the author relied on "the topographic knowledge and artistic skill of a gentleman recently returned from the rich silver mines" to describe Nevada communities in terms appealing to potential investors.[39] These were the "ridiculously" named Virginia City, Silver City, Devil's Gate, Carson City, and Genoa. Each town was described in terms of its population, its chief enterprises, the surrounding topography, and sometimes its history, however brief. In several cases, the author took a condescending tone, as in his recital of the by-now-legendary tale of Virginia City's founder, James Finney: "coming at length upon the worthless *blue stuff*, as he termed it, but in reality the rich sulphurets, he became disgusted with this luck, and not being longer able to make whiskey money, parted with his claim, selling it . . . [for] an ancient horse of thin flesh and a short dock."[40] Readers would immediately contrast this with the contemporary selling prices of five, seven, and ultimately forty thousand dollars each for the divided shares of the Comstock Lode.

In addition to the James "Old Virginny" Finney myth, the author described various wonders of the Comstock Lode, including the mining works in operation and Virginia City's shortcomings in terms of water and wood, and then moved on to describe the other towns. All received similar levels of praise, save for Genoa, which contained too many Mormons for the author's liking: "Adhering to their peculiar notions, and still cherishing in secret the fatal dogmas of their religion, they do not readily affiliate with the Gentiles around them, nor is there a likelihood of any cordial feeling ever existing between the two classes."[41]

Most significantly, this article described the inhabitants of "western Utah" as rather unintelligent, backward souls, lacking the mental capacity to exploit their own resources fully. The legendary tradition establishing the earliest prospectors as fools had additional import within the context of publication. For the California, and especially San Francisco, readers of *Hutchings' California Magazine*, the obvious implication of this tale would be that the Washoe Country's residents needed help. Specifically, they needed the help of capitalists, who flattered themselves that their exertions would not only yield themselves profits, but would also elevate the social and cultural milieu of the communities in which they invested. This fiction had legs: throughout the rest of the nineteenth century and in nearly every published depiction of mining areas meant to attract capital, one can find variations on the James Finney myth.

In the context of San Francisco's developing regional power structure, "Notes and Sketches" contributed to the cultural and economic colonialization of California's eastern neighbor in several ways. The author, in describing the historical narrative of botched progress, encouraged the idea that wise capitalists with foresight would better manage the resources than the benighted souls who actually lived there. In identifying Virginia City's need for timber and water, the article must have awakened entrepreneurial fantasies, for meeting those needs would ultimately call forth vast feats of engineering to draw the water and timber of the high Sierra to Mount Davidson.[42] In casting Nevada as either virgin territory or one fumbling about in the earliest stages of progress, these depictions invited and encouraged San Francisco readers to imagine themselves taking charge of the terrain. This imaginary act soon became quite real as San Francisco investors took charge of the Comstock and drew most of its wealth into their Nob Hill mansions.

As George Henderson notes for a later era of California development, the "geographical imaginations" of print culture were significantly interwoven with the "real" course of economic development unevenly spread over the landscape.[43] Before Californians could actually strike out and create their hinterland economies, they had to imagine themselves able to do so. Californians inherited a long tradition, going back to the earliest eras of European colonialism, of imagining territories fully inhabited with indigenous people as "empty," yet bursting with resources, awaiting the princely kiss of capital and Christian civilization to awaken from near-death slumber. This cultural practice of deterritorialization is as visible in Hutchings' travel and tourism pieces as it is in the almanacs and other publications. Not only do Hutchings' travel narratives contribute to a sense of place and identity rooted in specific landscapes, they simultaneously provide the cultural framework in support of San Francisco's imperial ambitions.

In October 1859, Hutchings published an extended narrative of the excursion to Yosemite he organized that year including photographer Charles Leander Weed, Ferdinand C. Ewer and wife, and Marianna Neill.[44] This article was significant on several counts. Weed was the first photographer to capture Yosemite's landscapes in a reproducible form. Hired by Hutchings and under his direction, Weed made several large-format and stereotype images. The illustrations accompanying "The Great Yo-Semite Valley" were engraved prints taken from Weed's photographs. Additionally, this article formed the core of Hutchings' future travel guides—laying out the route, distances, prices for travel and accommodations, and sights to see along the way. Hutchings took pains to minimize the imagined dangers and discomforts of this foray into the Sierra. Rather, any discomforts translated into contrasts that would only enhance the charming and salubrious features of the trip:

> The picturesque wildness of the scene on every hand; the exciting wonders of so romantic a journey; the difficulties surmounted; the dangers braved, and overcome; put us in possession of one unanimous feeling of unalloyed delight, so that when we reached the foot of the mountain, and rode side by side among the shadows of the spreading oaks and lofty pines in the smooth valley, we congratulated each other upon looking the very picture of happiness personified.[45]

Hutchings' 1859 party was one of the first to visit the first "real" hotel in the valley, Gus Hite's "Upper House," a 20 × 60-foot, two-story frame building that housed women on the top floor, men below (see photograph on p.

C. L. Weed photograph, "Upper House, Yosemite Valley," 1859. Charles Leander Weed ncluded the image of Hutchings' future hotel in the first photographic tour of Yosemite Valley. (Courtesy Yosemite Research Library, Yosemite National Park)

103). Five years later, Hutchings would purchase this hotel when he moved into the valley. During the four years since Hutchings' initial visit with Ayres, local entrepreneurs had been busy building roads, trails, and crude hotels to accommodate a small but growing number of tourists each year. In the summer of 1856, one year after Hutchings' initial visit, two trails ran into the valley. One, built by the Mann brothers, connected the town of Mariposa with the valley through a southern route, while the second connected Coulterville to the valley on a northerly route. By 1857, a third route followed the Old Mono trail from Big Oak Flat to join the Coulterville Trail at Crane Flat. These trails began the competition for tourist dollars among the principal "gateway communities" to Yosemite that continues to this day: Coulterville, Big Oak Flat, and Mariposa.[46] In the spring of 1856, a few entrepreneurs began erecting buildings to accommodate visitors, although it would be another few years before the crude shacks could really be called hotels. The "Lower Hotel" began as an 18 × 20-foot structure that primarily served as a tavern—most visitors slept outside the building. Gustavus Hite opened the "Upper Hotel" for business in the spring of 1857—a large canvas tent about seven-tenths of a mile from the Lower Hotel. A year later, Hite began construction of the building that would finally be finished in 1859, just in time for Hutchings' party.

And so, as Hutchings created the cultural infrastructure for tourism to Yosemite in his many publications, articles, and guided tours for other influential mavens to experience (then to broadcast) the wonders of the place, locals built the physical structures to accommodate those visits. Despite their work and investments, visitation to Yosemite remained low through the end of the 1850s—averaging around eighty-five visitors per year. This is unsurprising. Travel to Yosemite was expensive and exhausting, as historian Hank Johnston describes:

> From San Francisco, most Yosemite-bound travelers embarked on an all-night, mosquito-plagued ship ride up the San Joaquin River to Stockton. Arriving at 6 a.m., the groggy passengers immediately set out on a jostling, dust-filled one- or two-day stage ride over bumpy foothill roads to the end of the line at Mariposa, Coulterville, or Big Oak Flat, depending on one's itinerary. Then came two or three more days of rigorous horseback riding over steep, narrow trails to reach the rim of Yosemite Valley. The final descent down a chancy cliff-side route to the Valley floor itself gave even the most intrepid traveler cause for concern.[47]

In 1859, Hutchings accounted a cost of approximately $240 for a party of five to travel to the valley and spend eight days there, but this did not include the steamship fare, overnight accommodations on the way, or accommodations in the Upper Hotel. With these factored in, the cost could be close to $100 per person—very steep, especially during one of California's frequent economic downturns. Hutchings recognized that the most likely tourists would be wealthy urbanites as his articles frequently alluded to escaping the "peck of troubles" of city life.

Fracture Lines

At the end of the 1850s, the vast majority of Californians had to remain content to enjoy Yosemite as armchair tourists, consuming the wonders of the valley through printed word and image or in the oratory of ministers like Scott and Ferdinand Ewer. That Yosemite's iconography remained in the realm of culture and imagination does not negate the growing power of this icon of sublimity in the context of San Francisco's expanding imperialist structure. Traditional narratives, and our contemporary understanding, of sacred places like Yosemite posit that they are islands apart from the urban and industrial nature of modernizing America. But, as we have seen, narratives and images of Yosemite were made possible by and were completely bound up in the technological, ideological, and cultural apparatus that also fueled the expanding control over hinterland resources giving rise to San Francisco's industrial, imperial economy. Similarly, actual tourism to the place began and would continue along the transportation lines and network of towns that developed to colonize California's rural areas for the capitalist economy controlled by Sacramento and San Francisco. What is perhaps less obvious, but no less important, is the critical cultural role Yosemite played for San Franciscans.

Just as Miriam Leslie eased her shock over hydraulic mining's destructive impact with the psychic balm of a visit to Belmont's gardens, nineteenth-century urbanites read multiple affirmations into the symbolic vision of Milton's Eden in their backyard. Yosemite was divine sanction for San Francisco's white, Protestant elites; its geology a symbol of correct social order to settle the unrest of working-class laborers; its sacred landscape an antidote to the landscapes sacrificed in the course of mining, bonanza agriculture, and lumbering. Even the narrative of the difficult journey ending in the peaceful valley Paradise functioned as an allegory of California's future destiny after the difficult and chaotic period of the gold rush and subsequent economic volatility. These connotations served to validate and reinforce California's emerging residential elite and middle classes around particular understandings of California's landscapes. In the hands of Hutchings and other writers, artists, and publishers, Yosemite served as an anchoring image in an emerging sense of place to help settle California's transient Anglos and focus disparate energies toward the vision of a civilized metropolitan empire on the rim of the Pacific.

However, just below the surface of this narrative, actual social, racial/ethnic, class, and gender tensions continued to strain California society. Like the political turmoil over slavery pulling the rest of the nation apart at the seams, the internal contradictions of California's social reality continually threatened to overturn the bourgeois mythologies carefully crafted and purveyed by Hutchings and his friends. In 1860, the trajectories of both California and the rest of the United States would converge in the crucible of war. Unsurprisingly, Yosemite would be at center stage.

Part III
Yosemite and the National Sublime

Nine years after his first visit to Yosemite, James Mason Hutchings packed up his new family and left San Francisco to build a home in the mountain valley. Though he continued to publish tour guides through the 1860s and 1870s, after 1864 his career focused more on building the infrastructure to support the rising tide of Yosemite tourists and delivering illustrated lecture tours. Moving from behind the curtain of the stage he had set for Yosemite's developing iconography, Hutchings became a central figure in the drama initiated by the Yosemite Grant, the act passed by Congress just two months after Hutchings' move, to set aside the valley as a public park "for public use, resort, and recreation . . . inalienable for all time."[1]

The Yosemite Grant initiated a powerful new force that constituted a tipping point in American environmental history; the moment when the right combination of individuals, contextual transformation, and ideological change hit a nerve in the broad social psyche of a time and launched a new environmental understanding.[2] That new understanding included a new role for the U.S. government in managing public lands—one that recognized certain landscapes for scenic value and sought to restructure the economic and policy approach to such landscapes. This new understanding also recognized the power of tourism as both a communication tool and an economic strategy to fund the administration of these scenic landscapes. Within a decade, this initial step would coalesce into the national park idea, giving birth to one of America's most significant lasting environmental legacies and launching the creation of sacred

Carleton Watkins' stereograph, "Yosemite Falls #2," 1861. Stereograph images of Yosemite gave a wide audience access to its sublime imagery. (Courtesy California State Library, Sacramento, CA)

spaces across the nation. By combining the power of the federal government to manage lands for conservation with the economic power of commodity landscape tourism, the Yosemite Grant laid the critical foundation for over a century of environmental conservation politics and policies that would follow.

The powerful resonance of Yosemite's landscape features in the context of the Civil War and its aftermath gave the place an entirely new significance on the national stage as an icon of postwar unification in the aesthetic framework of northeastern values and institutions. So potently did the images of Yosemite speak to some Americans at the time that it quickly became a cultural container or crucible where many Americans could work out or elide some of the deepest hopes and anxieties of the age.

However, as Hutchings' career illustrates, the process by which Yosemite shifted from a regional to national icon was contested and complex. His legal challenge to the Yosemite Commissioners took the matter of federal control over public lands to the U.S. Supreme Court, with long-term implications for postbellum national land policy. Both Hutchings and the commissioners simultaneously waged public-relations campaigns to bolster credibility with the American public while further promoting Yosemite. Hutchings' challenge also sealed his own fate as a marginalized figure in the history of Yosemite. A fresh look at the origins of Yosemite that balances Hutchings' case with that of the Yosemite Commissioners raises new questions and complications about the origin of Yosemite, the national park idea, and American conservation policy more generally.

At the same time, Hutchings continued to promote the valley's scenic wonders to the general public through his hotel keeping, tour guide publishing, and illustrated lectures given to audiences of thousands. In the process, Hutchings also hosted, sponsored, or otherwise assisted new generations of photographers, artists, writers, theologians, and scientists in their visits to the valley. The works of these intellectuals serve as cultural maps to the changing meanings of the Yosemite iconography as the wrenching transformations of the Second Industrial Revolution shook the nation.

Five years after Hutchings' move to the valley, the transcontinental railroad linked San Francisco with the rest of the nation, and John Muir took up residence as Hutchings' employee. The two events were instrumental in another step of the tipping point: the transformation of Yosemite from a place valued primarily for its spectacular scenery into a national symbol of wilderness that would shape the cast of twentieth-century American environmentalism. The railroad not only caused a leap in Yosemite tourism, it bound San Francisco and California more tightly into the industrializing national economy. As the United States progressed through the Second Industrial Revolution, Yosemite as an idea and an image expanded to frame new ideas, hopes, and anxieties, including widespread national concerns about class, gender, race, and national identity.

And John Muir's transcendental vision of nature as the site for individual renewal transformed Americans' relationship with the environment into the wilderness idea that became a central philosophy of twentieth-century environmental politics. Muir's concept of wilderness focused on the discrete individual's relationship with nature, shifting the older notion of scenery as a communal spectacle into alignment with more modern and urban understandings of experience. While history's characterization of Hutchings and Muir has stressed their rivalries to the point of casting them as environmental opposites, some reflection on their more complex relationship yields a more nuanced understanding of their shared values and mutual roles in the ongoing evolution of American environmental ideas.

Yosemite and the Crucible of War

It was during one of the darkest hours, before Sherman had begun
the march on Atlanta or Grant his terrible movement through the
Wilderness, when the paintings of Bierstadt and the photographs of
Watkins . . . [gave] the people on the Atlantic some idea of the
sublimity of the Yo Semite.
    —Frederick Law Olmsted. *Yosemite and the Mariposa Grove: A
    Preliminary Report, 1865*

Encamped on Yosemite's valley floor in August 1865, five of the
Yosemite Grant's first commissioners gathered to hear their chair,
landscape architect Frederick Law Olmsted, read these words as part
of his "Preliminary Report on the Yosemite Valley and Mariposa Big
Tree Grove."[1] Olmsted's report reminds us how important the Civil
War context was to contemporary understandings of Yosemite's national significance—it was at the height of this war that the U.S.
Congress passed legislation setting aside the Yosemite gorge and
Mariposa Big Tree Grove to be granted to the State of California "inalienable for all time," launching the iconography of Yosemite onto
the national stage, where it would become infused with nationalistic symbolism.[2]

During the Civil War, Olmsted had worked for the Union as the
principal administrator of the U.S. Sanitary Commission, and his
most famous achievement—New York City's Central Park—was
completed in 1863. Previously a well-known journalist and author in
New York City, Olmsted was also deeply connected with the literary elite of the urban Northeast. Olmsted was working as the manager of the Mariposa Estate in the foothills west of Yosemite in 1864

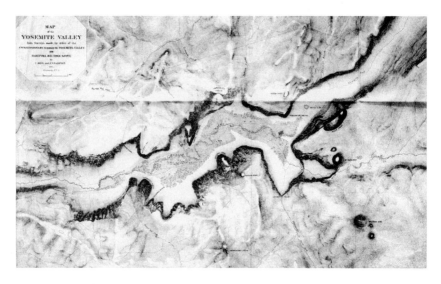

"Map of the Yosemite Valley," C. King and J. T. Gardner, 1865. From Josiah D. Whitney,
Yosemite Guide-Book, *1870.*

when Congress passed the grant, and later that year California Governor Frederick H. Low appointed him as chair of the administrative body designed to manage the Yosemite Grant.

James Mason Hutchings may very well have been in Olmsted's audience. It was his second summer of playing "mine host" to the tourists, scientists, artists, and other visitors to the mountain valley, having purchased Gus Hite's Upper Hotel and moved from San Francisco to Yosemite the year before. Nevertheless, despite his decade of promoting the place and working to make it accessible to the public, Hutchings was not among the group of men appointed to the first Yosemite Commission. And, though he would continue to spend the rest of his life tirelessly promoting Yosemite and advocating for the environmental conservation of the Sierra, by the twentieth century he would be dismissed in the stories of Yosemite's origin as a selfish entrepreneur standing in the way of enlightened progress.

Hutchings' absence from Yosemite's origin story may seem a trivial detail at first, but it points to deeper forces at play in Yosemite's transition from a regional to a national icon. While it is true that the decision to set Yosemite aside as a sacred, iconographic landscape marked a watershed in American environmental history, the decision itself was not uncontested. Faced with the loss of his investments in the tourist infrastructure of Yosemite, Hutchings opposed the commissioners all the way to the U.S. Supreme Court. In the end, Hutchings' lawsuit gave the court an opportunity to clarify the power of Congress over public lands and helped to pave the way for additional battles in the so-called "war of incorporation" playing out over western regions during the second half of the nineteenth century. Incorporating Hutchings' experience into the analysis of Yosemite's national iconography illuminates many parallels with the process of appropriating other western lands for national purposes—as Supreme Court Chief Justice Stephen J. Field clearly spelled out in the 1873 ruling against Hutchings.

Popular and scholarly history have tended to dismiss Hutchings and his protest as a retrograde act by a self-interested businessman, in the process reifying the position of the Yosemite Commissioners and Field Court and oversimplifying the complexities of the case. This historic marginalization of Hutchings' perspective also supports the assumption that Yosemite's creation was divorced from the political, economic, and ideological processes of the time and simultaneously that it was a prescient gesture of wilderness protection by selfless idealists and a benign federal government. Indeed, the story of Yosemite's origins—as told in tourist publications as well as professional histories—reads twentieth-century preservation impulses back into the unproven motives of the unidentified men who originally proposed the grant idea. "It is quite safe to assume," wrote Hans Huth in 1984, "that . . . the group of men promoting the interests of Yosemite did so for idealistic reasons."[3] However, such assumptions do not help us understand the complex political, economic, and cultural circumstances giving rise to the Yosemite Grant and the nationalistic iconography to flow from that act.

Olmsted's report points to the importance of the Civil War and national anxieties about regional difference that prompted many leading culture makers to see in Yosemite a symbol of postwar unification. Intended to acquaint the California State Legislature with the philosophy behind and intended purpose of the Yosemite Grant, Olmsted's document was never published as an independent whole in the nineteenth century but reached audiences in the form of excerpted newspaper and journal articles. Nevertheless, Olmsted's report is an excellent expression of the ideology that motivated the Congressional appropriation of the dramatic gorge in California's Sierra Nevada for "public use, resort, and recreation . . . inalienable for all time."[4] "The power of scenery to affect men is . . . proportionate to their degree of civilization," wrote Olmsted, so that the effect of Yosemite's scenery would, in theory, en-able all Americans to achieve comparable "degrees of civilization." Olmsted was one of the nineteenth-century's chief architects of the idea that landscape and society had the power to shape social character: his Central Park was an explicit effort to "corral and contain the energies of New York's working classes."[5]

Olmsted couched his vision for Yosemite in strikingly democratic terms: "It is the main duty of government, if it is not the sole duty of government, to provide means of protection to all citizens in the pursuit of happiness against the obstacles, otherwise insurmountable, which the selfishness of individuals or combinations of individuals is liable to interpose to that pursuit."[6] Olmsted's philosophy specifically addressed the matter of private property as an institution that would gather the benefits of scenery to the few who could afford it, rather than making it available to the masses who most needed it. This became the theoretical groundwork for the public case against Hutchings.

Paradoxically, aside from the matter of private property, the administrative design of the Yosemite Grant relied on midcentury theories about private enterprise and the social utility of scenic landscapes. That many Americans were already familiar with landscape as a symbol for national identity made the particular landscape of Yosemite an easy sell. That culture makers like Hutchings and W. A. Scott in California and leading northeastern writers like Thomas Starr King, Samuel Bowles, and Horace Greeley had already begun to interpret Yosemite through the lens of divine sanction for middle-class institutions in California and the orderly progress implied in the imperial expansion of San Francisco meant that Yosemite was a landscape already invested with social and political meaning. Finally, as Niagara and other iconographic destinations had demonstrated, tourism to national icons could be a profitable venture, but one that had to be carefully managed for full effect.

The Yosemite Grant pulled together various strands of nationalistic hope and anxiety, economic ambition, and national policy to forge a powerful dynamic that linked together consumer tourism, landscape iconology, and nationalism in America's first efforts to conserve landscape almost exclusively for its scenic value. Yosemite in the nineteenth century was not an environmentalist cause, as many of us like to assume. It was not about preserving an undisturbed "nature." Olmsted, like Hutchings, saw Yosemite as "a literal work of art," a spectacle that would unite the American people in reverent and therapeutic contemplation of its aesthetic beauty. In setting aside this landscape, Congress transformed San Francisco's hinterland Eden into a national icon that would help to consolidate a new, postwar national identity.[7]

The American Civil War was the culmination of many decades' tension between Northern and Southern states over the practice of slave-holding and the power relationship between states and the federal government. Western expansion exacerbated these tensions, as incoming states affected the congressional balance of power. California's admission as a free state into the union in 1850 flared hostilities even further since it geographically violated the Mason-Dixon line that had maintained an uneasy balance between North and South since 1821. The compromises of 1850 that attempted to restore a sense of balance inflamed rather than soothed tensions, leading to the outbreak of hostilities in December 1861. The war itself was more destructive and deadly than all other military engagements of the United States combined, and left a permanent imprint on the nation's psyche.

For the Union, national authority and sovereignty was *the* critical issue of the war, and during and after it the Union congress enacted policies to strengthen federal power and bind America's disparate regions more tightly to national authority. As men like Frederick Law Olmsted, Josiah Whitney, California Senator John Conness, and Supreme Court Justice Steven J. Field addressed national challenges during and after the Civil War, chief among their concerns was the potential for remote regions to develop cultural, economic, and political autonomy from the Atlantic seats of power—Washington, D.C., New York, and Boston. Such autonomy, many felt, threatened to continually destabilize national power and economic consolidation. In this context, images of Yosemite's dramatic gorge reminded many observers of the nation split apart by war, while the sublime waterfalls and lush valley suggested divine sanction for postwar unification. Perhaps most importantly, Yosemite was a place that all in the nation could identify with. During and after the war, fueled, in part, by passionate attachment to local place rather than to an abstract nation, the idea of a symbolic landscape that could inspire the sentimental devotion of all Americans had great cultural potential for building a new, postwar national identity.

In the opening paragraphs of his report, Olmsted dramatized the context of the Civil War as the backdrop to Yosemite's first major media appearance in the eastern states. By the end of the 1850s the promotional efforts of James Mason Hutchings, James Weed, Carleton Watkins, and other California publicists had attracted the attention of artists, photographers, scientists, and journalists from beyond California. Indeed, it was not only the "paintings of Bierstadt" and "photographs of Watkins" that brought Yosemite to national attention in this era, but articles by Horace Greeley of the *New York Tribune* in 1859 and Thomas Starr King in the *Boston Evening Transcript* during the winter of 1861–1862 that publicized the spectacular landscape to northeastern audiences at the exact time that sectional political strife was driving the nation into secession and war. The timing was not lost on contemporary observers, who immediately contrasted the horrors of modern, industrial warfare with the sublime scenes described by King and Greeley. The contrast became strikingly visible in 1862, when the 30 mammoth plate (22 × 18 inches) and 100 stereo views of Yosemite photographed by Carleton Watkins in 1861 went on display at Goupil's New York Gallery. Watkins' photographs depicting views of the cliffs and waterfalls around the valley followed close on the heels of an exhibit from the Mathew Brady Studio of the war dead from Civil War battlefields, cementing the contrast between the destruction of war and the healing potential of Yosemite's landscape. "A shattered nation looked west, well beyond the conflagration, to peaceful environments not torn asunder by war."[8]

But the process of transforming Yosemite from a symbol of metropolitan San Francisco's bourgeois identity into a national icon of postwar unification and divine sanction was neither automatic nor uncontested. In the context of war, where old symbols took on new meaning, Hutchings' efforts to promote California identity through landscape placed him at odds with those who would "save California for the Union."

Although California was geographically distant from the conflict, it was touched by the war in several ways. Many historians have argued that California's statehood disrupted the delicate political balance between slave and free states in Congress, and that the "compensatory" legislation meant to balance this disruption—the Fugitive Slave Act and territorial "popular sovereignty" policies—furthered the lines of opposition between slave and free and accelerated the violence that led to war.

As Californians struggled to define themselves in relationship to the conflict, some cultural elites from the East worried about another regional secession. There were sensationalistic news accounts accusing Southerners of instigating the occasional outbursts of armed Indian resistance. While these beliefs were probably unfounded (as the native Californians had plenty of their own reasons for resisting Anglo expansion), influential Southerners, such as Senator William Gwin and his "chivalry" party, had wielded considerable political influence in the state during the 1850s. Furthermore, some Californians were beginning to chafe under their semicolonial status in relationship to Washington, D.C., and other Atlantic seats of power. In 1857,

Congregational minister Charles Edward Pickett captured this sentiment when he called for the establishment of an independent Pacific Republic.[9]

In 1860, Thomas Starr King, pastor of Boston's Hollis Street Unitarian Church, answered the call to become minister of San Francisco's First Unitarian Church. King was a gifted orator and had already established a deep interest in the religious interpretation of landscapes through a series of discourses and published articles on the White Mountains. King had read Horace Greeley's accounts of his 1859 trip to Yosemite in the *New York Tribune* and almost immediately made the trip to Yosemite upon arriving in California. The following year, King published a series of articles celebrating the wonders of the valley for the *Boston Evening Transcript*. These articles, which reached a wide audience of Northern elites, appeared between December 1, 1860, and February 9, 1861, the exact period during which the Southern states protested Abraham Lincoln's presidential election by seceding from the United States.[10]

Once in California, King responded to the national crisis with his campaign to "save California for the Union," raising funds for Olmsted's U.S. Sanitary Commission in a series of statewide lecture circuits. Touring through the Pacific Slope and speaking to packed audiences, King used national geography as a metaphor for the Union and urged Californians to think beyond their provincial boundaries to recognize that their regional identity was as an integral component of an indivisible Union, ordained by God. Yosemite played a critical symbolic role in this campaign, as King emphasized the spiritually and politically redemptive qualities of the spectacular Sierra gorge to underscore his central message. Evidence of the success of King's campaign to more clearly align California's political identity with that of the Union is demonstrated, in part, by the fact that California led the country in contributions to this commission.[11] King's success also conclusively demonstrated the rhetorical power of Yosemite as a unifying symbol.

King's vision for California was not only political and religious, but intensely cultural as well. In 1863, he delivered a series of lectures entitled "The Chief Poets of America," promoting New England poets as part of his wider effort to "Northernize" California. As he wrote to his old Boston friends James T. and Annie Fields of Ticknor and Fields publishing house, King sought to transform California culture by promoting New England cultural institutions: "Schools, *Atlantic Monthlies*, lectures, N. E. preachers [and] Library Assoc[iations]." Such efforts demonstrate King's assumption that both landscape and print culture were powerful tools for shaping a collective identity. At the same time, King expressed a low opinion of the literary culture already flourishing in California, where "we raise bigger trees & squashes than literati & brains."[12]

King's religious, cultural, and political campaign may have won the hearts and minds of Californians, but it was not the only vision for the state in response to the Civil War. Pickett's vision of the independent Pacific Republic was one alternative. Others hoped California could remain neutral—a haven for both Northerners and Southerners during the war. One of the most vocal proponents of the latter idea was Hutchings' friend, Presbyterian minister William Anderson Scott, formerly of New Orleans. In public addresses to his congregation, Scott hoped that California might offer a site for the realization of the South's best qualities: "a love of sun and genial skies and flourishing estates, a sense of responsibility for the *res publica*, manners, the code, and physical courage." Scott preached tolerance and pluralism and vigorously opposed the secular ambitions of New England churches, including the enforced reading of the Bible in public schools. Presumably, he would not have been too happy with King's efforts to "Northernize" the state. Although Scott had been a popular minister and prominent member of the San Francisco elite for several years, when he offered prayers for both American presidents in 1861, he was hanged in effigy and exiled from the state.[13]

Scott's fall from grace occurred in the same year that Hutchings' very active San Francisco publishing career terminated abruptly with his last issue of the *California Magazine* in 1861.[14] In later years, Hutchings recalled that failing health prompted this move: "The family physician . . . gave emphatic enunciation to the opinion that unless we left the city at an early day, we should soon do so from the world."[15] But there is little other evidence that he suffered ill health at that time in his life—he continued to take excursions into the mountains and eastern California. He may also have been disappointed in the financial health of the magazine: throughout the last volume, he exhorted readers to increase their subscriptions. However, it is also possible that Scott's fate had something to do with this departure. Hutchings had witnessed enough vigilante "justice" in California, including the actions of both Vigilance Committees in San Francisco, to understand the implications of mob violence, and may have feared that his friendship with Scott put him at risk as well.

At any rate, Hutchings' efforts to promote California culture through his own publications did not exactly line up with the pro-North ideology sweeping the state. King's comment about squashes and literati appears to have been an almost calculated personal affront against boosters like Hutchings, for whom the size of trees and squashes (and other produce, not to mention mountains and waterfalls) formed such a consistent theme in his own promotion of California. Hutchings did not agree with Scott on all things, and he was definitely pro-Union in the last issues of *Hutchings' California Magazine*. But Scott's vision of California as a place of tolerance (within certain Anglo-Protestant boundaries) and a haven for both North and South seems consistent with Hutchings' own ideas about the state. Although he promoted institutions and values akin to those of the northeastern middle class, Hutchings' emphasis on printing original California material would have put him at odds with King's campaign to promote "Ticknor-and-Fields-ism" exclusively. Hutchings' efforts to define, interpret, and promote California culture, landscapes, and society to create a specifically Californian identity would have run counter to those of King and Greeley to define California for the Union through the aggressive promotion of New England culture. At the same time, King's promotion of New England culture must have caused Hutchings mixed feelings. However insulting King's slight against indigenous Anglo California culture might have been, his promotion of education and literary institutions meshed well with Hutchings' own advocacy of schools and his role as a bookseller who carried eastern titles. Nevertheless, as a publisher and businessman, he might have perceived the potential for damaging competition from leading Atlantic publishing houses in the pro-North fervor gripping the state. At any rate the ever-adaptive Hutchings had his eye on a new venture anyway.

Hutchings Moves to Yosemite

In his autobiography and memoirs, Hutchings suggests that he departed San Francisco to move directly to Yosemite, where he purchased possessory right to two preemption claims, one containing the Upper Hotel built by Buck Beardsley and Gus Hite, in 1863.[16] However, Hutchings actually spent much of 1862 and 1863 as partner and supervisor of the San Carlos mine in Owens Valley, in the eastern scarp of the Sierra Nevada range, while making expeditionary winter trips into Yosemite to determine whether it were habitable year-round. During the 1850s, seasonal residents managed tourist accommodations in Yosemite during the summer months and lived in Central Valley homes over the winter. In his autobiography, Hutchings wrote that popular belief held that "no one could ever make a permanent winter home in Yo Semite, inasmuch as snow from the surrounding mountains drifted into it, as into a deep railroad-cut, and filled it half full."[17] Prior to purchasing his hotel, Hutchings wanted to ensure that he and his family could become full-time residents, so he set out to test the possibility with two winter excursions to the valley. He may also have returned to mining to earn some extra cash toward the Yosemite venture, while escaping some of the political heat of San Francisco. At any rate, in 1862 and 1863 Hutchings worked with Henry Hanks to establish the temporarily successful mining operation San Carlos Exploring and Mining Company during the Owens Valley Indian Wars and returned by the year's end to San Francisco with samples of ore to report their success to the other members of their company.[18]

Although San Carlos had a brief boom with a proposed smelting furnace in the works, Hutchings left Owens Valley in the spring of 1864 to settle in Yosemite.[19] On May 19, 1864, Hutchings, his wife, Elvira, her sister Lucy, and her mother, Florantha Sproat, moved into the Upper Hotel at Yosemite and renamed it "Hutchings' House." The two sections of land included in Hutchings' purchase were governed by preemption laws, longstanding legal traditions supporting frontier homesteads. Preemption acts encouraged settlement on unsurveyed land, where settlers could file a claim and, as long as they lived on the land and worked to improve it by building structures, clearing trees, farming or raising livestock, could expect to gain title to that land once it was surveyed. Confident that the law of the land would return their investment, the Hutchings began over a decade of hotel keeping, stock raising, trail building, and otherwise managing the material needs of Yosemite's tourist trade as well as building their own home and starting a family.

Simultaneously, however, events transpired in San Francisco and Washington, D.C., that would directly impact Hutchings' new career. In February 1864, Israel Ward Raymond, of the Central American Steamship Transit Company, wrote to California Senator John Conness urging that the Yosemite Valley and the Mariposa Grove of Sequoias be permanently set aside as a public park. On March 28, Conness introduced the famous bill, and Congress deliberated briefly before passing the act in June, granting the valley and grove to the State of California "on the express conditions that the premises shall be held for public use, resort and recreation and shall be inalienable for all time," and establishing the Yosemite Commissioners as the governing body responsible for its management.[20]

Yosemite Grant and the Origin of American Conservation Policy

Although public parks of various sorts had existed in America prior to 1864, the Yosemite Grant was the first time the federal government had set aside a landscape for purely scenic and recreational purposes. While the grant created little debate or publicity in the midst of the Civil War, in retrospect it has been hailed as the unprecedented act of selfless, idealistic California gentlemen and a uniquely foresighted Congress. Many historians agree with Alfred Runte's analysis casting the Yosemite Grant as the precursor to the national park concept initiated with Yellowstone eight years later.[21] As the point of origin for "America's Best Idea," the Yosemite Grant deserves recognition as an important moment of transformation in modernizing America's relationship with the environment.[22] Through the late nineteenth and especially the twentieth century, hundreds of thousands of acres of stunning scenery, unique ecosystems, and cultural treasures have been preserved from most forms of development for the edification and enjoyment of millions of visitors from around the world. While recognizing the important value of these conserved lands to the nation and the world, it is no less important to suggest that the historic impulses launching this conservation movement turn out to be far more complex and contradictory than most histories of the grant suggest. Restoring Hutchings' perspective to the story reveals some of these complexities while suggesting even more questions for further research.

The creation of Yosemite as a national icon depended upon a complex of technological, cultural, political, and economic forces in play before, during, and after the Civil War. As for the actual genesis of the grant idea, it was apparently the brainchild of Israel Ward Raymond, California representative of the Central American Steamship Transit Company of New York, and a number of other influential gentlemen whose names have been lost to history, identified only as "gentlemen of fortune, of taste, and of refinement" in Senator John Conness' letter to Congress.[23] After some discussion among this group, Israel Ward Raymond wrote to Conness in February 1864, urging him to take Congressional action: "I think it important to obtain the proprietorship soon, to prevent occupation . . . and that it may be accepted by the legislation and its present session and laws passed to give the Commissioners power to take control and begin to consider and lay out their plans for the gradual improvement of the properties."[24] Raymond's phrasing raises many questions. What, for example, did he mean by "occupation," when people had been living in Yosemite and operating tourist facilities for eight summers? Was it the prospect of year-round residency that he was referring to? If so, then he may have been specifically responding to Hutchings, who publicized his efforts to determine Yosemite's winter conditions for the purpose of living there full time. It is also clear that Raymond and Conness had discussed this plan previously; the reference to "Commissioners" indicates that they and whoever else participated in the planning stages had already sketched out the structure of the grant's administration. And his use of the word "proprietorship," connoting a business venture, together with the comment about "laying out plans for the . . . improvement of the properties" suggests that the gentlemen of "fortune, of taste, and of refinement" had their own intentions for the park's economic development.

Historians have speculated about the identities of the remaining individuals involved in this plan. John Sears guesses that Thomas Starr King and Horace Greeley, powerful and respected voices with widespread appeal, were involved (King died in March 1864, just two months before Congress passed the Yosemite Grant act). Hans Huth is probably right that the men initially named as Yosemite Valley Commissioners were the same individuals who planned the congressional bill with Conness: landscape architect Frederick Law Olmsted, California State Geologist Josiah D. Whitney, surveyor William Ashburner, Raymond, E. S. Holden, Alexander Deering, George W. Coulter of Coulterville (who built the toll Coulterville trail for tourists to enter the valley), and Galen Clark, owner of Clark's station near the valley's entrance at present-day Wawona.[25] In his letter to the commissioner of the General Land Office, Conness suggested an additional name: Stephen J. Field. Field had just served six years as justice of the California Supreme Court and was beginning one of the longest-running Supreme Court justiceships in American history. He had been a powerful force in California legal practice during the 1850s and was well known for incurring enemies along the way. Although Field did not become a Yosemite Commissioner, Conness' suggestion implies that he, too, may have been one of the early instigators of the Yosemite Grant idea. As luck would have it, Field was still on the Supreme Court when Hutchings' lawsuit came through and wrote a ringing rejection of Hutchings' case.

Whether or not the Yosemite Commissioners were the exact same "gentlemen of taste and refinement" who had generated the grant idea, they certainly were influential in the early administration of the park. While many of these individuals did have broad social interests in mind, it does not necessarily follow that such interests would negate any personal or economic ambition. At least two of these men had clear business interest potential in controlling the development of Yosemite's commercial tourism. George W. Coulter was one of the founders of Coulterville, which continues to act as a "gateway" community to Yosemite. Coulter built one of the first trails into the valley and purchased the lease on Hutchings' hotel after Hutchings' eviction. Israel Ward Raymond's prominent position in one of the most extensive transportation companies in the Pacific would have given him plenty of economic reasons to have an interest in Yosemite's development as a destination resort, in addition to his passion to preserve the spectacular scenery.[26]

As geologists and surveyors, Ashburner and Whitney may have seen the Yosemite Grant as an opportunity to further their own scientific pursuits in the Sierra. As we have seen, Thomas Starr King and Horace Greeley were keenly interested in the nationalist implications of Yosemite as a symbol of divine ordination for the Union in the postwar era.

The point here is not to suggest that these mysterious gentlemen were completely craven robber barons cloaking their schemes in false do-gooder gestures. The point is that the men who created the Yosemite Grant, like many leaders of their day, had *multiple* motives—lofty and far-sighted idealism *as well as* economic and/or ideological self-interest. Hutchings was stamped of the same cloth: independent entrepreneur and self-made man, there is no doubt he hoped to profit from the tourist trade he had worked so hard to generate in print. But this profit motive does not negate his sincere passion for the mountains of the Sierra and the uplifting power of Yosemite's divine inspiration. It is only through the bifurcated lenses of twentieth-century politics that we see profit and preservation as polar opposites—a perspective also rooted, at least in part, in the nineteenth-century politics of the Yosemite Grant itself.

The combination of nationalist cultural politics, personal economic ambition, and the broader context of postbellum incorporation were all forces directly or indirectly affecting the early administration of the Yosemite Grant. Additionally, and more immediately, was the question of how to create the infrastructure needed to support the growing numbers of Yosemite tourists. In response to this question, the Yosemite Grant simultaneously drew on traditional assumptions about development while taking tentative steps toward creating a new system of land management. Given the voluminous negative opinion of the tourist developments around Niagara Falls, it is likely that part of the concept behind the grant itself and the creation of the Yosemite Commission is that there should be *some* kind of regulatory body to mitigate the worst effects of private development.

At the same time, neither the nation nor the state was prepared to subsidize the development of the Yosemite Grant with taxpayer funds. In order to support the creation of tourist infrastructure there, Congress designed the grant so the Yosemite Commissioners had authority over permits and "leases not exceeding ten years [that] may be granted for portions of said premises." The system intended to allow private developers to build infrastructure in anticipation of recouping investment from tolls, fees, and other charges to the consumer tourists visiting the valley, though the grant also specified that "incomes derived from leases of privileges . . . be expended in the preservation and improvement of the property, or the roads leading thereto."[27] Therefore, private entrepreneurship was designed from the outset to drive and shape development of the park.

Even Frederick Law Olmsted, who tended to be more philosophically inclined than his contemporaries, recognized the central importance of the profit motive in Yosemite. He pointed to the broader economic benefit of tourism to scenic sites as a key rationale for setting aside and preserving the Yosemite landscape. Turning to Switzerland and Bavaria as case studies, he wrote:

> Travelers [to the Swiss Alps] alone have caused hundreds of the best inns in the world to be established and maintained . . . have given the farmers their best and almost the only market they have for their surplus products, have spread a network of rail roads and superb carriage roads, steamboat routes, and telegraphic lines all over the country, have contributed directly and indirectly for many years the larger part of the state revenues, and all this without the exportation or abstraction from the country of anything of the slightest value to the people.[28]

Strikingly similar to the rhetoric of booster tracts promoting resource development, Olmsted's argument for the economic benefits of scenic tourism underscores the profit potential Yosemite's founders saw in the development of its scenery for visitors. Although Olmsted did argue for "the preservation and maintenance as exactly as is possible of the natural scenery," it is clear that he also supported the idea of private enterprise in developing Yosemite's tourist infrastructure. The management philosophy of the Yosemite Grant assumed that the market demands of the tourist industry would reward entrepreneurs for their investments, provide enough revenue for any costs incurred in the management of the grant, and thereby release the state from all but nominal fiscal support for the park.

This system was very much in keeping with the dominant land-management and economic philosophy of antebellum America, where the primary duty of the Government Land Office was to move land into private ownership as quickly as possible, with the belief that free market forces and private enterprise were the most efficient mechanisms to drive development for the benefit of all. Really, the only sticky wicket in the whole plan was the matter of private property in the form of existing preemption claims and the initial built environment of Yosemite's infant tourist infrastructure. In introducing the Yosemite Grant Act to congress, Senator Conness neglected to mention these preexisting claims.

Thus, the structure of the early decades of Yosemite development rested for the most part on widespread assumptions about the appropriateness of private enterprise for profit as the best way to accomplish development in a short period of time. Just as the postbellum federal government underwrote the development of western lands through preferential treatment to various businesses and combines, the Yosemite Commission intended to guide the growth of tourism development in Yosemite with permits, leases, and grants that in some cases encouraged competition among developers and in others awarded exclusive contracts. Unfortunately, the idea in practice fell short of the elegance expressed by Olmsted. For one thing, Hutchings' lawsuit kept open the question of the commissioners' authority to control development for eight years. The practice of awarding leases and permits opened the commissioners to charges of favoritism and corruption as well, and they were further hampered by the state legislature's hostility and reluctance to allocate funds to park development. Nevertheless, in the first decade of the Yosemite Grant, the commissioners encouraged the expansion of hotel facilities, bridge and ferry building, the creation of trails (with tolls) and other structures such as the Vernal and Nevada Falls ladders and stairs, nearly all of which carried fees, tolls, or encouraged the use of hired guides—and later were decried as blights on the landscape.

Although the Yosemite Grant was created by an act of Congress, it was submitted to the State of California for authority and administration. However, the Yosemite Commissioners often acted more like agents of the federal, rather than state, government, unsteadily balanced in the shifting gaps between state and federal powers in the Reconstruction era. One of the commission's first acts was to notify Hutchings and James Lamon (the only other person holding preemption claims on valley property) that their preemption claims were invalid and that they could now choose to lease their properties from the commissioners for a period of ten years, or move elsewhere. Given that so much of the Yosemite Grant depended on private entrepreneurship, one wonders why Hutchings' and Lamon's property claims mattered so much to the commissioners. Later arguments on behalf of the commissioners' opinion held that property owners would deface the sacred landscape just as tourist sharks had done at Niagara. However, these arguments are weakened by the damage wreaked by lease- and permit-holders over the several decades of the grant. If rampant development were such a grave concern, it seems that the act itself could have given more explicit authority to the commissioners to regulate it, whether leasehold or property owner, though the failure of Conness to mention the property holders to his fellow Congressmen did nothing to encourage such foresighted action. Given the general hubris of the postwar era, and the social and professional ties that linked Olmsted, King, Whitney, and other culture makers into the elite networks of Boston and New York, Hutchings was probably the victim of good old-fashioned New England chauvinism. Until more evidence emerges in the historic record, however, any additional reasons or motives for the curious anti-property stance of the commissioners remains speculative.[29]

Private Property and the Yosemite Grant

In his efforts to claim and develop private property in Yosemite as well as to interpret and publicize the valley, Hutchings found himself caught up in the ideological aftermath of the Civil War and the incorporation of the West into the nation. Together with James Lamon, Hutchings had filed preemption claims on property within the boundaries of the grant prior to congressional action and inhabited and improved that property, according to all the relevant requirements of the law. This fact was never mentioned in any of the Congressional deliberations prior to signing it into law. Those who supported the grant idea may have hoped that these land claims would be easily dealt with, but the process turned out to be fraught with many of the same tensions that would emerge in the era of Reconstruction between individuals, states, and the nation.

In the spring of 1866, the Yosemite Board of Commissioners informed Hutchings and Lamon that they no longer had legal title to their preemption claims and would be able to lease their lands from the commission. Hutchings, "under the beguiling hallucination" that his prior claim to the Yosemite lands constituted a more solid title than did the newly invested authority of the Yosemite Commission, refused this option and convinced Lamon to join him. The commissioners responded with a suit of ejectment. Hutchings and the commissioners carried this dispute through the courts to the U.S. Supreme Court, and through the legislature to the U.S. Congress. In all, it would be ten years before the commissioners' suit finally ousted Hutchings from Yosemite.[30]

While the Hutchings case percolated through Mariposa County District Court, the California state legislature voted in February 1868 to surrender the state's right and title to the quarter sections claimed by Hutchings and Lamon. This move was sustained over Governor Henry H. Haight's veto, but was framed as a memorial to the U.S. Congress and required ratification by that body to become effective.[31] In his book, *In the Heart of the Sierras*, Hutchings reported that the act passed the House of Representatives unanimously, but was defeated in committee during Senate hearings. Meanwhile, the district court ruled in favor of Hutchings; the Yosemite Commissioners appealed to the California Supreme Court, which reversed the decision; and Hutchings appealed to the U.S. Supreme Court, which heard the case in 1872 and decided against him in 1873. Justice Field wrote the court's opinion in language that strongly indicated this case's broader implications for federal land policies in the postwar era of incorporation and Reconstruction:

> If [the preemption laws] deprive Congress of the power to devest [*sic*] [public lands] by grant to another party . . . it must operate equally to deprive Congress of the power to reserve such lands from sale for public uses of the United States, though needed for arsenals, fortifications, lighthouses, hospitals, custom-houses, court-houses or for any other of the numerous public purposes for which property is used by the government . . . [The laws] do not . . . impair in any respect the power of Congress to dispose of the land in any way it may deem proper; . . . It is the only construction which preserves a wise control in the government over the public lands, and prevents a general spoliation of them under the pretense of intended settlement and pre-emption.[32]

The legal wrangling over Hutchings' and Lamon's preemption claims reveals tensions similar to those raised by other land-disposal acts of the federal government in the age of western incorporation. As the state of California attempted to uphold the residents' land claims, the Yosemite Commissioners responded that the State had no such rights, being bound by the terms of the original congressional grant, alluding to the newly expanded powers of the federal versus state governments in the postbellum context. Although appointed by the governor of California, the commissioners positioned themselves as protectorates of a decidedly *national* treasure. At the same time, however, traditional land practices, if not the law itself, favored Hutchings' position. And Hutchings aggressively marketed his case, traveling for several years at the end of the decade to press his claims in Washington, D.C., and financing his trips with illustrated lectures up and down the Atlantic seaboard (continuing to publicize Yosemite to the nation in the process). Hutchings' extensive knowledge of the Sierra, his engaging lecture style, and the persuasive tenets of his case garnered a good deal of sympathy, both locally and abroad—as his success with the California legislature and the House of Representatives illustrates. To bolster their own claims to legitimacy, the Yosemite

Commissioners launched a campaign to cast themselves as selfless defenders of the national icon over against the rapacious instincts of a private developer, bent on turning Yosemite into "another Niagara."

In his *Yosemite Guide-Book*, California Geological Survey chief Josiah Whitney echoed Olmsted when he wrote that private landowners in the valley would necessarily use their position to pursue profit (conveniently ignoring that the grant was contingent on such effort by leaseholders): "and the Yosemite Valley, instead of being 'a joy forever,' will become, like Niagara Falls, a gigantic institution for fleecing the public."[33] As early as the 1830s, "Niagara Falls" had become a metaphor for one of the paradoxes of scenic tourism: those who travel need shelter and food. But the material acts of providing these necessities—building hotels, roads, and raising stock for food and transport—often disrupted or directly challenged the sublime experience some travelers were conditioned to expect. The fact that those who provided food and shelter for tourists did so for a profit was especially irksome to some Niagara visitors, who called them "hucksters," and "tourist sharks."[34] Whitney's reference to Niagara, then, conjured the image of a despoiled national treasure, with which educated northeastern readers were probably quite familiar. By implicitly casting Hutchings as a "tourist shark," Whitney countered Hutchings' appeals to property rights and identified the Yosemite Commissioners as defenders of a national trust.[35]

This public relations battle has left a deeper imprint on our collective perceptions of this time than most historians probably realize. Hutchings' legal defeat marked a pyrrhic victory for the commissioners, whose unpopularity at the time would lead to their dismissal *in toto* in 1880. However, over time most historians have adopted the position of the commissioners as articulated in their campaigns to discredit Hutchings. Peter Blodgett casts the Yosemite Commission as hapless but completely well-intentioned managers with a "single, overriding dilemma: how . . . [to] foster development in the valley for the benefit of visitors without irreparably damaging the valley's unspoiled character." The commissioners' "long, bitter struggle" against Hutchings implicitly arrays the latter in opposition to this balancing act. Elsewhere Blodgett links the building of hotels in Yosemite to the "entrepreneurial energy that characterized the gold rush," suggesting that it was an equally destructive practice. Alfred Runte likewise adopts the position that the commissioners and their supporters defeated Hutchings' claims on the basis of preservationist instincts, arguing that a win for the landholders (Hutchings and Lamon) against the Yosemite Commissioners "would irreparably compromise all future attempts to establish scenic parks on the public domain."[36]

Sympathy to the Yosemite Commissioners in historic interpretation implicitly or explicitly reads support for twentieth-century management practices back into the historic record. Many of the historians who have uncritically accepted the perspective of the Yosemite Commissioners have gone further to make sweeping statements on behalf of the unknown "gentlemen of taste" who originated the grant idea in 1864. Hans Huth adamantly declares, without evidence, that in writing to Conness, Israel Ward Raymond "certainly did not take this step to further any of his business interests."[37] "It is quite safe to assume," wrote Huth, "that . . . the group of men promoting the interests of Yosemite did so for idealistic reasons," without documentation and in direct opposition to the clear business interests that men like George Coulter had in controlling access to Yosemite tourism.[38] Yosemite historian Carl P. Russell represents an alternative view more sympathetic to Hutchings. While acknowledging that "millions of Americans today are indebted to the board of commissioners who pursued the case to a settlement favorable to the people," Russell noted that "no man had done more than J. M. Hutchings to call attention to the fact that the Yosemite was . . . worthy of the distinction bestowed upon it by the state," and that the vast collection of Hutchings' writings fail to reveal "the commercialism and selfishness with which [he] . . . has been charged."[39]

However strongly one feels support for twentieth-century preservationist policies, the historic record does not support the majority view's leaps of logic. In his opinion for the Supreme Court's decision against Hutchings, Stephen J. Field mentioned all kinds of government land disposal practices that might be threatened by similar land claims. Not one of them included or even suggested a continuing role for Congress in establishing and maintaining "scenic parks on the public domain." Preemption laws, he wrote, do not "impair in any respect the power of Congress to dispose of the land in any way it may deem proper . . . It is the only construction which preserves a wise control in the government over the public lands." Far from being an endorsement of later environmentalist policy, Field's decision marked a significant transformation in federal land-disposal philosophy. Where once the ideal for western settlement was to transfer land into the hand of yeoman farmers who would carry American institutions to the frontier, now the power of Congress was paramount.[40]

In 1869, the completion of the transcontinental railroad not only brought more tourists to the valley (visitation rose from 600 to 1,122 that year), it also bound California and San Francisco more tightly into the industrializing national economic system.[41] Hutchings welcomed California's incorporation into the United States. In *Hutchings' California Magazine*, he repeatedly called for the completion of the transcontinental railroad, an achievement he could only have welcomed more with his new career in promotional tourism. However, just as the Yosemite Grant ultimately spelled disaster for Hutchings' plans to live and work in Yosemite, the transcontinental railroad caused widespread economic depression in California. Eastern factories that had geared up for wartime production dumped low-cost goods on the California market, undermining the state's own industrial production. California farm products for the most part could not survive the trip east and even when they could, freight rates disproportionately favored eastern producers, so Californians could not compete in eastern markets. The incorporation of the West into the national economic and political fabric did not always benefit those residents of the formerly more independent regions.

The western impact of the Civil War and Reconstruction extended far beyond cultural battles for the loyalties of California residents. With Southern opposition absent from Congress, the Union passed several legislative acts that radically affected the fate of the Far West, laying the legal infrastructure for accelerated expansion into western territories and the rapid growth of industrial capitalism that would bind regions more tightly into the economic and political frameworks dominated by northeastern cities. Until 1877, many states in the South and much of the Far West were not represented in Congress due to Reconstruction restrictions in the South and the territorial status of most western land. The Homestead Act of 1862, the Timber and Stone Act of 1878, and other similar land legislation facilitated western settlement while the legislation enabling the transcontinental railroad construction gifted thousands of acres of western lands to railroad corporations as incentive. Additionally, the Constitutional amendments passed during Reconstruction not only firmly asserted the power of the federal government over that of the states, they also granted corporations the legal status of individuals while limiting liability, enabling the rapid expansion and consolidation of large-scale monopolies and combinations in the postwar era.

After the Civil War, America's resource-rich western lands became extractive hinterlands, with raw materials flowing into industrial cores and finished goods back out again via railroad transport. Alan Trachtenberg calls this era the "age of incorporation": referring both to the economic phenomenon of corporate growth and the regional transformation whereby once-independent regions became more tightly bound into the cultural, political, and economic framework of the nation.[42] For California, Hutchings, and Yosemite, this Civil War legislation became the catalyst initiating a series of struggles over the appropriate use and meaning of western lands. These struggles took place in courtrooms and legislatures, in the pages of newspapers, and clothed in scientific debates. In some cases, such as Mussel Slough California in the 1880s, armed conflict erupted from disputes over changing notions of appropriate land use.

As was true for Hutchings, in many instances the public lands given over to corporations and combinations were already inhabited by settlers who had filed preemption claims on the land and were working to improve it, according to the pre–Civil War law. Preemption reflected the antebellum faith in the individual "yeoman farmer" as the primary agent to settle distant lands. However, Field's language in the Hutchings decision illustrated the postwar shift from this older view: "It is the only construction which preserves a wise control in the government over the public lands, and prevents a general spoliation of them under the pretense of intended settlement and pre-emption."[43] The formerly noble yeoman farmers are now cast as suspect characters whose claims mask the intent to "spoil" public lands. Ironically, given their shared connection with the Yosemite Grant, Field's legal interpretation also belied Olmsted's claim in 1865 that "it is the main duty of government . . . to provide means of protection to all citizens in the pursuit of happiness." Many of the struggles that ensued during the "western war of incorporation" occurred in places where such preemption settlers faced eviction in the face of competing subsequent claims from the railroads and other corporate interests favored in the post–Civil War era of national economic expansion.[44] Ironically, the federal land-grant practices that facilitated more rapid extraction of minerals, timber, and agricultural resources from western lands did far more to "spoil" those lands than the actions of individual farming families. The battle over Hutchings' claims in Yosemite thus played into the political economy whereby the federal government manipulated public lands to support some kinds of economic activity over against others.

Although it is true that Congress had never set aside land for scenery and recreation prior to the Yosemite Grant, traditional histories have focused on the "unprecedented" quality of this event to the exclusion of the complex historical contexts surrounding it, as if to suggest that the grant were somehow not a product of its time and place. However, attention to the broader national context reminds us that during and after the Civil War, *all* the land acts passed in Congress were "unprecedented." Several of these acts focused on western lands and expressed national (that is, Union) sentiment toward these lands: the Homestead and Morrill acts of 1862, for example, defined western lands as places to promote the Jeffersonian vision of yeoman farmers and miners and explicitly *not* as places where slavery could take root or spread. Olmsted's point that by preventing the park from falling into private hands the government secured the "pursuit of happiness" for all Americans was indeed a noble idea. However, the fact that the *practice* of that idea meant commodification of the landscape for tourists who could afford it ensured that it would remain a pleasure park for those with the economic means to demonstrate the appropriate "degrees of civilization." And by 1872 when the matter came before the Supreme Court, the need to clarify and uphold Congressional power and authority over public lands trumped even Olmsted's democratic plea for the "sole duty of government . . . to [protect] all citizens in the pursuit of happiness."[45]

Tipping Point: Yosemite and Environmental Conservation

In making the grant of Yosemite Valley to the State of California, Congress and President Lincoln put national law and policy in the service of landscape conservation for the first time in history. In designing the Yosemite Grant to stimulate and benefit from the tourist industry, the federal government and Yosemite Commissioners linked that preservation to the dominant economic ideology supporting private enterprise. With this act, a powerful force arose in American environmental history—the interlinked dynamic of consumer tourism, preservation, and national policy. This force would gather momentum over the next century to become the fundamental framework of American environmentalism in practice—though ideas, values, and trends would shift, the idea that environmental goals were best served through a combination of national policy and consumer tourism to sacred spaces remained a powerful concept through the end of the twentieth century. Although the term "environmentalism" is anachronistic when talking about the Yosemite Grant itself, it does apply to the ideas that evolved later. Both Yosemite and later Yellowstone were set aside to preserve "scenery," not nature or the environment. But the ideas of American environmentalism would emerge within the architecture created by the Yosemite Grant—quite literally, as John Muir, founding philosopher of American en-

Carleton Watkins' photograph "Hutchings' House" (undated) depicts Hutchings' hotel with the Merced River in the foreground. (Courtesy Yosemite Research Library, Yosemite National Park)

vironmentalism, came to his insights about nature and wilderness while living and working in Yosemite and its backcountry.

"Mine Host"

Meanwhile, Hutchings welcomed tourists to his hotel, and like other Yosemite entrepreneurs, aggressively expanded the tourist infrastructure during the 1860s. He started the first saddle train operation in 1866, and by 1875 was able to provide full outfits of saddle and pack animals as well as experienced guides for hire to parties wishing to camp out and hunt in the high Sierra. He raised cattle to provide milk and butter for his hotel guests, as well as establishing a fruit orchard and a five-acre vegetable garden. Hutchings' daughter Gertrude recalled "the orchard was a short distance below the old saw mill near the foot of Yosemite Falls . . . An irrigating ditch carried water to the barn and side ditches watered the vegetable garden . . . I remember well Spitzenberg, Winesap, King, Rhode Island Greenings and Northern Spy." But Hutchings' crowning horticultural achievement was the famed strawberry patch, which took four separate shipments of plants before he could obtain viable rootstock. The thirteen small roots increased to thousands of plants, some of which produced nearly two hundred berries each.[46]

In good preemption fashion, Hutchings continuously worked to expand and improve his dwellings. In the fierce winter of 1868, a "Mono wind" blew through the valley, knocking down hundreds of trees. Hutchings imported a sawmill to take advantage of the lumber but could not get it to operate until the arrival of John Muir and Harry Randall a year later. Hutchings hired Muir to build and operate the sawmill for ninety dollars a month, plus room and board, and Muir's work led to the rapid expansion of Hutchings' holdings. In addition to the cabin he built for himself, Muir replaced the muslin partitions dividing the rooms of the Hutchings' House, added porches and a new kitchen to Hutchings' cabin, and built a number of cottages to house the increasing number of guests. Muir wrote, "I had the good fortune to obtain employment from Mr. Hutchings in building a sawmill to cut lumber for the cottages . . . thus I secured employment for two years, during all of which time I watched the varying aspect of the glorious Valley."[47] Additions to the Hutchings House included the famous Big Tree Room, a combination kitchen and sitting room built around a large incense cedar. Hutchings later recalled,

This cedar, 175 feet high, was standing there when the room was planned. I had not the heart to cut it down, so I fenced it in, or rather, built around it . . . The base of the tree, eight feet in diameter, is an ever present guest in that sitting room . . . The large open fireplace was built with my own hands . . . Travelers from all climes and countries welcomed the sheltering comfort and blazing log fire of this room.[48]

Hutchings' House became the destination resort for many of the genteel tourists of the day. Though he charged a dollar more per day than other hotels in the valley, and the quality of cooking was allegedly inferior (usually involving strawberries and trout), many visitors came to be entertained by Hutchings himself.

Nineteenth-century celebrities who stayed at Hutchings' House included

Helen Hunt Jackson, Ralph Waldo Emerson, Horace Greeley, Louis Prang, and Carleton Watkins.[49] J. W. Boddam Wetham echoed a common refrain in describing Hutchings the hotelier:

> Mr. Hutchings himself is a poet, author, and philosopher; presumably, therefore, extremely ill-suited for the post of hotelkeeper, an employment requiring more practical qualifications. When Mr. Hutchings is up in the clouds, and dreaming of nature and her grandeur, he smilingly and thoughtfully assents to whatever you may have to say, and the next moment forgets all about you and your pleadings and philosophically returns to the contemplations of the magnitude of his waterfalls, but Mr. Hutchings' good nature and desire to please, make ample amends for any little discomforts.[50]

Hutchings and Yosemite's Consumer Tourism

While working as a hotelier, fathering three children, and traveling to defend his land claims, Hutchings continued to publish California travel guides. Between 1860 and 1876, he produced at least eight editions of his *Scenes of Wonder and Curiosity in California: Illustrated with over One Hundred Engravings. A Tourist's Guide to the Yo-Semite Valley.* The first two, in 1860 and 1861, were published under the imprint of Hutchings & Rosenfield. Hutchings issued two other editions under the imprint of J. M. Hutchings & Co. He published a London version under the imprint of Chapman and Hall in 1865, and subsequent editions (1870, 1871, 1872, and 1876) in New York and San Francisco under the imprint of A. Roman and Company. Much of the material in *Scenes of Wonder* was reprinted from articles and illustrations previously published in *Hutchings' California Magazine*, with some updated material relevant to the changing mechanics of travel.[51]

Hutchings' role as hotelier clearly structured many of his recommendations to tourists. He repeatedly counseled readers to take their time while staying in the valley, and to alternate days of exercise and rest in order to become "sufficiently toughened" for increasingly more difficult excursions. "Quiet, rest-giving rides, with intervals of physical toil, should give us all time to *feel* as well as to see, its infinite glories." Clearly, such a strategy would not only increase guests' physical endurance, but also lengthen their stay in his hotel.[52]

Throughout the Yosemite chapter of his guidebooks, Hutchings influenced the visitor's response to the valley's scenic wonders. At Yosemite falls, "if man ever feels his utter insignificance at any time, it is when looking upon such a scene of appalling grandeur." "We . . . stand, awed, in the immediate presence of such untold and bewildering majesty as that now rewarding our toil." At the same time, however, Hutchings also offered repeated disclaimers about the impossibility of adequately describing them: "It is impossible to describe the magnificent panorama that is here spread out before us," "we can only give a few plain facts and leave you to 'do the sublime.'" Ironically, Hutchings usually followed these disclaimers with at least a paragraph of very detailed description, including the appearance of the sky, the feel of the air, and perhaps some Indian lore, historical background, or seasonal variations. As fulsome as these descriptions were, they accentuated the inadequacies of secondhand experience by emphasizing colors, scents, and the sensations of air, altitude, and temperature. Regardless of the quality of photograph, engraved illustration, or printed text, none would be able to capture the full experience of actually being there.[53]

The commercial dimension of consumer tourism that Hutchings developed as hotelier after 1864 was not distinct from the cultural work that he and others engaged in to express the sublimity of Yosemite throughout the second half of the century. In reality, consumer tourism was a logical philosophical, as well as economic, extension of the cultural work that Hutchings had been engaged in while publishing in San Francisco. In his published works, Hutchings had joined the dynamic field of landscape representation, which ranged from the enormous paintings of the Hudson Valley school exhibited in urban galleries, to traveling panoramas and the lithographic prints and woodcut engravings such as the ones he crafted in his publications. As representational technology changed rapidly in the midcentury, the mammothplate photographs and stereographic slides of Watkins and other photographers joined the range of formats for depicting the landscapes that held such cultural significance for midcentury Americans.

As media technology and economics evolved over the century, Americans gained an increasing variety of options for landscape consumption. Very wealthy patrons like Daniel Wadsworth of Hartford, Connecticut, could, of course, commission their own landscape paintings from the likes of Thomas Cole for their own use. Urban Americans could visit galleries and see such paintings on display from time to time. Middle-class Americans of some means could purchase photographs, stereographs, or lithographic prints and view them in their own homes. In the smaller towns and hinterland communities, traveling panoramas, long scrolls with landscape scenes painted on them and illuminated with lanterns, were shown, often with a lecture, to audiences who paid to come and watch the show. As transportation networks eased the burden of travel, actual visits to the special places depicted became yet another option in the range of landscape spectacles available to consumers. It is important to remember, then, that tourism to Yosemite was simply another dimension to the cultural work of landscape interpretation. Visitors came because they had been prepared, by hearing sermons and lectures, reading articles like King's and guidebooks like Hutchings', to encounter a landscape of great aesthetic, religious, and political import, now sanctioned by the federal government of the United States. Just as the guidebooks, narratives, lithographs, and stereographs transformed Yosemite's scenery into consumer goods, tourism to the park was structured around consumerism and commodification of landscape. Tourists to Yosemite had to pay to enjoy and be enlightened by the scenery—just as they do today. And while this economic exchange had begun with earlier sacred sites like Niagara, the Yosemite Grant codified it into national policy.

Even after the Supreme Court decision, Hutchings fought to keep his residence in the valley. The state of California awarded him $24,000 to quit his claim, a stunning amount considering that the state refused to provide more than a few thousand dollars to the management of the grant for the entire decade. Hutchings, however, felt that it was less than the property's real worth. When the commissioners advertised the property for lease, Hutchings published announcements in local papers that he would sue anyone who tried to lease his former property from the "so-called Commissioners." Only one person applied—George Coulter, one of the "gentlemen of taste and fortune" who comprised the charter group of Yosemite Commissioners. Though Coulter resigned before making the offer, the hotel was just the latest in a chain of money-making operations his family had been engaged in during the prior decade of the grant and illustrates his definite financial interest in the park.[54]

Hutchings' ongoing defiance of the commissioners was immensely popular with his neighbors in the valley. In the spring of 1875, Yosemite residents fired their guns into the air to celebrate Hutchings' return to his former hotel in spite of the Coulter & Murphy lease. When the sheriff evicted him from his place, Hutchings moved the telegraph apparatus, post office, and Wells Fargo office from his former hotel into a nearby unoccupied building and turned that into a hotel for the summer. Already suffering from much adverse publicity, the commissioners tolerated this arrangement during the 1875 tourist season. The Mariposa *Gazette* reported that Hutchings "promises to remain in his new abode until hell freezes over and the devil can take a trip to

Yosemite on the ice." Hutchings finally moved to San Francisco in the fall of 1875, ending the hotel-keeping phase of his Yosemite career.[55]

According to Olmsted, the highest purpose that the Yosemite Grant would serve was to fulfill the "political duty of grave importance" of the new republican government toward its people. Just as Abraham Lincoln's Gettysburg Address defined a new relationship between the government and citizens as "a new birth of freedom . . . for the people, by the people" in the context of war, so the Yosemite Grant articulated a new relationship between government and western lands. The various struggles to define and manage Yosemite during the decade after the Civil War illustrate how profoundly important Yosemite was becoming to national identity. Although our contemporary origin myth defines the Yosemite Grant as an "unprecedented" act by forward-looking visionaries anticipating the future of wilderness preservation, attention to the cultural politics surrounding its creation demonstrates the opposite point. In an era filled with "unprecedented" acts of Congressional authority, the Yosemite Grant is a perfect expression of the national impulse to subsume western lands—cultural icons and tourist destinations just as mineral veins and forests—into the dominant political and economic framework of the Second Industrial Revolution.

Hutchings, Muir, and the Modern Paradox of Wilderness

Hutchings' 1873 Supreme Court defeat signaled the end of the first stage of his Yosemite career. In 1875, as he was finally evicted from his home of eleven years, he planned a final flourish. In preparation for the great Centennial Exhibit, Hutchings led an expedition to the summit of Mt. Whitney that included W. E. James, the first photographer to visit the peak. A series of photographs depicting the ascent of the mountain, crowned by a panoramic view from the highest point in the United States, would surely confirm not only the national significance of the high Sierra, but also Hutchings' implicit authority to interpret it. Although no record of the planned photographic exhibit in either the national or California centennial fairs has surfaced, the 1875 expedition represents a turning point in Hutchings' career; launching the evolution from litigious hotelier to a regional and national advocate for the preservation of the high Sierra. Ironically, given his reputation, by the 1880s Hutchings argued to extend the very kinds of federal control he had fought so bitterly in his own court battles, joining with Muir and others to advocate for the creation of Yosemite National Park in 1890 and the creation of the Sierra Club in 1892.

But irony and paradox were built into Yosemite by the marriage of sublimity and commercialism that allowed the American Congress to set the land aside in the first place. In structuring the Yosemite Grant to run on commodity tourism, the government and commissioners facilitated increasing numbers of visitors to encounter the spectacular landscape and experience the elevating and therapeutic influence in the "occasional contemplation of Nature."[1] In witnessing the sublime spectacle of Yosemite, visitors and remote armchair tourists alike would coalesce a common identity through reverence and appreciation of the scene before them. At the same time, however, much of the perceived value of such activity was in the escape it offered from the worries and cares of ordinary life. Whether one visited a sublime scene as a religious experience, a patriotic gesture of admiration for America's symbolic landscapes, or purely for therapeutic recreation, *escape* from the daily concerns of life was key to the success of this experience. But Yosemite continued to be as interconnected with the forces of industrialization and urbanization in the latter part of the century as it had been since the days of the gold rush.

After the Civil War, waves of immigration brought new groups of people into America, many from Eastern and Southern Europe, who went to work in the rapidly expanding factories of northeastern cities. Many older Americans responded to these groups with nativist hostility similar to the anti-Irish and anti-Black movements of the antebellum era. Class anxieties intensified as factory workers attempted to unionize and were harshly suppressed with police action and violence. In 1873, the year of Hutchings' Supreme Court defeat, Europe and America entered the Long Depression, an economic deflation that intensified conflicts between workers and factory owners. Violence countered striking workers in eastern cities, culminating in the Great Railroad Strike of 1877. Meanwhile, cities grew more dense with factories, tenement districts, and increasing levels of crowding, pollution, and disease. Just as Olmsted had intended, tourists to Yosemite sought relief from the illness and social strife of the cities in the fresh air and open spaces of California's mountains. Yosemite did have fresh air and open spaces, but it also was home to people of different classes and ethnicities whose labor made tourism possible in the first place.

One of the most significant factors in the rapid industrialization of the country was completion of the transcontinental railroad, which had a direct impact on the numbers of Yosemite tourists. In 1984, the year of the Yosemite Grant Act, 147 visitors came to the valley, increasing to 369 in 1865. Each year after that, the number climbed by around 100 until 1869, the year that the transcontinental railroad was completed, when the number jumped to 1,122. By 1874, annual visitation had risen to 2,711, when numbers declined, probably due to the depression of the mid-1870s. Visitation rose again after 1879, until 1886, when over 4,000 tourists came to the park.[2] Though tourists came to the valley with varying agendas, all visitors to Yosemite had a few things in common: they made their livelihood elsewhere, and their travels to the valley were supported by transportation, agricultural, and architectural technologies as well as the labor of Sierra residents. Modern tourists required modern amenities like carriage roads, hotels with walls (and then running water and bathhouses), postal services, and entertainment. In the days before transoceanic barges and eighteen-wheel trucks could transport food, film, and tchotchkes into the valley (and garbage out of it), most basic tourist amenities had to be grown or manufactured in Yosemite of Yosemite materials. Furthermore, the tourists' expectations of and experience in Yosemite were mediated by commodity exchange, since the entrepreneurial design of the Yosemite Grant ensured that visitors' encounters with Yosemite required cash transactions—to stay, eat, climb stairs, ride pack mules or horses, enjoy guided walks, or play billiards.

The difference between those who paid money to enjoy Yosemite and those who were paid to facilitate that experience connected Yosemite to the sharpening class divisions throughout the country. These divisions also fueled important disputes over the future of Yosemite as Hutchings, Muir, and others advocated strenuously to extend the boundaries of the Yosemite Grant to protect the high country watershed—arguments that ultimately led to Yosemite's full designation as a national park in 1906. The preservationist cause at the end of the century marked the final stage of the long-shifting perceptions of Anglos about the Sierra high country. Initially the hunting and harvesting grounds of Amerindians for thousands of years, the Sierra crest became the fatal danger zone of the emigration era, then the grazing and lumbering "commons" of valley farmers, and finally, through development of the Yosemite Grant, the recreational zone of travelers and the scientific laboratory of university-trained scholars. Although Olmsted's republican vision of the Yosemite Grant was to make it accessible to all in theory, the costs of commodified tourism ensured that only those who could afford to do so would enjoy the place in practice.

Late-nineteenth-century Americans were disinclined to grapple with the deep contradictions their society produced, and the central paradox of sublime commodification in Yosemite was no exception to this rule. Rather, when confronted with evidence of Yosemite's connections to the problems they hoped to escape, observers either complained that it failed to meet expectations or, more often, learned to look the other way. Technological transformations in media representation fostered new ways of seeing that encouraged visitors to simply ignore the people and infrastructure that challenged the ideal purity of the sublime landscape. Even scientific debates contributed to this process, directing attention from the here and now toward geologic deep time. Some popular literature transformed questions of race and class in Yosemite into sensationalistic fiction. But arguably the most powerful and long-lasting effort was John Muir's creation of the wilderness idea, the pan-theistic spiritual philosophy that shifted the communal experience of spec-tacular scenery into an individual, deeply personal experience of the divine through intense, solitary communion with nature. Muir's philosophy dove-tailed into the turn-of-the-century shift to the psychological sense of self that characterized the industrial world's modernized, urban elite. His poetic and ecstatic writings redefined Yosemite into a spiritual symbol for the individu-ated, isolated self of the twentieth century, and fueled generations of envi-ronmental advocacy for the creation of wilderness preserves.

Muir developed his philosophy during the three years he lived in Yosemite Valley—most of that time working as Hutchings' employee and boarding daily with the family. Muir also developed close relations with Hutchings' children and, most controversially, Hutchings' wife, Elvira, at least partially contributing to the Hutchings' divorce in the late 1870s. These domestic trou-bles, coupled with Muir's rising popularity as the wilderness spokesman in the late century, led to friction between the two men and the standard historic explanation of their lasting enmity. That story reinforces the traditional in-terpretation of Hutchings' battle with the Yosemite Commissioners—by cast-ing him as Muir's opposite, the standard account places Hutchings on the side of economic profit seeking over against the spiritual appreciation of nature for its own sake. Once again, the traditional narrative oversimplifies histori-cal reality. Though there is no record that they completely reconciled their personal differences, Hutchings' advocacy for Yosemite paralleled Muir's throughout the 1880s and 1890s, and both men were founding members of the Sierra Club in 1892. Nevertheless, as the century drew to a close, the com-plexities of landscape perception became increasingly bifurcated: humans came to be juxtaposed against nature, economics opposed to spirituality, the modern and scientific separated out from the "primitive." John Muir's wilder-ness philosophy captured and elaborated this modernizing tendency. Hutch-ings, with his public stance on property and his love of the public, would be-come situated on the opposite edge of the widening gulf separating "human" and "economic" from "spiritual wilderness."

Stubborn, irascible, but inventive and ever-adaptable, Hutchings was far more intellectually nimble than his detractors have realized and a far more sympathetic advocate for the cause to set aside and preserve Yosemite than he has been given credit for. As hotelier, he energetically pursued the Yosemite Grant's spirit and letter, not only building accommodations and transport networks, but contributing to photography's technological revolutions, col-lecting documentary evidence for contemporary scientific debates, and even promoting the feminist "ride astride" cause. Even as strife and tragedy visited his family and his career crumbled, Hutchings managed to land on his feet, shifting his perspective at the same time. As lecturer and advocate, he passionately pressed thousands of Americans around the country to support the preservation of the sublime Sierra through increased federal control of public lands. Whether collecting seeds so gardeners could embrace California species, selling curricula and slide-shows to schools, or speaking to packed lecture halls, Hutchings never wavered in his devotion to the Sierra Nevada of California. Literally to his dying moment, he looked upon the walls of Yosemite as his home and heaven on earth. Meanwhile, just as Yosemite had provided symbolic reassurance to ambitious San Francisco elites and war-torn Easterners in the 1850s and 1860s, the place continued to offer images of divine sanction for bourgeois policies and values in the dramatic demographic changes wrenching the country in the 1870s and 1880s.

The Art and Technology of Sublime Tourism in the Yosemite Grant

In a rare composition that eschews the nineteenth-century conventions of landscape painting, William Hahn made tourists the focal point of his 1874 series of paintings depicting the trip to Glacier Point, the cliff-side perch that offers a panoramic view of Yosemite Valley and the surrounding high country. *Yosemite Valley from Glacier Point* provides unusual documentation of the tourist gaze. Framed by the view of Half Dome, Liberty Cap (Mt. Broderick), and Vernal Falls, a group of tourists, together with their horses and guides, survey the scene. In the center, a yellow-jacketed artist appears to be instructing a woman and young girl about the scene before them. To their left, five other members of the party lounge on the granite, looking out over the panorama. A dark-skinned man walks toward the party, carrying bottles and a lunch sack, while behind him lie the littered remains of the meal. A second man naps in the shade of the horses.

The woman at the center of the painting surveys the scene through an optical device, perhaps a Claude Lorrain glass. The Claude glass was a popular tool in the late eighteenth and early nineteenth century that allowed artists and landscape tourists to "see" the scene before them as a painting. A series of tinted lenses could be shifted around to modulate the harsh glare of sunlight and to arrange the scenery into near, middle, and far distance. A Claude glass could also focus the view on the scenic elements, blurring distracting features like roads, buildings, and staircases on the edge of the visual frame. It is a perfect metaphor for the way of seeing that became naturalized in the late nineteenth century. Just as the woman in the painting ignored the litter of her own lunch and the guides who had assisted her arrival at Glacier Point, so did landscape and wilderness tourists learn to ignore the technological infrastructure and human labor that made their sacred parks possible. Through the increasingly sophisticated technology of photography, sublime views became available to a mass market as stereographs and cartes de visite, small albumen print photographs affixed to cardboard backing, encouraging the notion of Yosemite as a place apart from the turmoil of industrializing and urbanizing America.[3]

Taking the View: Photography and Landscape in Yosemite

The photographic technology of 1875 was a far cry from the daguerreotype apparatus Hutchings carried through the California mining towns in 1854. That technology could not be reproduced—only producing one small image on mirrored glass or metal per exposure. But technology evolved swiftly over the next few decades. By the time Hutchings took photographer Charles Leander Weed into Yosemite in the summer of 1859, British inventor Frederick Scott Archer had produced the first usable glass photographic negative, from which multiple paper prints could be made.[4]

Although Hutchings had commissioned Weed's photographs and used the salt print and stereograph images as the basis for engraved illustrations for his *Hutchings' Illustrated California Magazine*, it was Weed's studio employer, R. H. Vance, who made the first photographic prints for display in his studio and stereographic images for sale. Stereograph prints were double images that created a three-dimensional effect when viewed through a stereopticon lens. For decades, middle-class families around the world entertained themselves by gazing into the lenses at lifelike images of famous sights around the globe. Yosemite quickly became a favorite subject, and many got their first glimpse of the waterfalls and cliffs of Yosemite through the lenses of a stereopticon.

Weed also used a single-lens camera with 10 × 14-inch sheets of glass, each weighing around 1.5 pounds. Wet-plate technology required photographers to mix chemicals directly onto the glass, expose the image, and then fix it in a dark tent with another chemical bath. Prints were made through direct contact, so the size of the negative dictated the size of the print. Wet-plate photography was famously cumbersome, but photographers made some of the most stunning images with it. Following Weed, another Vance photographer, Carleton Watkins, went to Yosemite to build his reputation in 1861. Watkins commissioned a new camera, capable of holding 18 × 22-inch glass-plate negatives and outfitted it with a wide-angle lens specifically to capture the massive scale of Yosemite's scenery. Additionally, by 1863, albumen replaced salt prints, giving the images a depth and richness lacking in the earlier, flatter images. The resulting "mammoth-plate" photographs stunned the world and garnered Watkins several international awards. His were the photographs displayed at Goupil's studio in New York that helped to persuade Congress to support Senator Conness' bill granting Yosemite to the state of California.

Yosemite photography quickly became a very competitive business, and despite their technical accomplishments, both Weed and Watkins struggled to make a living. It was especially difficult to maintain name recognition when the studios who commissioned their work frequently accepted credit for it without attribution and the images were easy to pirate. Professional and amateur photographers also joined the rising tide of visitors to the valley, proliferating images of scenes like Yosemite Falls that were quickly becoming cliché. Watkins continually sought new vantage points and visual topics for his photographs, often hauling his weighty camera, dark tent, and chemical baths to unimaginable heights in the days before asphalt roads. In 1867, English photographer Eadweard Muybridge journeyed to Yosemite and soon became another highly inventive image maker. In his efforts to produce new perspectives on the valley, Muybridge surpassed Watkins in his daring exploits to precipices where even his hired assistants refused to follow.

Photographers' efforts to stay ahead of the market and competition simultaneously reproduced customary ways of visualizing landscape and created new perspectives. Watkins' photographs were classical compositions. Many followed painterly conventions, just as Ayres' drawing for the lithographic print of "The Yo-Hamite Falls" had, by including a foreground to anchor the composition. In framing his compositions, Watkins reinforced the image of sublime wilderness through the new medium of photography. At the same time, the clarity, depth, and enormous scale of Watkins' photographs imbued the sublime aesthetic with a new technical precision. His images were equally valuable as scientific documentation as they were as works of visual art: California State Geologist Josiah Whitney included twenty-four of Watkins' photographs in his 1868 *Yosemite Book.*[5] Muybridge, however, produced several images taken from heights such as Glacier Point, gazing down onto features of the valleys below, with the foreground eliminated altogether.

Carleton Watkins, "Mt Broderick and Nevada Falls," mammoth-plate albumen print, 1861. Watkins' photographic compositions drew on the conventions of landscape painting, with the foreground included. (Courtesy California State Library, Sacramento, CA)

These images imbue the viewer with the sensation of soaring or hovering above the subject, an impression Muybridge deliberately encouraged when he named his equipment wagon "The Flying Studio."[6]

Watkins' 1861 series of Yosemite photographs was a powerful agent in convincing Congress and East Coast elites of the importance of setting aside Yosemite. Images of Yosemite, contrasted with those of Civil War battlefields, echoed Olmsted's theory of the redemptive potential the landscape held for postwar nation rebuilding. Likewise, the photographic images that he, Muybridge, and other artists produced in the second half of the nineteenth century continued to reinforce bourgeois assumptions about the best use of spectacular western scenery. Though the photographers employed new technology, their most famous compositions echoed older, painterly traditions that constructed the wilderness and the artist/viewer's relation to it in mythic terms by erasing the physical traces of civilization, thereby eliding contentious questions of power and ownership raised by controversies such as Hutchings' preemption claim.[7] Photographers, like painters before them, produced Yosemite

Eadweard J. Muybridge, "Cloud's Rest, Valley of the Yosemite, No. 40," mammoth-plate albumen print, 1872. Muybridge's images create the illusion of soaring by eliminating the foreground from his compositions, contributing to the "panoptic sublime." (Courtesy Bancroft Library)

icons that shifted attention away from controversial conflicts, thereby serving to "internalize power relations . . . at a profoundly unconscious level."[8]

At the same time, as photographers and then tourists ascended the higher points around Yosemite, they were able to experience a specific form of sublime, what Alan Wallach calls "the panoptic sublime": "Having reached the topmost point in an optical hierarchy, the tourist [or artist] experienced a sudden access of power, a dizzying sense of having suddenly come into possession of a terrain stretching as far as the eye could see."[9] Such experiences, whether through the lenses of a stereopticon, a gallery display of mammoth prints, or actual visits to Sentinel Dome and Glacier Point in Yosemite, reinforced the ideal of natural landscapes whose aesthetic value is defined, in part, by the absence of human habitation. This ideal, in turn, informs the emerging notion of "wilderness": that "island in the polluted sea of urban-industrial modernity," where visitors could not only encounter, possibly, the divine but also reenact the moment of "discovery"; the powerful illusion of being the "first" to witness spectacular nature in its pristine, "original" state.[10] As Kevin DeLuca and Ann Demos have argued, in addition to naturalizing a "particularly classed way of seeing nature," the vision of pristine wilderness also contributed to the evolving understanding of what it meant to be white in America.[11]

While the nexus of sublimity and commodification produced tensions and internal contradictions, it was also a powerful generative force, as the rapid transformations in photographic technology and imagery demonstrate. The market forces driving tourism and creative production pushed artists and photographers to seek new subjects and perspectives, innovating new technologies in the process. Weed, Watkins, and Muybridge also shot images of tourists, Yosemite residents, and buildings and structures, but these images failed to reach the critical acclaim of those landscape compositions that upheld and extended the cultural perspectives linked to visions of pristine, uninhabited nature. Thus, the expectations of consumers and critics also mediated the artists' range of interpretive experimentation. Yosemite's natural features, the administrative structure of the grant, and the evolving experience of tourism itself all combined to encourage visitors to attempt their own artistic or poetic interpretations of the place. Yosemite was not so much a blank canvas onto which visitors projected their hopes and anxieties, as it was a crucible to inspire artistic expression. And while the voluminous writings, sketches, paintings, and photographs to pour forth from Yosemite usually upheld dominant cultural perspectives, occasionally the art or insight would turn in fresh, new directions.

When Hutchings brought W. E. James along on the Whitney expedition, the photographer carried a stereo camera and produced about seventy-five prints. Hutchings himself was not a professional photographer, or at least there is no record of his continuing to take his own photographs after his daguerreotype images in the early 1850s. However, by providing the funds and the marketing expertise to initiate photographic expeditions, Hutchings provided important support to early photographic developments, helping to foster innovation and technological change in Yosemite photography. Contrary to the common practice of the day, Hutchings tended to credit his photographers, even when they supplied the basis of illustrations. Photography remained central to Hutchings' public campaigns, as he illustrated his East Coast lectures in the 1860s and 1872–1873 with mammoth prints and later used lantern slides. Additionally, when Hutchings brought his "seeing eye for beauty" to the Yosemite Valley, he directed the artists and photographers to capture views he knew would tap into the culturally recognized vision of meaningful scenery. Despite their technical innovations, Watkins' and even Muybridge's dazzling visual accomplishments built upon the frameworks Hutchings had established, rather than challenging them directly.

Class, Race, and Playing with Fire

Long, long ago—before dapper tourists quickened their sluggish blood, and tore their kid gloves by clambering their way into this home of gigantic beauty—before "commissioners" had been appointed to protect nature from the vandalism of art, or the Californian ladies used the spongy bark of the mammoth trees for pincushions . . .

So begins the tale, *Forked Lightning—or, Gonza the Brigand. A Wild Tale of the Yosemite Valley,* John P. Cowan's 1872 dime novel published in Ornum and Company's series of "Indian Novels."[12] Where Watkins' artistic compositions of uninhabited western spaces obliquely hinted at questions of power, race, and class through visual codes established over several decades; *Forked Lightning*'s alternate tale of Yosemite's discovery plays out racial fantasies in direct and lurid detail. The melodrama pits Walt Tyler, the New England–born son of a wealthy merchant, against Rafael Gonza, a Californio outlaw who kidnaps Tyler's Mexican wife, Astola, and their baby from a foothill mining village. With his band of Mexican and "Mohave" Indians, Gonza takes Astola into the fastnesses of the Yosemite Valley. The "Forked Lightning" of the title is an Indian prince who befriends Tyler and leads him into Yosemite to rescue Astola and the child. Cowan plays on every imaginable racial stereotype in populating the tale with treacherous Indians and crafty Mexicans, not to mention the noble Walt Tyler and his graceful, fair-skinned Señora. The plot is a twisting series of near-misses and mistaken identities. It finally lurches to a halt when Forked Lightning rescues the heroes by killing Gonza but loses his balance and falls from a precipice in the process. Yosemite is thus freed from the suspect motives of the Mexican bandit as well as of the redeemed Indian prince, whose selfless sacrifice makes the valley available to the New England businessman and his band of trusty miners.

Forked Lightning's narrative was structured more by the literary conventions of dime novels than by concern for historical accuracy, of course. These cheap, ephemeral publications were priced to appeal to the mass audience and became especially popular with young boys in the 1870s. Frequently set in the Far West, dime novels and their independent heroes offered imaginary escape from the increasingly dirty and crowded industrial cities. Romance, adventure, mystery, and suspense were the driving forces of dime novels, so it should come as no surprise that Cowan's tale included impossible exaggerations, such as the giant halls carved from hollowed-out Sequoias where the "Mohave" held banquets and rituals. At the same time, and perhaps inadvertently, the story pointed toward race and class issues connected with Yosemite in ways that tour guides and other, more genteel publications would not.

By the 1870s, Yosemite was home to a diverse population, reflecting California's continued racial and ethnic diversity. The Flores family operated a laundry in the Lower Village, and their son, Manuel, worked as a packer and trail guide for Hutchings. Teams of Chinese stonemasons laid the walls for hiking trails and wagon roads into the valley. To satisfy the tourist demand for food, herders ran sheep and cattle on meadows planted with timothy for forage, and Joel Westfall operated a slaughterhouse and butcher shop for the hotel trade. The packers and herders were usually first-generation European immigrants and Amerindians integrating their traditional seasonally migratory lifeways with the new tourist economy. Amerindians frequently transported water from the Merced River to the hotels. As mentioned in the chapter 2 discussion of the Mariposa Battalion, many Amerindians returned to or made Yosemite their home in the second half of the nineteenth century. Tribal members not originally from Yosemite were drawn in by the promise of seasonal subsistence in the tourist economy. Many were able to combine traditional seasonal lifeways with some pecuniary reward for providing Yosemite hotels with fish, water, and the mail.

Although Hutchings was one of the original authors of California's race-based hierarchy, he and his mother-in-law, Florantha Sproat, maintained friendly relations with the Miwok, Mono, and Awahneechee, who lived in or moved through Yosemite Valley. Amerindian women taught Florantha to predict the weather and practice medicine with local herbs. The Hutchings children grew up with Amerindian playmates, and the family relied on the assistance of "Indian Tom" as well as numerous other seasonal workers who helped with haying and sheepherding and acted as tourist guides. Tom taught Hutchings to gather seeds and cultivate indigenous plants, an indispensable role in Hutchings' nursery business of the late 1870s. Hutchings was known to keep a jar of Mono Lake brine shrimp, an Amerindian delicacy repugnant to most whites, on a windowsill in his cabin as a gift for Native American visitors.[13]

However, the coexistence between Amerindians and the Yosemite tourist population was fraught with tension. Commissioners and other park managers continually attempted to "clean up" Amerindian settlements, and at the end of the century, U.S. Army cavalry were brought in to evict sheepherders, many of whom were Amerindian (or partly so), from the high country. Many genteel Yosemite observers agreed with Samuel Bowles, who wrote in 1868: "We know they are not our equals . . . We know that our right to the soil, as a race capable of its superior improvement, is above theirs; [therefore,] let us act directly and openly our faith . . . Let us say: you are our ward, our child, the victim of our destiny, ours to displace, ours to protect."[14] Whether through the classical compositions of Watkins or the melodramatic ending of *Forked Lightning*, the Anglo story of order and progress eclipsing the chaotic wilderness and its indigenous inhabitants continued to appeal to ever-widening audiences of middle-class and elite Americans.

While Walt Tyler's marriage to the Mexican Astola would have been scandalous to upper-class readers in 1872, intermarriage was a regular practice in California as in other parts of the country. Yankee traders had married Californio women during the Mexican period, though unlike Tyler they adopted Spanish names and Mexican lifestyles. Though Cowan had clearly never visited Yosemite, he did accurately capture pre-1855 Anglo fears about the place, that it was a "stronghold" or "fortress" where Amerindians could gather strength for attacks on foothill settlements. And his tongue-in-cheek introduction alludes to the vision of Yosemite as the domain of dapper tourists in kid gloves. Despite Olmsted's eloquent rationale for a park accessible to all people, the cost of commercial tourism to the valley ensured that tourism to it would remain the privileged playground of the well-to-do.

"To Take Charge of the Ladies:" Women and Class in Yosemite

In 1884, Hutchings wrote and published his culminating work, *In the Heart of the Sierras*. Over 400 pages, offered in gilt-stamped cloth or split calf binding, the volume was clearly intended for an audience quite different from the one meant to consume *Forked Lightning*. Hutchings also intended the semiautobiographical book to be read as a documentary, not a fiction. As with his other publications, Hutchings wove together new material with old, some of which dated to his earliest scrapbooks and diaries. Reading *In the Heart of the Sierras* as the culmination of over thirty years of publishing is like moving through a textual palimpsest, in which illustrations and text originally produced during the California gold rush were interleaved with the most advanced photographic reproductive technology and discussion of the latest scientific controversies. Where Hutchings' earliest publications pressed California land-scapes into service to frame an emerging social order in California, Hutchings used landscape in *In the Heart of the Sierras* to shape a vision of himself.

Among other topics, Hutchings romanticizes his domestic experiences: the building of a winter cabin, familial pastimes during the long winters, the planting of orchards and his beloved strawberry patch. Hutchings described his own family life as a perfect idyll of domestic bliss—surrounded by intense scenic beauty, the Hutchings family discovered the secret of true happiness as they gathered around the hearth, knitting and reading with the snow drifting outside the windows. However, Hutchings' recourse to sentimental tropes of domesticity elided his more messy family life, just as photographs, paintings, and travel narratives glossed over his land disputes and the working people and landscapes of Yosemite.

Given Hutchings' preoccupation with the proper role of women in the pages of his *California Magazine*, it is perhaps ironic that both his daughters became notorious as athletic, convention-defying women. Floy (Florence) was born shortly after the Hutchings moved to Yosemite, in August 1864. The most dramatic of the two sisters, she consistently wore men's clothing, smoked, and climbed mountains whenever she could. Cosie (Gertrude), born three years later, was also an independent spirit and an excellent equestrian and mountaineer, if slightly less rebellious than her older sister. Willie Yo Semite Hutchings was born with a twisted back and was relatively frail as a child, though as an adult he continued the old family tradition of working as a cabinetmaker, and accompanied the survey of Mt. Conness in the 1890s.

The independent spirit of Hutchings' daughters suggests that he learned to forego at least one of his Victorian cultural predispositions in Yosemite—the idea that women should be retiring, frail creatures relegated to the domestic realm. Not only did his own daughters grow to be convention-defying women, but he communicated this value to Yosemite tourists as well. For women who traveled to Yosemite and expected to enjoy themselves, it was necessary to defy conventional images of middle-class physical delicacy. Many writers expressed their delight at this necessity: author Grace Greenwood (Sarah Jane Lippincott) exulted in her freedom to race John Muir's pony up and down the valley in 1871. Several articles made much of the matter of riding astride. Middle-class women in the nineteenth century were trained and encouraged to ride sidesaddle, presumably to help maintain their sense of virtue. But sidesaddle was uncomfortable for the riders and injurious to the horses or mules they rode upon. Sidesaddles shifted the weight of the rider to just over the animal's kidneys. On the steep and rocky trails that descended several thousand feet to the valley floor, the unbalance of the sidesaddle put horses and mules in even more danger of losing their footing than already existed. Hutchings, who for many years managed Yosemite's livestock in addition to his hotel and promotional efforts, recognized the potential damage of sidesaddle and waged an ongoing campaign to convince women tourists to "ride astride."

> Calculate to ride astride and dress for it. A woman who has only one leg, or has two on one side, may have some excuse for the unnatural, ungraceful, dangerous and barbarous side-saddle. The last word was prompted by remembering the raw back of the beautiful horse which carried Miss [Dorothea] Dix into the valley, under the old, conventional side-saddle. The lady is, unquestionably, a noted philanthropist, but that poor horse probably never suspected it. Anna Dickinson rode in man-fashion, arrived fresh and strong, and so did her horse. Ask her animal if he wants to carry that lady again, and he'll never say nay (neigh).[15]

Hutchings laid in a supply of divided skirts for rent at Tamarack Flat, for many years the last stop for wagon and coach trips on the Big Oak Flat Road. Here travelers switched to saddle for the last 5 miles and 2,000-foot descent into the valley. That Hutchings' efforts to protect his investment in stock inadvertently supported a feminist cause is somewhat ironic, but the "ride astride" issue points out that the practical experience of Yosemite tourism occasionally allowed visitors to challenge, or at least depart from, existing social norms.

The ride-astride matter illustrated one of the ways in which travel to Yosemite encouraged (or mandated) that genteel middle- and upper-class women defy gender conventions. However, Yosemite did not function in the same way for all women. The tourist-consumers who came to Yosemite needed to be fed, housed, and transported. And so, the production of Yosemite landscapes was not merely a cultural one that took place in books, articles, and photographs: it was also a material one that transformed the economy and ecology of the valley a century ago and continues to do so to this day. From 1856 forward, the tourist industry depended upon the energies of women and men who chose to make Yosemite their home, at least for part of each year. And if the act of tourism allowed the middle- and upper-class tourists to defy gender convention, it appears that the act of producing for the tourist economy did not have the same effect on the lives of women and men who lived and worked in the valley. By all accounts, and with a few notable exceptions, most of the people who labored for the tourist economy did so largely along gendered lines.

"By all accounts," because workers in Yosemite were far less likely to write about their own experiences than were tourists. The most visible of women laborers were those wives of hotel keepers who worked as cooks. Food was every bit as important to tourists as sublime scenery, and so women such as Mary Peregoy, Emily Snow, and Isabella Leidig received written praise from hungry travelers for their abilities in the kitchen. Wives were apparently so essential to the success of hotels that in 1869 Yosemite Guardian Galen Clark, charged with overseeing the park's development, selected Edwin Moore as his partner in Clark's station "because I wanted a partner who had a wife."[16] The range of work these husband-and-wife teams engaged in illustrates the impact of the tourist economy. Men built hotels, trails, corrals, ladders, and other structures; raised and slaughtered livestock, and farmed to raise food for their guests. Women cooked, reared their children (Isabella Leidig gave birth to eleven children in Yosemite), kept house, cleaned, did the laundry, gardened.

Attention to the activities of workers and residents in Yosemite highlights yet another dimension of the role of class distinctions in the transformation of Yosemite into a national landscape for recreational tourism. By contrasting the experience of women tourists with that of the women residents who helped to feed and shelter them, the divide between the tourist consumers and resident producers becomes more clear. Beyond the quality of the food they placed in front of the hungry visitors, the productive lives of Yosemite women were as invisible to visitors and to later historians as were those of the Chinese trail builders, Mexican launderers, and Miwok water bearers. Hutchings perched somewhat precariously between the two ends of the Yosemite tourist economy. As a writer and publisher, he knew how to appeal to the educated elite and did so throughout his professional life. As hotelier, he managed the mundane business of producing for the tourist trade and built long-term relationships with those "invisible" Yosemite residents. The relative invisibility of nonwhites and working-class whites in Yosemite was analogous to the sublime aesthetic that framed spectacular nature to erase human presence, with far-reaching implications for America's emerging environmental consciousness.

The image of domestic bliss that Hutchings painted in *In the Heart of the Sierras* belied more than the rebellious spirit of his daughters. During their years in Yosemite, the Hutchings' marriage became increasingly strained.

Hutchings' young wife, Elvira, suffered from depression, loneliness, and isolation after their move to Yosemite. A dreamy, artistic woman, Elvira could not adapt to the constant round of domestic chores that the celebrated cooks of other Yosemite hotels mastered. Her mother, Florantha, stepped into that role with aplomb, prepared by her years of keeping the boardinghouse in San Francisco. During their eleven years of year-round Yosemite residence, Hutchings was frequently away from home, whether advocating for his property rights or arranging business matters. But Elvira was as miserable if not more so when he was home. In 1873, she confided to Jeanne Carr: "O Mrs. Carr, I feel sick for the kind of love he has for me. I believe that I should never have thought of the word separation if he had not spoken of it first in regard to my physical incapacity of satisfying him sexually. He needs a strong, passionate woman."[17]

In the fall of 1869, Hutchings hired John Muir and Harry Randall to help manage his business affairs and "to take charge of the ladies" while he traveled east to press his property claims in Congress. Muir had been sent by Jeanne Carr, his lifelong mentor and confidante. When Jeanne's husband, Ezra, took a position at the University of California, Berkeley, the couple visited Yosemite in the spring of 1869 where they met James and Elvira Hutchings. Jeanne recommended Muir to Hutchings and encouraged him to seek employment there. The men boarded with the Hutchings family and became friends with the children and Florantha and Elvira. In her loneliness and depression, Elvira turned to Muir and developed romantic feelings for him. Over the next four years, while Hutchings was frequently away on business, Elvira and John Muir developed a close relationship, although the exact nature of it remains a mystery. The two frequently went botanizing and hiking together, and both characterized their relationship as deeply spiritual. Muir wrote, "Mrs. Hutchings is always kind to me, and the clearness of her views on all spiritual things is very extraordinary."[18] Elvira and Muir both confided about this relationship to Jeanne Carr, though only a fraction of their correspondence remains.

Hutchings most likely had suspicions much earlier, but Elvira confessed her feelings in the spring of 1873 to him and Florantha: "I have spoken frankly of *all* to my mother and Mr. Hutchings." Her mother could not understand but thought separation might be best. Elvira wrote to Jeanne: "O, Mrs. Carr. Mr. Hutchings knows all, knows how my friend [Muir] feels toward me, furthermore he wishes us not to see or correspond with one another while I am his wife." If they separated, Hutchings said he must keep the children.[19] In May, Elvira Hutchings traveled to Oakland to meet with Jeanne. After the visit, on the same day of Elvira's departure, Carr wrote Muir to ask him frankly what his feelings were and told him that he had to respect Elvira's role as wife and mother:

> All your work, more your glorious possibilities, are nothing to me, John, if you are not great enough to put yourself in Mr. Hutchings' place. I am greatly distressed about this and fear to do you injustice in my estimate of affairs, and I will say no more. I must know whether Mrs. Hutchings' statements are colored by her own wishes or yours . . . I believe the very spirituality of your love has blinded your judgments and dulled your conscience, and made you see both her and yourself, so to speak, above the laws of duty to one's neighbors.[20]

She mentioned that she had planned a trip to Yosemite with Albert Kellogg and painter William Keith, but she wrote, "I do not wish to see you or the valley at present, lest I should say repentable things."[21]

The outcome of this exchange is lost to the historic record. Muir responded to Jeanne in June but that letter was expunged from her papers at his request. Elvira returned to Yosemite from her visit with Jeanne Carr in June, and Jeanne did go through with her summer trip to Yosemite, with Muir as guide for most of the time. Muir spent most of that summer in the high country, permanently leaving Yosemite in September 1873. Elvira stayed with Hutchings until the Mt. Whitney expedition, which she left early to return to San Francisco. Elvira joined the Swedenborgian movement, and at least by 1879 had moved to Portland to live with her sister. On January 1, 1880, the *San Francisco Chronicle* noted that Hutchings had been granted a divorce from his wife the day before "on the grounds of desertion."[22] Scattered reports of her later years indicate that Elvira became increasingly withdrawn and she eventually died of dementia at her daughter Cosie's home in Vermont.

Most of the letters that might have documented Muir's perspective in this relationship were destroyed by him and his descendents. Thus, the historic consensus remains that Muir did not return Elvira's affections and that their friendship remained platonic. Even so, it would be difficult for Hutchings not to blame Muir for their divorce when Elvira left him and their three children after the family was evicted from Yosemite. After Hutchings and Elvira separated, he continued to live with her mother, Florantha Sproat, and the three children. By 1879, Hutchings had married the artist Augusta Sweetland, who became stepmother to Hutchings' two daughters, Floy and Cosie and to his son, Willie. Hutchings remarried three times. Both his second and third wives died shortly after their marriage, his fourth wife, Emily, survived his death in 1902.

The Whitney Expedition: Science and the Higher View

The summer of 1875 was Hutchings' last as "Mine Host" and hotel keeper in Yosemite Valley. While entertaining reporters, neighbors, and tourists with his antic defiance of the commissioners, he also organized a two-month expedition to King's Canyon and to take the first photographs on the summit of Mt. Whitney, the highest peak in the United States. The Whitney expedition seems an ambitious plan for a fifty-four-year-old man whose life had just been thrown into personal and professional turmoil. But for Hutchings, it was simply another expression of the creative entrepreneurial spirit that he had developed during the gold rush, and was the first of a series of mountaineering expeditions he would take over the next several summers.

Dragging photographers to the summits of Sierran peaks was one of Hutchings' favorite pastimes, continuing his lifelong fascination with emerging technologies of visual representation, from the daguerreotype of the 1850s to the "solar stereopticon" he would invent in the 1890s. He may very well have been scoping out the southern Sierra for another hotel site. The summit expeditions also gave Hutchings opportunity to continue his ongoing amateur scientific pursuits by observing and recording geological, climatic, and botanical phenomena. In the decades after the Yosemite Grant, science joined sublimity as a dominant organizing framework for interpreting and publicizing the importance of sacred places. Hutchings had ample opportunity to converse with leading scientists and to conduct his own observations and experiments. The combination of scientific and sublime appreciation of the high Sierra marked the work of such famous scientists as Clarence King, first president of the U.S. Geological Survey, and Hutchings' erstwhile employee, John Muir.

En route to Whitney's summit, Hutchings conducted experiments in barometric pressure, made geological observations, reached the summit of Mt. Ritter, and explored the Devil's Postpile basaltic columns. The party included Al Johnson, the guide who had led the first ascent of Whitney in 1873; photographer William James; Albert Kellogg, Hutchings' old botanist friend; nephew Edmund Bedford; C. B. White, the resident doctor from Camp Independence; George P. Stanley; John F. Connell; James Fleming; and two soldiers from Camp Independence. Originally Elvira Hutchings, Yosemite packer Manuel Flores, and "Mr. Boericke of S.F." were also in the party, but

Hutchings sent Flores as guide to accompany Elvira and Boericke when they decided to turn back. "They wanted to start out alone," he wrote, "but I just as soon have thought of sending two children out alone. They would have been lost in less than half an hour."[23]

The Hutchings party reached the summit on Sunday, October 3. In addition to his explorations around Mt. Whitney and writing the first recorded description of the Kern River Golden Trout, Hutchings directed James to photograph fissures in the earth left by the Lone Pine earthquake of 1872. He may have hoped to contribute evidence to the debates over the formation of Yosemite. Josiah Whitney, Yosemite commissioner and director of the California Geological Society, held that Yosemite had been formed by a cataclysmic subsidence, not the slow forces of erosion and glaciation. In 1865, Whitney articulated the cataclysmic theory in his California Geological Survey report and developed it further in the 1868 *Yosemite Guide-Book*.[24] On March 26, 1872, one of the largest earthquakes in recorded California history struck Lone Pine on the eastern scarp of the Sierra. Based on the extent of its damage, scientists today guess that it would have registered between 7.5 and 8 on the Richter scale, equivalent to the San Francisco quake of 1906. Lone Pine caused a series of massive rockfalls in Yosemite, made famous by John Muir's ecstatic description:

> It was a calm moonlit night, and no sound was heard for the first minute or so [after the earthquake], save low, muffled, underground, bubbling rumblings, and the whispering and rustling of the agitated trees, as if Nature were holding her breath. Then, suddenly, out of the strange silence and strange motion there came a tremendous roar. The Eagle Rock on the south wall, about a half a mile up the Valley, gave way and I saw it falling in thousands of the great boulders I had so long been studying, pouring to the Valley floor in a free curve luminous from friction, making a terribly sublime spectacle—an arc of glowing, passionate fire, fifteen hundred feet span, as true in form and as serene in beauty as a rainbow in the midst of the stupendous, roaring rockstorm.[25]

Lone Pine added credence to the Whitney theory of Yosemite's cataclysmic origins, but observations by Muir and others pointed toward a growing body of evidence in favor of glaciation. Though Yosemite is not the characteristic U-shape of most glaciated valleys, it does bear striated marks and moraine piles. Clarence King observed glacier-formed striations in Yosemite's granite walls but changed his mind to support Whitney, then his professional superior. The man most often cited in opposition to the Whitney interpretation is John Muir, who persistently argued for the glaciation theory. Hutchings was a vocal proponent of this idea as well, popularizing the debate for his readers over several pages of *In the Heart of the Sierras.* In his descriptions of trails around the Yosemite basin, he pointed out places where readers/visitors could see for themselves evidence of glacial action.

Hutchings' position in the scientific argument rested on his long familiarity with the valley, together with his knowledge of and response to the scientific theories of the day. In popularizing scientific debates to his tourist/readers, Hutchings continued his lifelong interest and the work he had begun with his *California Magazine,* which had functioned in the 1850s as a forum for early founders of the California Academy of Science, such as geologist John B. Trask, and other amateur scientists to publish their findings. Hutchings developed lifelong friendships with several of these men. His friend Albert Kellogg was a medical doctor whose interest in botany led him to become one of the early experts in California plants, wrote a series of articles on endemic species of California wildflowers for *Hutchings' California Magazine.* Hutchings and Kellogg went on botanizing trips together; Kellogg credited Hutchings with the discovery of a species of penstemon, "in a recent tour of the mountains." He also accompanied Jeanne Carr on her 1873 summer tour with Muir as guide.[26]

By offering a forum where California's first scientists could publish the results of their studies, *Hutchings' California Magazine* performed a valuable service in promoting scientific study in the state. The magazine also served as a reference and resource for later scientists and surveyors. In Yosemite, Hutchings supported the work of survey parties, offering the services of Florantha and Elvira to type the California Geological Survey notes in 1865. But by the 1870s, the heyday of the amateur scientist, which Hutchings exemplified, was being replaced by the rise of professional science, with its emphasis on educational background, disciplinary divisions, and institutional or bureaucratic association. So, scientific observation, survey, and debate became a discourse for understanding Yosemite and the high Sierra that engaged educated classes across the country in the decades after the Civil War.

The Whitney expedition reminded Hutchings of his love for mountaineering. He was among the first to ascend Mt. Shasta in 1855, and in 1871 he had just missed being the first to climb Mt. Lyell by ten days (A. T. Tileston was the first). Hutchings descended the Tuolumne River Canyon from Tuolumne meadows in 1873, and was the first white man to descend Tenaya Canyon from Tenaya Lake to Mirror Lake in Yosemite Valley. After 1875, freed from the duties of hotel keeping, he and his family spent the next several summers in the high country around Yosemite. In 1877 he and several women climbed a series of mountains, including Half Dome. The party included Florantha Sproat, her widowed sister, Matilda Ladd Hedrick, Augusta Sweetland (who would become Hutchings' second wife), Miss Whaley, and Hutchings' children Cosie and Willie. As part of this tour, Hutchings climbed the summit of Mt. Starr King together with George Anderson and Jean Baptiste Lambert. The next day, they repeated the climb with Cosie, Augusta, and photographer S. C. Walker.[27]

From 1875 to 1881, Hutchings lived on Pine Street in San Francisco and led tours of Yosemite and the high country mountains in the summers. He also launched a seed business concentrating on California native plants, drawing on his many botanizing hikes with Tom. During these years he increased the frequency of his illustrated lecture circuits around the region. Once again, Hutchings found himself in the center of shifting cultural norms and values. San Francisco in this period was a hotbed of political agitation over Chinese labor, the wheat trade, and other issues that led to the return of vigilance committees in 1876 and the restructuring of California's state constitution in 1879. The root of many of these controversies was once again land, the struggles between the working class and corporate combines and the proper role of government in managing competing interests over land. Although Hutchings had his day in court over the priority of small-holding private property, his views began to shift in the years after leaving his hotel behind. In his lectures around the state, he began to advocate for increasing government protection of the Sierra high country, joining with Muir and other scientists in a heated critique of those who would destroy it. But this critique was not levied against the corporate interests behind industrial-scale lumbering nor the hydraulic mines that continued to lay waste to the Sierra landscape. Rather the targets of the grant-extension advocates were the livestock herders: voiceless and itinerant immigrant and Native American sheepherders.

Grant Extension: Class, Technology, and Politics

In 1879, California adopted a second state constitution, which included a provision for replacing the Yosemite Board of Commissioners, widely seen as corrupt and ineffective. This new board of commissioners initiated an investigation into the possibility of extending the Yosemite Grant's boundaries to protect the valley's surrounding watershed. Hutchings supported this idea, suggesting that the increased tourism would defray the cost of the grant. Several prominent advocates came forward to add their support, including California State Engineer William Hammond Hall, Frederick Law Olmsted, and, of course, John Muir. The grant extension cause brought many people together who would go on to support the creation of Yosemite National Park in 1890 and form the Sierra Club, America's first environmental advocacy organization, in 1892. In the ensuing debates, class and technology became inextricably bound up in conservationist discourse:

> When I seek to hold loving communion with God, and nature, and steal away into these inspiring solitudes, and there find that sacrilegious and vandal hands—yes, those of the herder—have set on fire these glorious forests; as I look at the dense smoke curling up through the blackened and burning stumps, or listen to the crackling of the blaze, and see the sheets of flame leaping from tree to tree, licking their beautiful foliage with devouring tongues, I cannot but make the unchristian-like confession that I execrate the act and feel neither respect nor patience with the doers.[28]

Advocates for the extension of the Yosemite Grant found a *bête noir* in the humble Sierra sheepherders, who were often Amerindians hired by stock owners or first-generation immigrants from Portugal or the Basque country. As Hutchings' diatribe suggests, it was not only the grazing that raised conservationists' ire, but especially the deliberate annual burning of meadows and underbrush to encourage the growth of forage. Sheep had come to California as early as 1841, and the Euro-American emigrants to Nevada and California began raising sheep in the early 1850s. They "followed the spring," driving flocks up from valley ranches on both sides of the Sierra to graze in meadows at increasingly higher elevations as the snow melted. Contrary to the impassioned arguments of conservationists, grazing sheep reduced brush in the high country meadows and increased soil fertility with their manure. Basque shepherds frequently were paid in a percentage of the flock's increase, until they gained enough to establish their own farms and could sponsor another relative from the old country. At the season's end, following the ancient practice of Amerindians, shepherds of all ethnicities would burn the meadows as they descended back down to the valley. The burning practice protected the meadows from brushy incursion, encouraged the growth of new forage, and actually helped to protect the forests from catastrophic wildfire by eliminating the dead grasses and windfall branches that can kindle a lightning strike.[29]

The ecological benefits of sheepherding and particularly annual burning are only slowly being understood in the twenty-first century, after a century of fire suppression policy has wreaked its own ecological damage. In the nineteenth century, the literate, scientifically educated elites could not see it at all. Hutchings joined forces with Muir who wrote in 1879 that "all the gardens and meadows were destroyed by a hoard of hoofed locusts, as if swept by a fire." The term "hoofed locusts" became Muir's favorite catchphrase for the allegedly horrific impact of sheep-grazing in the California mountains and a powerful rationale for extending federal control over more Sierra territory. Even today, "grazing by domestic sheep in the Sierras is considered a 'classic example' of 'market failure, which requires collective action to remedy,' the most vivid California example of the tragedy of the commons."[30] However, the alternative forest management structure proposed by professionals trained in eastern universities was fire suppression, a policy now widely acknowledged to have increased the vulnerability of mountain ecosystems to disease and catastrophic wildfire.

Professional foresters, scientists, and environmental conservationists like Hutchings and John Muir derided the controlled burning as "Paiute Forestry," indicating the ancient roots of the practice. Sierran ecosystems had co-evolved with the hunter-gatherers, who practiced seasonal burning in addition to judicious pruning, seed-scatter, and other techniques to maximize food sources, open the woods to facilitate travel and hunting and promote the growth of plants used in tool-making. With the demographic disasters wrought by virgin soil epidemics, forced removals, and outright genocide in the 1850s, Sierra ecosystems lost the majority of their human caretakers. At the same time the native bighorn sheep were also decimated by diseases introduced by the domesticated European sheep. Although there were episodes during the nineteenth century where sheep did overrun the Sierra meadows, these usually resulted from a convergence of factors, such as drought combined with a sudden upswing in sheep populations due to market conditions (as happened the year Muir first recorded the "hoofed locust" phrase), rather than established practices. Aside from these episodes, the sheepmen's practice ironically kept the forests and meadows close to their ancient patterns for another few decades. But the derisive term "Paiute Forestry" points to the central role of class and ethnic bias underpinning supposedly objective scientific observation and policy design.

Despite the fact that words such as *conservation, preservation,* and *restoration* imply some kind of protection of a pristine environment, the practical fact is that the creation of wilderness parks has always meant the privileging of one kind of development over another. While Yosemite's landscapes were protected from mining, logging, and commercial agriculture, they were intensively manipulated to provide access to tourists. Road- and trail-builders borrowed dynamiting techniques from the mines and railroads to blast granite walls into roadbeds and support walls. Hutchings and others maintained extensive stock operations to bring tourists and supplies into the valley. There were butchers, photographers, and a saloon in the valley. In other words, Yosemite's tourist industry was indeed an *industry*, complete with resource extraction, hierarchical labor systems, and top-down management structure. And although preservation language continually emphasized the "public good," the practical effect of the conservation efforts in the 1880s and 1890s was to wrest the high Sierran forests and waters from the voiceless and powerless itinerant sheepherders and into the hands of scientific managers.

The initial Yosemite Grant extension proposal met with vociferous opposition from local residents, particularly those in the San Joaquin Valley who recognized their dependence on the mountain ranges and timberlands for economic survival. As in the *Forked Lightning* introduction, class issues became explicit when San Joaquin Valley residents protested that the extension would serve "four-eyed tourists and funny business for ever." The debate over Yosemite's grant extension shares many characteristics with a parallel development in the Adirondacks. In 1883, a powerful alliance of recreational sportsmen and industrialists in New York wishing to ensure the flow of water to their mills created the Adirondack state park. They replaced local traditions of land use with bureaucratic management based on principles of scientific rationality and enforced by ever-increasing numbers of "foresters" with police powers. Like the Basque and Amerindians of Yosemite, the 15,000 ethnically diverse residents of the Adirondacks found their traditional patterns of forage and timber harvesting illegal under the new rules and regulations. With their economic livelihoods threatened, they were increasingly forced into the wage-based labor that serviced the tourist trade. Middle-class and urban advocates of the park, like their California counterparts, regarded the residents as wasteful and selfish threats to the natural environment, just as sheepherders were seen by Muir, Hutchings, and others. California farmers and sheepmen managed to defeat the extension in the early 1880s, but the issue only fueled the fight to shift control of Yosemite into federal hands.[31]

Whether or not they had direct ties to industry, professional scientists tended to address problems with a zeal for technology characteristic of industrial forces at the end of the century. After the high country surrounding Yosemite Valley was designated as a national park (the valley remained under the control of the State of California) in 1890, Head Forester of California

Allen Kelly wrote a proposal to restore the Yosemite waterfalls with a system of reservoirs and flumes. Writing for the national periodical *Harper's Weekly*, Kelly argued that doing so would ensure that the waterfalls, and by implication the tourist season, would continue to run in full through the summer instead of drying up by August: "The vast volume of Nevada Fall, that plunges in a broad sheet of foam 600 feet downward into a roaring, seething caldron . . . dwindles to an insignificant dribble in October." Kelly's proposal may seem preposterous to twenty-first-century understandings of the charm of wild nature. But it was consistent with the emerging theories of forest conservation favored by progressives and professionals. Drawing on the assumptions of George Perkins Marsh and Charles Sargeant, Kelly blamed the short waterfall season not on the natural cycles of drought and flood in Sierra watercourses, but on the damage to high-country forests wrought by sheepherders. Allen Kelly's proposed system of reservoirs, canals, and flumes would "restore" the watershed to its imagined "natural" state while the forests took the necessary time to heal from the perceived depredations of high-country sheep. This scenario, of using hydraulic mining technology to protect and restore the natural and scenic beauty of Yosemite's waterfalls, illustrates the industrial and technological focus of the scientific managers who rushed to assert the power of their expertise over the time-worn practices of the working people who had lived in the mountains for generations.[32]

In addition to launching the Grant extension proposal in 1879, the new board of Yosemite Commissioners also elected to appoint Hutchings Guardian of Yosemite Valley in 1880, a position that allowed him to return to his old residence and gave him responsibility for overseeing the park's management. Returning triumphantly to his "Old Cabin" by Yosemite Falls would have marked the crowning achievement of Hutchings' life, had tragedy not struck his family. About a year after they moved back to the cabin, Florence was killed in a climbing accident, and Augusta died six weeks later after a lung hemorrhage. In 1883, Florantha Sproat, Hutchings' indomitable mother-in-law and de facto business partner, also died. After Florence died, Hutchings adopted his Mono employee, Tom, and dedicated *In the Heart of the Sierras* to him. Descendents of Tom Hutchings claim James Mason as their ancestor.

Hutchings' tenure was marked not only by personal tragedy but also (perhaps unsurprisingly) contentious disputes with the commissioners over park management. His advocacy for the grant extension cast him in opposition to many of his former neighbors over the propriety of government oversight. A dispute with Executive Secretary Briggs over the hiring of Briggs' relatives led to Hutchings' dismissal from the Guardianship in 1884. He left Yosemite for San

Francisco, where he wrote and published *In the Heart of the Sierras*. Though he continued to visit, botanize in, and advocate for Yosemite over the next eighteen years, Hutchings would never return as resident to the valley again.

Between 1884 and his death in 1902, Hutchings continued to advocate for Yosemite and the Sierra through his illustrated lecture tours and often passionate correspondence to administrators, politicians, and newspapers. In 1892, Hutchings married for the fourth time to English-born Emily Ann Edmunds. Co-principal of the San Francisco Van Ness Seminary, Emily may have been the "strong and passionate woman" Hutchings had been looking for. She called him "Mason" and worked with him to organize his lecture series and joined in his public complaints about the mismanagement of Yosemite. Later in the decade, the two took on the responsibilities of managing the Calaveras Grove Hotel. In 1902, Hutchings and Emily decided to retire from the hotel business and move back to San Francisco. They traveled by way of Yosemite in the fall. At the point where El Capitan first comes into view, Hutchings stopped the wagon and stood up, exclaiming, "It is like Heaven." One of the horses bolted, throwing Emily to the ground. Twenty feet further, James was also thrown out of the carriage, striking his head on the rocks. Whispering, "I am very much hurt," he died in Emily's arms a few moments later.

John Muir and the Transition from Scenery to Nature

Although Hutchings continued as political advocate for Yosemite and lectured widely on behalf of the valley up until his death, his role as primary spokesman for the sacred landscape came to be superseded by John Muir. Because the nature philosophy that Muir developed is far more familiar to twenty-first-century Americans than Hutchings' older view, it is worth reflecting on the mutual influence the two perspectives had on each other. Additionally, because Hutchings and Muir have implicitly or explicitly been defined against each other in historic interpretation, a reconsideration of Muir in light of Hutchings can clarify the complexity of their joint "fatherhood" of Yosemite.

John Muir first visited Yosemite Valley in the spring of 1868, and after a short visit returned to the foothills to find work. First, he tended sheep through the winter of 1868–1869 for an Irishman named "Smoky Jack" Connel, then went to work for Pat Delaney during the summer of 1869. This job took Muir into the high country beyond Yosemite Valley, and gave him ample opportunity to explore the mountains that would inspire him for the rest of

Taber Photographic Co., "J. M. Hutchings of Yo Semite," ca. 1890. This photo was taken near the time that Yosemite National Park was created, when Hutchings was approximately 70 years old. (Courtesy California State Library, Sacramento, CA)

his life. John Muir's biographer Donald Worster described the summer of 1869 as the moment of Muir's conversion to the religion of nature, awakening in him "the deepest and most intense passion of his life, a long moment of ecstasy." Unfortunately, Muir threw away the journal that he kept during that year, so what remains is the heavily revised version, which he published in 1911 as *My First Summer in the Sierra*. Though a "much-labored over and retrospective account," *First Summer* contains some of Muir's most poetic expressions of his nature religion—a passionate elaboration of pantheism, where everything was connected: "When we try to pick out anything by itself, we find it hitched to everything else in the universe."

Worster notes that Muir's ideas themselves were hitched to many other things in the transcendentalist spiritual universe: "the intellectual landscape of Britain and America in the nineteenth century was scattered with species, near-species, and assorted varieties of a common transcendentalist or pantheistic genus." Muir's particular version of this pantheism, which he would work out over the course of the next decade or so, included four key elements:

> Behind the beautiful material face of nature breathes a world-controlling power called "God," "Beauty," or "Love." Humankind is out of synchrony with that power—an alienation that must be healed by direct experience of wild, natural beauty. Humans are not naturally corrupt or fallen but only strayed away from the true source of happiness and virtue. Science was his mode of reestablishing contact with the world spirit.[32]

Muir descended from the mountains in September, again looking for work. He decided to try Yosemite in the winter and connected with Hutchings in the fall. Hutchings may have initially perceived Muir as a kindred spirit, as both men shared the religious perception of mountains. However, whatever positive feeling may have existed between the two initially was never recorded and was fairly quickly replaced with friction. Although working for Hutchings paid well and gave John Muir a home in Yosemite Valley and plenty of time to conduct his own travels, scientific studies, and writing, Muir only stayed on for three years. But he continued his friendships with the rest of Hutchings' family, writing favorably of Florantha's knowledge of weather patterns and befriending the sisters Cosie and Floy.

Beyond the matter of Elvira, Muir gained popularity as a tourist guide in the 1870s, particularly with the elite writers and scientists who often sought him out specifically (some sent there by Jeanne Carr). In 1872, Therese Yelverton gave Muir's public persona a romantic boost when she published the novel *Zanita: A Tale of the Yo-semite*, wherein the hero "Kenmuir" was modeled directly on John Muir. It would have been a bitter pill for Hutchings, who had labored for twenty years to bring Yosemite to the attention of America's cultural elite, to witness as his millwright became the darling of eastern literati just as he, Hutchings, was being evicted from his home of nine years. However, the real-life rivalry between the two men has received disproportionate attention from historians who fixate on these extreme differences while ignoring the broad areas of common interest and passion the two men shared over their long lives.[34]

First and foremost, both men shared a deeply religious appreciation for the Sierra mountainscapes. Hutchings' very first writings of Yosemite cast the valley in biblical terms, and he clearly saw Yosemite as a spiritual alternative for the Californians for whom "religion was a by-word and a reproach." Like Hutchings, Muir built a home in Yosemite and sought to support his passion for the mountains with work that would return a decent living—and that work was serving the tourist industry. Hutchings agreed with Muir against Whitney and other professional scientists in the debate over subsidence versus glaciation as Yosemite's geological origins, and popularized Muir's views (though without attribution) in his writings and lectures. In the 1880s, Hutchings and Muir joined forces to support the grant boundary extension against the depredations of the "hoofed locusts" and other local interests. Occasionally the two men even gave public lectures together. Hutchings was also an avid and skilled mountaineer, and the two shared many friendships, including with scientists like William Brewer and Albert Kellogg, Jeanne and Ezra Carr. Hutchings was, with Muir, a founding member of the Sierra Club, and as Guardian of Yosemite fought to limit the expanding damage of the tourist industry on the valley itself. Whether or not the two men directly reconciled their differences is not known, but in 1891 Muir named a mountain in King's Canyon after Hutchings.

Despite the broad area of common ground between the two men, they have most often been cast as opposites in historical narratives of Yosemite. Hank Johnston wrote that Hutchings and Muir had an "enduring bitterness for each other," based on the observation that Hutchings never mentioned Muir in *In the Heart of the Sierras*. Thurman Wilkins describes their acrimony as grounded in Hutchings' resentment of Muir's popularity with tourists. Other Muir scholars mention Hutchings only in passing, as the owner of the sawmill where Muir worked. Worster wrote that Yosemite "was privately and intimately [Muir's] own, more so than it was for the litigious, deed-hungry Hutchings or for the summer tourists who passed through the park on a three- or four-day stopover." For Worster, as for so many other Muir scholars, it is difficult to cast a critical eye after reading Muir's lyrical and ecstatic nature writing. To those of us who came of age in the twentieth century, any critique of the wilderness idea or its most eloquent champion feels like a political challenge to the entire environmental movement of the late twentieth century.[35]

Muir was indeed one of America's most insightful writers and clearly established, as had not been done before, the modern idea of wilderness—a place apart from the problematic modern world of urban alienation and industrial pollution. Wilderness, in Muir's writing, was a sanctuary to which Americans could escape and find communion with the God of Beauty, finding redemption from the ills of modern, industrial, urban life. Muir's philosophy carries many of the earlier strands of the sublime view of spectacular scenery forward into more modern contexts, but one of the key differences is that Muir's nature was a solitary pursuit. Muir taught his readers to engage with nature as discrete individuals, lonely pilgrims setting out to escape the noise of society to find the "still small voice" of the divine in the sounds of forest and river.

Muir's nature, ostensibly apolitical, differed in many respects from the spectacular scenery that had inspired Hutchings, Olmsted, and the United States Congress at midcentury. The scenic spectacle created a communal spectator—in the aftermath of the Civil War, the nationalistic agenda that spurred the Yosemite Grant reified Yosemite's iconographic power to move Americans into appreciation for and identification with the federal government. During the subsequent conquest of the West, Yosemite's spectacular features captured in the photographic artistry of Watkins and others again helped Americans forge a common identity, this one sympathetic to the extension of federal control over western lands and people.

Muir's intensely individualized *spiritual* relationship with nature extended and internalized the process of removing the material relationships between humans and their environment from the discourse of environmental consciousness. From Muir's perspective, physical comfort, the society of fellow companions, and other material or social needs were distractions from the solitary ecstatic appreciation of wilderness. In order to commune with nature, humans had to subsume themselves into it. And before they could do that, they had to imagine themselves free from other humans, from the material trappings of civilization, including money and technology. In the language of postmodern theorist Bruno Latour, Muir's philosophy finally completed the process of purification by which Americans constructed an ideal perception of "human" and "nature" as binary opposites. Despite the appeal of imagining modern society as a discrete entity separated from "nature," "the primitive," and most forms of physicality, reality, according to Latour, is actually comprised of hybrids that combine all dimensions of physical, spiritual, technological, political, and cultural activity. The separation between Human and Nature at the heart of Muir's wilderness philosophy contributed to the process of what T. J. Jackson Lears calls "evasion": "By denying the dilemmas posed by modernization, [evasion] provided both a source of escape from unprecedented conflict and a means of legitimizing continued capitalist development in a liberal polity."[36]

As American environmental consciousness matured into this bifurcated realm, the myth of Yosemite's origin began to take hold and shape the future directions of federal control over public lands. Muir continued to gain popularity and influence as the "Apostle of Wilderness"—the hero of the narrative. Every hero has to have his antagonist, and Hutchings, who continued to entertain the public, to defend tourists, and to be honest about his entrepreneurial pursuits, became that opposite. More to the point, Muir's literary persona became identified with the dehumanized concept of "nature," while Hutchings, the people person that he always was, remained tied to "humanity." With his legal struggle to validate his land claims and investments as evidence, Hutchings became the emblem of the self-centered businessman, whose only interest in Yosemite was to make a quick buck off the tourist trade.

Just as this shallow characterization of Hutchings denies the complex richness of his life and contributions to American environmental history, the elevation of Muir to the status of wilderness saint denies his own complex and sometimes contradictory humanity. Muir was a sheepherder who campaigned against sheepherding. "The California sheep owner is in haste to get rich, and often does," he wrote derisively, but then he made enough in two summers of sheepherding that he could afford to loan five hundred dollars to his brother David, a considerable sum in 1869. Though he criticized others for seeking after wealth, he would become a very wealthy man himself. Muir left Yosemite after a few years to live in San Francisco and to cultivate friendships with wealthy and influential members of elite American society, including railroad magnate Edward Harriman and Robert Underwood Johnson, publisher of *Century Magazine*. In addition to publicizing his nature philosophy through magazine articles, in 1880 Muir married the wealthy Louise Strentzel and took over management of her family's Martinez farm, turning it into a very successful enterprise over the next twenty years. His friendships and financial success gave him entrée into the upper echelons of American society just as Mark Twain's "gilded age" came into fruition. And though Muir is forever associated with Yosemite, unlike Hutchings he did not live there very long. After he left the valley in 1873, he only returned, like so many others, as a temporary sojourner.

The frugal Scotsman would continue to build wealth throughout his life, leaving behind an estate worth $241,137 at his death in 1914, equivalent to $4 million in twenty-first-century dollars. Over his many years of writing magazine articles, books, and speeches, Muir had built up a literary persona for himself modeled after the ascetic Henry David Thoreau—a man in "shirts sailed ragged and buttonless," worn-out shoes, and a belt of grass who marched off to conquer mountaintops with nothing but a bag of tea and a handful of oatmeal for sustenance. This persona was juxtaposed against the "blank fleshly apathy" of tourists and the corrupting influence of materialism on the human spirit. So effectively did Muir's ascetic persona saturate the public understanding of him that the size of his estate befuddled observers at his death. Arno Dosch wrote for the *San Francisco Chronicle* that "A large sum of money did not seem to fit somehow with the popular conception of the naturalist passing months idealistically in the mountains."[37] Demonstrating the proof of Dosch's observation, most Muir scholars prefer to ignore his financial success. Even Worster, after painstakingly recording Muir's ongoing relationship with money, concluded that it meant little to him. Tellingly, Worster's logic rested on a comparison with the fortunes of robber barons: "Compared to the great fortune makers of his day—Rockefeller, Harriman, J. P. Morgan, Vanderbilt, Carnegie—his estate was rather modest."[38]

That Worster would explain away Muir's wealth by comparing him with captains of industry, including some of his personal acquaintances, points to some of the deepest ironies that Muir's nature philosophy has imprinted on American environmental history. Though he proclaimed the mountains as cathedrals free from the hierarchical constraints of conventional religion, and eschewed the formalities of traditional society, his vision of an intense personal relationship with nature became especially appealing to the captains of industry. As William Cronon put it, "the very men who most benefited from urban-industrial capitalism" were the ones who most passionately pursued the wilderness idea and became its political and economic champions in the late nineteenth century. Some of Muir's most effective work in getting the wilderness idea institutionalized through state and federal policies was in developing personal relationships with those capitalists who had the power and influence to get legislation passed. Initially, his friendship with Jeanne and Ezra Carr gained him entrée into this society, including meeting the Strentzels. His own financial success, though not on a par with the mega-wealthy he rubbed shoulders with, was enough to maintain comfortable relations with them. Of course, it also made possible his continuous travels and scientific studies. Muir's deepening relationships with the San Francisco elite (as well as those of the East Coast) ensured that Yosemite's fate continued to be a direct product of the nation's ongoing economic expansion at the turn of the century as it had been of San Francisco's metropolitan growth in the 1850s.[39]

Muir's literary persona of the ragged wilderness wanderer as well as his elaboration of the dehumanized wilderness myth taught Americans to ignore the role of wealth in creating wilderness just as they had learned to ignore the role of the working-class people in sustaining the park. Indeed, wealth, or the making of it, became antithetical to the idea of wilderness at the precise historical moment that celebrating wilderness became an activity primarily for well-to-do city folks. Thanks to the early republican bent of the Yosemite Grant, those who advocated that increasing acres of public land be set aside for wilderness preserves could imagine they were doing so on behalf of all Americans, but in fact elitism remained a feature of twentieth-century environmentalism until late in the century: "Today's noisy, littered campgrounds, inhabited by people motivated by low fees, concerned with 'partying' or 'having a good time,'" wrote Thomas and Geraldine Vale in 1998, "are in many respects worse than the sheepherder's camp, and with no excuse."[40]

Hutchings' attitudes toward fire and his advocacy of the Yosemite Grant extension in the 1880s continued his long practice of using landscape to reinforce middle-class visions of social order. Both Muir and Hutchings shared the class biases of the late-century intelligentsia with regard to the enclosure of forest lands for recreation and science. The twentieth-century environmentalist movement's adoption of Muir as the favorite poster child for wilderness preservation also suggests the movement's blindness to matters of class and race. As environmental justice advocates point out, traditional environmentalism in the twentieth century was less concerned with the grave environmental issues facing the poor and minorities than with creating wilderness "preserves." Such emphases have continued uncritically the nineteenth-century understanding of wilderness as a refuge and haven for urban elites, an understanding rooted not only in class and ethnic bias but integrally tied to the extension of urban power over countryside and hinterland areas; and, in the case of Yosemite, in the extension of federal control over western lands.[41]

As William Cronon's critique of the wilderness idea points out, the creation of wilderness preserves in the high Sierra, Wyoming, and other scenic areas did little or nothing to curb the environmental destruction of the industrial revolution and rapid urbanization in the latter decades of the nineteenth century. Indeed, just as Miriam Leslie in the 1870s had sought to ease the psychic pain of hydraulic mining's environmental destruction by visiting the gardens of Belmont, later captains of industry sought refuge in wilderness parks. Indeed, most of our high country reserves would not have come into being without the political advocacy of men like Edward Harriman, Southern Pacific magnate and close friend of John Muir's—just as the interconnection between consumer tourism and national policy made the Yosemite Grant possible. A more radical environmentalism that directly challenged industrialization and modernization simply would not have been tenable at the turn of the twentieth century. Nevertheless, Yosemite and other national parks have continued to function as sources of inspiration and as crucibles for new environmental ideas for each succeeding generation.[42]

A clearer understanding of Hutchings' role in the cultural production of landscape complicates the clear-cut bifurcation between nature and humanity that Muir's wilderness idea depended upon. Hutchings' historical legacy forces a reconsideration of comfortable assumptions about the historic relationships between American landscape and human society more broadly. Hutchings, as we have seen, attempted to fuse his own appreciation of nature and landscape with his entrepreneurial ambitions. He appreciated California landscapes *both* for their aesthetic qualities *and* as cultural resources for the tourist economy. He attended both to the material needs of tourists and to their intellectual, spiritual, and aesthetic appreciation of California scenery, without turning up his nose at them behind their backs. While Hutchings' sympathies definitely rested with the middle classes, he did not require that wilderness be emptied of humans in order to carry symbolic value. Indeed, for both Muir and Hutchings, it was necessary to bring the right kind of humans into contact with the scenic wilderness so it could be transformed into the iconographic symbol of national power and sublimity. Only for Hutchings, the "right kind of people" was a much broader swath of the general public than it was for Muir.

Perhaps, in the end, it was Hutchings' independent and more democratic tendencies that sealed his fate in the history of Yosemite. Unlike Muir, Hutchings did not cultivate relationships with mentor/patrons who could provide entrée into the parlors of gilded-age capitalists. A classic American self-made man, Hutchings remained fiercely independent to his dying days. Although Hutchings was not above constructing highly idealized versions of his own history, he was unable or unwilling to go to the extremes of Muir's purified wilderness. The Sierra was his adopted home, and his struggle to keep that home while promoting it as a national icon, landed him smack in between the human-nature dichotomy that yawned ever wider as the century wore on. Like most men, Hutchings had many contradictory characteristics, but till the end of his days he steadfastly maintained his passionate attachment to the Sierra Nevada where he worshipped his God, built his home, and invited the world into his parlor.

CONCLUSION:
DISCOVERING OUR PLACE IN
NATURE

Hutchings' life project "to make Yo-Semite known to the public eye" was a phenomenal success that expanded far beyond his time and place. In the twenty-first century, Yosemite continues to be a source of artistic and literary inspiration and a laboratory for scientific study, continually yielding new perspectives and insights. Yet, if Hutchings' story challenges the traditional understandings that support the continuation of Yosemite and other national parks as preserved landscapes, what are the implications for the present and future of these American icons now? Indeed, what insight or wisdom can the generations of the twenty-first century glean from a new vision of Yosemite's origin, one that encompasses the complexities raised by Hutchings' story? To some degree, this question is impossible to answer at the moment. This study is only one part of a much larger discourse that challenges the dualistic understandings of Human and Nature that gave rise to wilderness parks in the late nineteenth century. It cannot hope to predict the outcome of this discourse. At the same time, the work of restoring Hutchings' place in Yosemite's historic narrative has taken place against a strong cultural shift in American environmental thinking, from the "death" of environmentalism to the rising awareness of global climate change and widespread efforts to imagine a sustainable future for humankind on the planet. The new narrative of Yosemite's origin may offer some historic precedents as part of that evolving discourse.

Yosemite's Origin Myth

As mentioned in chapter 5, the story of Yosemite's origin as the anonymous act of beneficent "gentlemen" generated widely accepted but unproven (and unprovable) assumptions: that the Yosemite Grant was a foresighted act of a benign federal government bent on protecting the pursuit of happiness for all Americans, that the Commissioners were defending this action, and that all who opposed it stood only for selfishness, greed, and the right to exploit the environment. Of course, it is equally impossible to prove any alternate narrative, given the sparse historic record. With the arrival of

John Muir on the scene, Yosemite's status as a holy wilderness and Miltonic Eden gained its modern spokesman. Yosemite's origin story, the battles with "developers" like Hutchings, and the ultimate triumph of the National Park movement have all become part of the ideological fabric supporting twentieth-century environmental politics, a politics oriented in large part toward protecting wilderness, "the nation's most sacred myth of origin."[1] To challenge the origin myth of Yosemite, then, seems a challenge to all environmental politics of the twentieth century, indeed to the very rationale for treasuring sacred landscapes like Yosemite altogether.

It is not necessary to assume that Yosemite's value to America is diminished by a more complex and historically nuanced understanding of its origin. We know that the works of Michelangelo and other Renaissance artists were commissioned by thoroughly corrupt popes and paid for with the sale of indulgences, yet that knowledge does not diminish the value of the art itself. In the same way, we must appreciate Yosemite, Yellowstone, the Grand Canyon, and other American icons as fabulous works of nature and culture combined, regardless of the forces that brought them into being. In Amy Scott's brilliant turn of phrase, we can continue to visit Yosemite and "encounter nature, but see a work of art."[2] As Paul Schullery and Lee Whittlesey argue in their analysis of the "campfire story" origin myth of Yellowstone, national parks have become "great experimental laboratories in which to test ideas of nature and culture and how they connect," and this dynamic view of sacred landscapes in America continues to hold tremendous value and potential for the future.[3]

But the myth of Yosemite's origin and the wilderness idea that it became subsumed into has been a powerful force in modern American politics, and myths do have value. Origin myths like that of the American idea of wilderness "convey a society's sense of its particular identity . . . becom[ing], in effect, a symbolic model for the society's way of life, its world view,"[4] and this is distinctly true for the idea of wilderness and its most eloquent hero, John Muir. But what values, precisely, are embedded in this myth, and what function have they played in modern society? William Cronon explores this question in great detail, concluding that, while the wilderness idea allows Americans to imaginatively reenact archetypal moments of frontier discovery, it does little to assuage the environmental damage of our modern industrial infrastructure. Wilderness allows moderns to ignore the "intricate and all too invisible networks with which [civilization] shelters us." Worse, says Cronon, "in its flight from history, in its siren song of escape, in its reproduction of the dangerous dualism that sets human beings outside of nature—in all of these ways, wilderness poses a serious threat to responsible environmentalism."[5]

What would "responsible environmentalism" at the dawn of the twenty-first century look like? For Cronon, as for many others, it begins by re-imagining the human place in nature. If we are to solve our most serious environmental problems, "we need an environmental ethic that will tell us as much about *using* nature as about *not* using it."[6] Creating such an ethic is an exciting and monumental challenge, one that ought to draw environmental historians together with anthropologists, writers, technicians, entrepreneurs, landscape designers, artists, city planners, and all professionals whose work links the human and natural together, to shoulder the task of redesigning that relationship through narratives and transit routes, food systems and artistic representation, dwellings and macroeconomics. But what has any of this to do with Hutchings?

Hutchings, with all his many flaws and imperfections, dedicated his life to creating a sense of place for California residents. And, while he lived and worked in Yosemite, he strove to weave together his sense of Yosemite's sacred value with a daily life built on local resources. Yes, he planted exotic species in Yosemite's soil, yes, he pastured mules and horses in its meadows. And yes, his landscape vision upheld a social ideal predicated on the superiority of white, middle-class Protestant values in a hierarchical society. To see the value of Hutchings' life in our own day, we must get over the perfectionist demands that insist only on the purest of heroes. Such standards feed back into the dangerous dualism that only undermines efforts toward a realistic transform-ation in our material relationship with the environment. Like all Yosemite residents, Hutchings created a live-work system that did not require a long, polluting commute or the importation of consumer goods from halfway around the world. He communicated about the value of nature and scenery, hoping to educate his adopted country *and* make a satisfactory living at the same time. If we are to imagine our own sustainable future, finding a way to marry our aesthetic and spiritual appreciation for the value of the nature that sustains us with our need to flourish is a critical first step. Hutchings' life may be an imperfect model for us to start that step, but it is still a model, a potential starting point.

Another dimension of Yosemite's origin myth that deserves attention in this discussion is the largely invisible role of wealth, entrepreneurship, and business more generally in the creation of sacred landscapes. While it is important enough to challenge the dualistic mythology that divides the making of money from the preservation of landscape, it is even more important to ask why we divided these two activities so strenuously in the first place. What ideology or interest is served in the fiction that wealth and industry are completely antithetical to scenic or wilderness preservation? Clearly, industry and the wealth it generated for a few have been primary culprits in the extraction of resources, pollution of our atmosphere, and the extension of urban control over small-town and rural hinterlands, so perhaps it is obvious that such forces are antithetical to wilderness preservation— except that, historically, they were intimately bound up in precisely that preservation. Again, it is our modern "need" for a purified dualism that perpetuates the mythic division between the business world and wilderness environment. But at a cost: by eliding the role of industry and entrepreneurship in helping to protect certain kinds of environments, we implicitly reinforce the fiction that business has no responsibility toward the environment.

The cost of dividing the economic world from the world of environmental protection is evident in the environmentalist confusion over the efforts of businesses and corporations to adopt sustainability practices, embodied in the term "greenwashing." While it is surely true that many corporations cynically adopt environmental standards only as marketing tools, it is also true that the business world desperately needs to reconfigure its relationship to the environment, and that the energy and innovation needed to build a sustainable future will not come about solely through legislation or regulation. The story of the beneficent federal government defending the highest values of the American people is indeed a noble and hopeful vision for our nation; but it ultimately disempowers ordinary people from taking necessary steps toward transforming their own communities, workplaces, and the corporations that do business there. The pressing environmental problems of the twenty-first century are not served by the dualistic myth of government protecting sacred environment from the profit-hungry corporations. *All* entities must become active agents of sustainable change, and part of that change involves discovering and crafting new narratives of the intersections between humans, nature, economics, and policy, in an effort to discover and create "an ethical, sustainable, *honorable* human place in nature."[7] It is my hope that this book offers one small step in the process of rethinking the narratives of our environmental future.

NOTES

INTRODUCTION: YOSEMITE AND THE TIPPING POINT IN AMERICAN ENVIRONMENTAL THOUGHT

1. Donald Worster, *A Passion for Nature: The Life of John Muir* (Oxford: Oxford University Press, 2008), 167; Ken Burns, *The National Parks: America's Best Idea* documentary film, 2009; William Cronon, "The Trouble with Wilderness; or Getting Back to the Wrong Nature," in *Uncommon Ground: Rethinking the Human Place in Nature*, William Cronon, ed. (New York: W. W. Norton, 1996), 69–90.
2. James Mason Hutchings, "The Great Yo-Semite Valley," *Hutchings' California Magazine* 4 (October 1859) in Hutchings, *Scenes of Wonder and Curiosity from Hutchings' California Magazine, 1856–1861*, ed. R. R. Olmsted (Berkeley, CA: Howell-North, 1962), 284.
3. Mark Stoll, "Milton in Yosemite: *Paradise Lost* and the National Parks Idea," *Environmental History* 13, no. 2 (April, 2008): 241.
4. Stoll, "Milton in Yosemite."
5. Malcolm Gladwell, *The Tipping Point: How Little Things Can Make a Big Difference* (New York: Little, Brown, 2000).
6. Drawn from a July 2000 search of the Modern Language Association Bibliography and America: History and Life databases. See also Samuel P. Hays, *Explorations in Environmental History: Essays by Samuel P. Hays* (Pittsburgh: University of Pittsburgh Press, 1998), xxiii.
7. Cronon, "Trouble with Wilderness," 69, 81.

PART I. THE MOUNTAINS OF CALIFORNIA

1. James Mason Hutchings, *Seeking the Elephant, 1849: James Mason Hutchings' Journal of His Overland Trek to California, Including His Voyage to America, 1848 and Letters from the Mother Lode*, ed. Shirley Sargent (Glendale, CA: Arthur H. Clark, 1980), 181.
2. Anon., "James Mason Hutchings," *Phrenological Journal of Science and Health* 52 (June 1871), quoted in Dennis Kruska, *James Mason Hutchings of Yo Semite: A Biography and Bibliography* (San Francisco: Book Club of California, 2009), 121.

CHAPTER 1. "TO CHEAT OURSELVES INTO FORGETFULNESS OF HOME"

1. Large sections of this chapter were originally published as "'Such Is Change in California': James Mason Hutchings and the Print Metropolis, 1854–1862." *Proceedings of the American Antiquarian Society* 114, pt. 1 (2004): 35–85, and much of the research was supported by the Stephen Botein Fellowship at the American Antiquarian Society in November 1998.
2. M. Kat Anderson, *Tending the Wild: Native American Knowledge and the Management of California's Natural Resources* (Berkeley: University of California Press, 2006); Mary Hill, *Gold: The California Story* (Berkeley: University of California Press, 1999); Robert Kelley, *Gold versus Grain: The Hydraulic Mining Controversy in California's Sacramento Valley* (Glendale, CA: Arthur H. Clark, 1959).

3. John Sunderland and Margaret Webb, comps. and eds., *Towcester: The Story of an English Country Town: The Celebration of 2000 Years of History* (Towcester, UK: Towcester Local History Society, 1995), 146–149; on the development of turnpikes in the expansion of transportation networks between English metropolitan areas, see R. A. Dodgshon and R. A. Butlin, eds., *An Historical Geography of England and Wales* (London: Academic Press, 1978), 406–407; B. J. Buchanan, "The Evolution of the English Turnpike Trusts: Lessons from a Case Study," *Economic History Review* 39, no. 2 (1986): 242–243.

4. Sunderland and Webb, *Towcester*, 199; Charles Dickens, *The Posthumous Papers of the Pickwick Club, Including Three Little-Remembered Chapters from Master Humphrey's Clock, in which Mr. Pickwick, Sam Weller & Other Pickwickians Reappear,* the Inner Sanctum Edition, ed. Clifton Fadiman (New York: Simon & Schuster, 1949), 711; Leonore Davidoff and Catherine Hall, *Family Fortunes: Men and Women of the English Middle Class, 1780–1850* (Chicago: University of Chicago Press, 1987), 48.

5. H. H. Horton, *Birmingham: A Poem in Two Parts* (Birmingham, 1851), cited in Davidoff and Hall, *Family Fortunes*, 368.

6. Sargent attributes this quote to Gertrude Hutchings Mills in her "Introduction," James Mason Hutchings, *Seeking the Elephant, 1849: James Mason Hutchings' Journal of His Overland Trek to California, Including His Voyage to America, 1848 and Letters from the Mother Lode,* ed. Shirley Sargent (Glendale, CA: Arthur H. Clark, 1980), 13.

7. Davidoff and Hall, *Family Fortunes*, 18–19; Eric J. Hobsbawm, *The Age of Capital 1848–1875* (New York: Charles Scribner's Sons, 1975), 2; see also Hobsbawm, *The Age of Revolution: Europe 1789–1848* (New York: New American Library, 1962).

8. Mark Billinge, "Hegemony, Class and Power in Late Georgian and Early Victorian England: Towards a Cultural Geography," in *Explorations in Historical Geography: Interpretive Essays,* eds. Alan R. Baker and Derek Gregory (Cambridge: Cambridge University Press, 1984), 28–67; see also Davidoff and Hall, *Family Fortunes*, 25–27.

9. Hutchings, *Seeking the Elephant*, 69; Martin Hewitt, "The Travails of Domestic Visiting, 1830–1870," *Historical Research* 71, no. 175 (1998): 198–203. See also Mary Poovey, *Making a Social Body: British Cultural Formation 1830–1864* (Chicago: University of Chicago Press, 1995); Gareth Stedman Jones, *Outcast London: A Study of the Relationship between Classes in Victorian Society* (Oxford: Clarendon, 1971).

10. Billinge, "Hegemony, Class and Power," 53–55; T. W. Heyck, *The Transformation of Intellectual Life in Victorian England* (New York: St. Martin's Press, 1982), 55; Mary Poovey draws links between the scientific methods of fact-finding and analysis and the creation of the New Poor Law Act of 1834 in *Making a Social Body*, 10; Nigel Everett makes a similar point in *The Tory View of Landscape* (New Haven, CT: Yale University Press, 1994), 3.

11. Angela Miller, *The Empire of the Eye: Landscape Representation and American Cultural Politics, 1825–1875* (Ithaca, NY: Cornell University Press, 1993), 249; see also Marjorie Hope Nicolson, *Mountain Gloom and Mountain Glory: The Development of the Aesthetics of the Infinite* (Ithaca, NY: Cornell University Press, 1959), 384–385.

12. Raymond Williams, *The Country and the City* (New York: Oxford University Press, 1973), 115–116; Davidoff and Hall, *Family Fortunes*.

13. Uvedale Price, *An Essay on the Picturesque, as compared with the Sublime and the Beautiful; and, on the Use of Studying Pictures, for the purpose of Improving Real Landscape* (London, 1810), cited in Ann Bermingham, "System, Order, and Abstraction: The Politics of English Landscape Drawing around 1795," in *Landscape and Power,* ed. W. J. T. Mitchell (Chicago: University of Chicago Press, 1994), 85.

14. Patricia Anderson, *The Printed Image and the Transformation of Popular Culture 1790–1860* (Oxford: Clarendon Press, 1994), 2.

15. Jon P. Klancher, *The Making of English Reading Audiences, 1790–1832* (Madison: University of Wisconsin Press, 1987), 48–50; Anderson, *Printed Image*, 2–3.

16. Benedict Anderson, *Imagined Communities: Reflections on the Origin and Spread of Nationalism* (London: Verso, 1994), 67–82; Anderson, *Printed Image, 53*.

17. Sunderland and Webb, *Towcester*, 149–181.

18. Sargent, "Introduction," in Hutchings, *Seeking the Elephant*, 13; Sunderland and Webb, *Towcester*, 199.

19. Hutchings, *Seeking the Elephant*, 37.

20. Ibid., 38.

21. J. S. Holliday, *The World Rushed In: The California Gold Rush Experience* (New York: Simon & Schuster, 1983), 34.

22. With no census figures or reliable data, exact demographic numbers are impossible to achieve. These estimates are the most recent historical guesses. Peter Blodgett, *Land of Golden Dreams: California in the Gold Rush Decade, 1848–1858* (San Marino, CA: Huntington Library, 1999), 55; Malcolm Rohrbough, *Days of Gold: The California Gold Rush and the American Nation* (Berkeley: University of California Press, 1997), 19; Holliday, *World Rushed In*, 42–43; Hobsbawm, *Age of Capital.*

23. Hutchings did not identify Butterfield's first name. Hutchings, *Seeking the Elephant*, 197.

24. Quoted in Holliday, *World Rushed In*, 321.

25. Fayette Robinson, *California and Its Gold Regions; with a Geographical and Topographical View of the Country, Its Mineral and Agricultural Resources . . .* (New York: Stringer & Townsend, 1849), 40.

26. Hutchings to John Wilson, March 22, 1850, in *Seeking the Elephant*, 200.

27. Arthur Quinn, *The Rivals: William Gwin, David Broderick, and the Birth of California* (New York: Crown Publishers, 1994), 37.

28. Rosemarie Mossinger, *Woodleaf Legacy: The Story of a Gold Rush Town* (Nevada City, CA: Carl Mautz Publishing, 1995).

29. See Albert L. Hurtado, *Indian Survival on the California Frontier* (New Haven, CT: Yale University Press, 1988).

30. U.S. Indian Commissioner J. Neely Johnson, "Speech to the Mariposa Battalion," in Hutchings, *In the Heart of the Sierras: The Yo Semite Valley, Both Historical and Descriptive: And Scenes by the Way . . .* (Oakland, CA: Pacific Press Publishing House, 1886), 48.

31. Gary Scharnhorst, "Introduction," in Bret Harte, *The Luck of Roaring Camp and Other Writings* (New York: Penguin Books, 2001), xvi.

32. James Mason Hutchings, "1855 Diary Transcript," comp. Gertrude Hutchings Mills (Yosemite Park, CA: Yosemite Research Library), 75, 24.

33. Hutchings, "1855 Diary Transcript," 75.

34. This rough schema outlines the "standard" evolutionary process of mining, described in the work of J. S. Holliday, *World Rushed In;* Rodman Paul, *California Gold: The Beginning of Mining in the Far West* (Cambridge, MA: Harvard University Press, 1947); Charles Howard Shinn, *Mining Camps: A Study in American Frontier Government*, 1884 Reprint (New York: Alfred A. Knopf, 1948); Rohrbough, *Days of Gold*; and Mary Hill, *Gold: The California Story* (Berkeley: University of California Press, 1999). However, Susan Lee Johnson points out that this only accurately captures the northern mines around Grass Valley and Nevada City. In many other districts, lack of water made hy-

draulic mining unfeasible, and in any case all mining techniques coexisted simultaneously because miners without capital could still work with the simpler techniques.
Roaring Camp: The Social World of the California Gold Rush (New York: W. W. Norton, 2000), 187–188.

35. Hutchings identified "Mr. Eastman of San Francisco" as "the artist for my commandments" in his diary. Hutchings, "1855 Diary Transcript," 147. According to
B. P. Avery, Eastman was the second engraver to begin working in California in 1849
and was still in business at the time of Avery's article in 1868. B. P. Avery, "Art Beginnings on the Pacific" (part 1), *Overland Monthly* 1, no. 2 (August 1868): 115.

36. Hutchings, "1855 Diary Transcript," 14. *Statutes of California*, 6th Session, 1855, pp.
50–51, 124–125, cited in Paul, *California Gold*, 312, n.2. Ralph Mann links the Sabbatarian movement firmly to the efforts of emerging middle-class leaders in Grass Valley and Nevada City to reform and control the unruly population of those communities. *After the Gold Rush: Society in Grass Valley and Nevada City, California,
1849–1870* (Stanford, CA: Stanford University Press, 1982), 56–58.

37. In his scrapbook, Hutchings pasted an unidentified newspaper article dated May 7,
1853, entitled "Laws of the Big Canon Mining District," summarizing the mining codes
of that district. James Mason Hutchings, "Scrapbook, 1853–1855," (Yosemite Museum
accession no. 6429), 59.

38. Charles Shinn applauded the legal efforts of these miners as spontaneous expressions
of their Anglo-Saxon racial predispositions to self-governance, but Rodman Paul
noted the Spanish and European origins of the mining codes. Paul, *California Gold*,
211–214; Shinn, *Mining Camps*, 126. The mining district codes came to be the law of
the land, with state and federal governments refusing to intervene for at least twenty
years. Maureen A. Jung, "Capitalism Comes to the Diggings: From Gold-Rush Adventure to Corporate Enterprise," in *A Golden State: Mining and Economic Development in Gold Rush California*, eds. James J. Rawls and Richard J. Orsi (Berkeley: University of California Press, 1997), 58. See also Donald J. Pisani, "'I Am Resolved Not to
Interfere, but Permit All to Work Freely': The Gold Rush and American Resource
Law," in *A Golden State*, eds. Rawls and Orsi, 123–173; Gordon Morris Bakken, "American Mining Law and the Environment: The Western Experience." *Western Legal History* 1, no. 2 (Summer/Fall 1988), 211–236.

39. Rohrbough, *Days of Gold*, 87–88; Paul, *California Gold*, 198–205; Bakken, "American
Mining Law," 216.

40. "The universal costume was a red or grey flannel shirt, old trousers, high boots that
were pulled up over the pant-legs, and a dilapidated slouch hat." Paul, *California Gold*,
69. Sheldon credits the illustrated paper *Wide West* with introducing the "familiar figure of the flannel shirted miner working in his claim" in 1853. Francis E. Sheldon, "Pioneer Illustration in California," *Overland Monthly* 2nd series, 11 (April 1888): 342.

41. Barbara Novak, *Nature and Culture: American Landscape and Painting, 1825–1875* (New
York: Oxford University Press, 1980), 34; Miller, *Empire of the Eye*; Nicolson, *Mountain Gloom and Mountain Glory*.

42. Jonathan Prude, "Town-Factory Conflicts in Antebellum Rural Massachusetts," in
*The Countryside in the Age of Capitalist Transformation: Essays in the Social History of
Rural America*, eds. Steven Hahn and Jonathan Prude (Chapel Hill: University of
North Carolina Press, 1985), 87.

43. Rex Burns, *Success in America: The Yeoman Dream and the Industrial Revolution*
(Amherst: University of Massachusetts Press, 1976), 1.

44. J. S. Holliday, *World Rushed In*, 50; Daniel Cornford, "'We All Live More Like Brutes

Than Humans': Labor and Capital in the Gold Rush," in *Golden State*, eds. Orsi and Rawls, 83; Rohrbough, *Days of Gold*, 2; David Goodman, *Gold Seeking: Victoria and California in the 1850's* (Stanford, CA: Stanford University Press, 1994); Mann, *After the Gold Rush*, i.

45. Paul, *California Gold*, 69; Sheldon, "Pioneer Illustration in California," 342.
46. David Beesley, *Crow's Range: An Environmental History of the Sierra Nevada* (Reno: University of Nevada Press, 2004).
47. Hutchings, "1855 Diary Transcript," 152.
48. Rand E. Rohe, "Man as Geomorphic Agent: Hydraulic Mining in the American West," *Pacific Historian* (Spring 1983): 5–16.
49. "Dame Shirley," the pen name of Louise A. K. S. Clappe, wrote the oft-quoted line, "gold-mining is Nature's great lottery scheme." *The Shirley Letters: Being Letters Written in 1851–1852 from the California Mines* (Salt Lake City: Peregrine Smith, 1970), 123.
50. Sunderland and Webb, *Towcester*, 199.
51. *Statutes of California*, 6th Session, 1855, pp. 50–51, 124–125, cited in Paul, *California Gold*, 312, n.2. Mann links the Sabbatarian movement firmly to the efforts of emerging middle-class leaders in Grass Valley and Nevada City to reform and control the unruly population of those communities. *After the Gold Rush*, 56–58.
52. "Notices," *Placerville Herald*, v1, n5 (May 28, 1853), 3.
53. April 9, Hutchings, "1855 Diary Transcript," 61. The notice appeared twice in the Placerville *Herald*, first on May 14, and again on May 28. It is the second version that Hutchings clipped, as it included the addition of a "Bingham" to the list. *Placerville Herald*, v1, n3 (May 14, 1853), 2; v1, n5 (May 28, 1853), 3. Newspaper Clippings, "Religious Notice," and "Movement for a Sabbath," Hutchings, "Scrapbook," 107.
54. "Ten Commandments . . . The Miners' Ten Commandments," *Placerville Herald*, v1, n6 (June 4, 1853), 1. Although Hutchings later remembered, and several historians have repeated, that he originally published this commandment alone, it does not appear out of the context of the whole anywhere in the short run of the Placerville *Herald*.
55. "A Saw—One of 'em" *Placerville Herald*, v1, n7 (June 11, 1853), 2. Hutchings, "Scrapbook," 102.
56. "For the El Dorado Republican," Hutchings, "Scrapbook," 103. The *Eldorado Republican* was the Placerville *Herald*'s chief rival. There are apparently no copies extant.
57. "A Chapter" *Placerville Herald*, v1, n9 (June 25, 1853), 2.
58. "The World in California," *Hutchings' California Magazine* 2 (February 1857): 338–344. Robert J. Chandler argues that Hutchings' lampoon in this article perpetuated damaging stereotypes of Jews. "A Stereotype Emerges," *Western States Jewish History* 21 (July 1989): 310–313. Hutchings began his partnership with Rosenfield, a Bavarian Jew who had lived in Mokelumne Hill, in 1856. This six-year partnership resulted in the most prolific publishing of both men's careers.
59. Gary F. Kurutz, "Popular Culture on the Golden Shore," in *Rooted in Barbarous Soil*, eds. Kevin Starr and Richard J. Orsi (Berkeley: University of California Press, 2000), 301–302. See also Tracy I. Storer and Lloyd P. Tevis, Jr., *California Grizzly* (Lincoln, NE: Bison Books, 1978), 152.

CHAPTER 2. "SUCH IS CHANGE IN CALIFORNIA"

1. James Mason Hutchings, "Original Diary 1854–5," (Washington, DC: Library of Congress Manuscripts Division, J. M. Hutchings Papers), March 31, 1855.
2. Joseph Armstrong Baird, *California's Pictorial Letter Sheets 1849–1860* (San Francisco: David Magee, 1967), 13–20.

3. James Mason Hutchings, "Commandments to California Wives," letter sheet (San Francisco: J. F. Larrabee, 1855); Hutchings, "Articles in a Miner's Creed" (San Francisco: James Mason Hutchings, 1855); Hutchings, "Hutching's [*sic*] Panoramic Scenes—Northern California," letter sheet (San Francisco: W. C. Butler, 1855); "Hutchings' Panoramic Scenes: California Indians," letter sheet (San Francisco: James Mason Hutchings, 1855); Hutchings, "Way-Side Scenes in California," letter sheet (NP: Anthony & Baker S.C., C. Nahl, Del, 1855); "Hutchings' Panoramic Scenes: The Mammoth Trees of California," letter sheet (San Francisco: James Mason Hutchings, 1855).

4. "Ione Valley," James Mason Hutchings, "Scrapbook, 1853–1855," (Yosemite Museum accession no. 6429), 104; "The Mammoth Tree," Hutchings, "Scrapbook," 20.

5. James Mason Hutchings, "1855 Diary Transcript," comp. Gertrude Hutchings Mills (Yosemite Park, CA: Yosemite Research Library), 49; "Hutchings' Panoramic Scenes—Northern California."

6. Thomas Ayres was born in New Jersey around 1816 and moved with his family to Wisconsin as a young adult. He arrived in San Francisco in August 1849 and spent the next five years sketching mining towns. His sketches of Yosemite, exhibited at the American Art Union in New York City, earned him a commission from *Harper's Weekly* to illustrate its series of articles on California. This promising art career was cut short when Ayres died in a shipwreck off the California coast in 1858. Katherine Church Holland, "Biographies of the Artists," in Janice T. Driesbach, Harvey L. Jones, and Holland, *Art of the Gold Rush* (Berkeley: University of California Press, 1998), 117–118. Edward Jump later produced at least one illustrated letter sheet of his own. Baird, *California's Pictorial Letter Sheets*, catalogue number 15.

7. Hutchings identified "Mr. Eastman of San Francisco" as "the artist for my commandments" in his diary, October 14, "1855 Diary Transcript," 147. According to B. P. Avery, Eastman was the second engraver to begin working in California in 1849 and was still in business at the time of Avery's article in 1868. B. P. Avery, "Art Beginnings on the Pacific" (part 1), *Overland Monthly* 1, no. 2 (August 1868): 115. On Charles Christian Nahl's prolific career, see Harvey L. Jones, "The Hessian Party: Charles Christian Nahl, Arthur Nahl, and August Wenderoth," in *Art of the Gold Rush*, eds. Driesbach, Jones, and Holland, 47.

8. George Baker had trained at the National Academy of Design before moving to California in June 1849. His first lithographic city view appeared in the *New York Tribune* that August. Like Hutchings, he engaged in several businesses at once, including running an express service, in addition to his work as an engraver and lithographer. Kuchel and Dresel emigrated from Germany and were among the most prolific lithographers in California in the 1850s. John W. Reps, *Views and Viewmakers of Urban America: Lithographs of Towns and Cities in the United States and Canada, Notes on the Artists and Publishers, and a Union Catalogue of their work, 1825–1925* (Columbia: University of Missouri Press, 1984), 165, 187.

9. According to Baird, most early letter sheets were lithographed, but a stereotype foundry did exist in San Francisco as early as 1855, so plates are a possibility. Baird, *California's Pictorial Letter Sheets*, 10–11; Advertisement, "California Stereotype Foundry, J. M. Burke & Co., 75 Davis," in R. H. Vance, *The Illustrated California Almanac* (San Francisco: R. H. Vance, 1855), 49.

10. Barbara Cloud, *The Business of Newspapers on the Western Frontier* (Reno: University of Nevada Press, 1992).

11. Hutchings, "1855 Diary Transcript," 194.

12. Gray Brechin, *Imperial San Francisco: Urban Power, Earthly Ruin* (Berkeley: University

of California Press, 1999), 33–35; Malcolm Rohrbough, *Days of Gold: The California Gold Rush and the American Nation* (Berkeley: University of California Press, 1997), 202–203; Rodman Paul, *California Gold: The Beginning of Mining in the Far West* (Cambridge, MA: Harvard University Press, 1947), 152–153.

13. Hutchings, "Articles in a Miner's Creed."

14. Hutchings, James Mason, *Scenes of Wonder and Curiosity from Hutchings' California Magazine, 1856–1861*, ed. R. R. Olmsted (Berkeley: Howell-North, 1962), 166.

15. Robert Kelley, *Battling the Inland Sea, American Political Culture, Pacific Policy, and the Sacramento Valley, 1850–1986* (Berkeley: University of California Press, 1989), 26–27; Brechin, *Imperial San Francisco*, 50. See also Kelley, *Gold versus Grain: The Hydraulic Mining Controversy in California's Sacramento Valley* (Glendale, CA: Arthur H. Clark, 1959).

16. Daniel Cornford, "'We All Live More Like Brutes than Humans': Labor and Capital in the Gold Rush," in *A Golden State: Mining and Economic Development in Gold Rush California*, eds. James J. Rawls and Richard J. Orsi (Berkeley: University of California Press, 1997), 93; Rohrbough, *Days of Gold*, 192; *North San Juan Hydraulic Press*, October 30, 1858, quoted in Paul, *California Gold*, 84.

17. Cornford, "'We All Live More Like Brutes,'" 94; Kelley, *Battling the Inland Sea*, 18–21; Brechin, *Imperial San Francisco*, 34–36.

18. Hutchings, *Scenes of Wonder and Curiosity*, 167.

19. J. S. Holliday, *The World Rushed In: The California Gold Rush Experience* (New York: Simon & Schuster, 1983), 402; Ralph Mann, *After the Gold Rush: Society in Grass Valley and Nevada City, California, 1849–1870* (Stanford, CA: Stanford University Press, 1982).

20. *Weekly Columbian* editorial, cited in Donald J. Pisani, "The Origins of Western Water Law: Case Studies from Two California Mining Districts," *California History* 70 (Fall 1991): 246.

21. Hutchings, "Saw Mill Railroad," *Hutchings' California Magazine* 2 (August 1857), 62–64; in the same issue, see also "More Water Wanted," "Editor's Table," 91.

22. For a discussion of a similar line of thinking in the *Lux v. Haggin* case of the 1880s, see David Igler, "When Is a River Not a River? Reclaiming Nature's Disorder in *Lux v. Haggin*," *Environmental History* 1, no. 2 (April 1996): 53.

23. Hutchings, "Way-Side Scenes in California."

24. Ibid.

25. Kimberly Johnston-Dodds, "The California Militia and Expeditions against the Indians, 1850–1859," in *Early California Laws and Policies Related to California Indians* (Sacramento, CA: California State Library California Research Bureau, September 2002), http://www.militarymuseum.org/MilitiaandIndians.html. An Act for the Government and Protection of Indians, April 22, 1850 (Chapter 133, Statutes of California, April 22, 1850); Dwight Dutschke, "American Indians in California," in *Five Views: An Ethnic Historic Site Survey for California*, California Department of Parks and Recreation Historic Preservation Office, 1988, available at http://www.cr.nps.gov/history/online_books/5views/5views.htm.

26. Kimberly Johnston-Dodds, "California Militia and Expeditions" http://www.military museum.org/MilitiaandIndians.html.

27. Warren A. Beck and Ynez D. Hasse, "California and the Indian Wars: Mariposa Indian War, 1851," in California State Military Museum: A United States Army Museum Activity *Preserving California's Military Heritage*, http://www.militarymuseum.org/Mariposa.html.

28. See, for example, Rosemarie Mossinger, *Woodleaf Legacy: The Story of a Gold Rush Town* (Nevada City, CA: Carl Mautz Publishing, 1995).

29. Gaylen D. Lee, *Walking Where We Lived: Memoirs of a Mono Indian Family* (Norman: University of Oklahoma Press, 1998).

30. Mark David Spence, *Dispossessing the Wilderness: Indian Removal and the Making of the National Parks* (Oxford: Oxford University Press, 1999).

31. Lafayette H. Bunnell, *Discovery of the Yosemite and the Indian War Which Led to That Event*, 3rd ed. (New York: Fleming H. Revell, 1880), ch. 3.

32. See, for example, Rebecca Solnit, *Savage Dreams: A Journey into the Landscape Wars of the American West* (Berkeley: University of California Press, 2000).

33. Lee, *Walking Where We Lived*; Spence, *Dispossessing the Wilderness*.

34. James Mason Hutchings, *Seeking the Elephant, 1849: James Mason Hutchings' Journal of His Overland Trek to California, Including His Voyage to America, 1848 and Letters from the Mother Lode*, ed. Shirley Sargent (Glendale, CA: Arthur H. Clark, 1980), 117–118.

35. Hutchings, "Scrapbook."

CHAPTER 3. "OPENING THE SEALED BOOK"

1. James Mason Hutchings, "The Great Yo-Semite Valley," *Hutchings' California Magazine* 4 (October 1859); quoted in Hutchings, *Scenes of Wonder and Curiosity from Hutchings' California Magazine, 1856–1861*, ed. R. R. Olmsted (Berkeley, CA: Howell-North, 1962), 284.

2. James Mason Hutchings, *In the Heart of the Sierras: The Yo Semite Valley, Both Historical and Descriptive: And Scenes by the Way . . .* (Oakland: Pacific Press Publishing House, 1888), 84.

3. Hutchings, *In the Heart of the Sierras*, 92.

4. James Mason Hutchings, "Original Diary 1854–5" (Washington, DC: Library of Congress Manuscripts Division, J. M. Hutchings Papers), August 18, 1855.

5. Now the location of the famous Transamerica pyramid building. An undated letter sheet illustration of the block of Montgomery Street between Clay and Commercial identified eight attorneys, three bankers, three merchants, one express agent, one stationer (Cooke and LeCount, who also produced lithographs), one daguerrean, and one dealer in distilled spirits. Joseph Armstrong Baird, *California's Pictorial Letter Sheets 1849–1869* (San Francisco: David Magee, 1967), cat. 177; Rosenfield Biographical File, California State Library.

6. Hereafter referred to as *Hutchings' California Magazine*.

7. Rev. W. A. Scott, *Pavilion Palace of Industry: California Industrial Exhibition, San Francisco 1857* (San Francisco: Hutchings & Rosenfield, 1857), advertisement, inside cover.

8. Richard Grusin, *Culture, Technology, and the Creation of America's National Parks* (Cambridge, UK: Cambridge University Press, 2004); Frederick Law Olmsted, *Yosemite and the Mariposa Grove: A Preliminary Report, 1865* (Yosemite National Park, CA; Yosemite Association, 1995), 12; Mark Stoll, "Milton in Yosemite: *Paradise Lost* and the National Parks Idea," *Environmental History* 13, no. 2 (April 2008): 238.

9. James Mason Hutchings, "Our Introductory," *Hutchings' California Magazine* 1 (July 1856): 1.

10. David M. Wrobel, *Promised Lands: Promotion, Memory, and the Creation of the American West* (Lawrence: University Press of Kansas, 2002), 4.

11. W. J. T. Mitchell, "Imperial Landscape," in *Landscape and Power*, W. J. T. Mitchell, ed. (Chicago: University of Chicago Press, 1994), 5–34, 9.

12. Hutchings, *In the Heart of the Sierras*, 97.

13. Clifford Merrill Drury, *William Anderson Scott: No Ordinary Man* (Glendale, CA: Arthur H. Clark, 1967).

14. See, for example, Scott, *Pavilion Palace of Industry*, and the several articles Scott wrote for *Hutchings' California Magazine* during its run.

15. Hutchings, "Original Diary 1854–5," June 3, 1855.

16. Malcolm Gladwell, *The Tipping Point: How Little Things Can Make a Big Difference* (New York: Little, Brown, 2002), 59.

17. Hutchings, "Our Introductory," *Hutchings' California Magazine* 1 (July 1856): 1. The original advertisement misspelled California as 'Califoairn.' Advertisement, *Hutchings' California Magazine* 1 (August 1856): back cover.

18. Francis E. Sheldon, "Pioneer Illustration in California," *Overland Monthly*, 2nd series, 11 (April 1888): 340.

19. "Monthly Chat with Contributors and Correspondents," *Hutchings' California Magazine* 2 (July 1857): 48; and *Hutchings' California Magazine* 2 (August 1857): 93; "To Contributors and Correspondents," *Hutchings' California Magazine* 4 (June 1860): 576.

20. James A. Silverman, "Uncovering the Snow Storm: Rescuing California's First Children's Poem from Obscurity," *California History* 63 (Spring 1984): 173. Shirley Sargent, *Pioneers in Petticoats: Yosemite's Early Women, 1856–1900* (Yosemite, CA: Flying Spur Press, 1966), 33–34.

21. Nicholas K. Bromell, *By the Sweat of the Brow: Literature and Labor in Antebellum America* (Chicago: University of Chicago Press, 1993), 29–34, 40–45. Stephen P. Rice, "Minding the Machine: Languages of Class in Early Industrial America, 1820–1860" (Ph.D. diss., Yale University, 1996), 25–91; Nina Lerman, "From 'Useful Knowledge' to 'Habits of Industry': Gender, Race and Class in Nineteenth-Century Technical Education," (Ph.D. diss., University of Pennsylvania, 1993), 158–224.

22. Scott, *Pavilion Palace of Industry*, cover, 1.

23. Ibid., 6.

24. See Bromell, *By the Sweat of the Brow*, 15–24; Bruce Laurie, *Artisans into Workers: Labor in Nineteenth-Century America* (New York: Hill and Wang, 1989); Sean Wilentz, *Chants Democratic: New York City and the Rise of the American Working Class, 1788–1850* (New York: Oxford University Press, 1984); Paul E. Johnson, *A Shopkeeper's Millennium: Society and Revivals in Rochester, New York, 1815–1837* (New York: Hill and Wang, 1984); Paul A. Shackel, *Culture Change and the New Technology: An Archaeology of the Early American Industrial Era* (New York: Plenum Press, 1996); Rice, "Minding the Machine."

25. Hutchings, *Scenes of Wonder and Curiosity*, 291, 308.

26. Nevada historian Phil Earl speculates that Henry DeGroot was the author of this article. Personal conversation, May 17, 2000.

27. Hutchings, *Scenes of Wonder and Curiosity*, 291.

28. James B. Snyder, Yosemite Historian, personal conversation, May 16, 2000.

29. Hutchings, *Scenes of Wonder and Curiosity*, 298.

30. Mitchell, "Imperial Landscape," 15.

CHAPTER 4. HUTCHINGS AND ROSENFIELD IN THE PRINT METROPOLIS

1. Large sections of this chapter were originally published as "'Such Is Change in California': James Mason Hutchings and the Print Metropolis, 1854–1862." *Proceedings of the American Antiquarian Society* 114, pt. 1 (2004): 35–85, and much of the research

was supported by the Stephen Botein Fellowship at the American Antiquarian Society in November 1998.

2. James Mason Hutchings, "1855 Diary Transcript," comp. Gertrude Hutchings Mills (Yosemite Park, CA: Yosemite Research Library), 89.

3. Including Adams & Co., where Hutchings had an account. Hutchings, "1855 Diary Transcript," 42.

4. Arthur Quinn, *The Rivals: William Gwin, David Broderick, and the Birth of California* (Lincoln: University of Nebraska Press, 1997), 177.

5. Hutchings, "1855 Diary Transcript," 42.

6. W. J. T. Mitchell, "Imperial Landscape," in *Landscape and Power*, ed. W. J. T. Mitchell (Chicago: University of Chicago Press, 1994), 14.

7. David J. St. Clair, "The Gold Rush and the Beginnings of California Industry," in *A Golden State: Mining and Economic Development in Gold Rush California*, eds. James J. Rawls and Richard J. Orsi (Berkeley: University of California Press, 1997), 190.

8. Gray Brechin, *Imperial San Francisco: Urban Power, Earthly Ruin* (Berkeley: University of California Press, 1999), 35.

9. Irving Murray Scott, "Hydraulic Mining Illustrated—I," *Overland Monthly* 12, no. 72 (December 1888): 576–585. Quoted in Brechin, *Imperial San Francisco*, 36.

10. Brechin, *Imperial San Francisco*, 50.

11. Miriam Leslie, *California: A Pleasure Trip from Gotham to the Golden Gate, April, May, June 1877* (New York: G. W. Carleton, 1877), 110.

12. Thomas R. Dunlap, *Nature and the English Diaspora: Environment and History in the United States, Canada, Australia and New Zealand* (Cambridge, UK: Cambridge University Press, 1999).

13. Edward C. Kemble, *A History of California Newspapers, 1846–1858*, reprinted from the Supplement to the Sacramento *Union* of December 25, 1858, ed. Helen Harding Brentnor (Los Gatos, CA: Talisman Press, 1962), 53.

14. Jen Huntley-Smith, "Territorial Enterprises: Print Culture and the West," in *Perspectives on American Book History: Artifacts and Commentary*, eds. Scott E. Casper, Joanne D. Chaison, and Jeffrey D. Groves (Amherst: University of Massachusetts Press, 2002): 276–278.

15. *California Pictorial Almanac for 1860* (San Francisco: Hutchings & Rosenfield, 1860); *California Pictorial Almanac for 1861* (San Francisco: Hutchings & Rosenfield, 1861).

16. Robb Sagendorph, *America and Her Almanacs: Wit, Wisdom and Weather 1639–1970* (Boston: Little, Brown, 1970), 7–17.

17. *California Pictorial Almanac for 1860*, 5.

18. Robert Greenwood, ed., *California Imprints 1833–1862; A Bibliography*, Seiko June Suzuki and Marjorie Pulliam, comps. (Los Gatos, CA: Talisman Press, 1961), 66–251.

19. Maureen Perkins, *Visions of the Future: Almanacs, Time and Cultural Change 1775–1870* (Oxford, UK: Clarendon Press, 1996), 16; see also David D. Hall, *Worlds of Wonder, Days of Judgment: Popular Religious Belief in Early New England* (New York: Knopf, 1989).

20. Shirley Sargent, "Introduction," in James Mason Hutchings, *Seeking the Elephant, 1849: James Mason Hutchings' Journal of his Overland Trek to California, Including His Voyage to America, 1848 and Letters from the Mother Lode*, ed. Shirley Sargent (Glendale, CA: Arthur H. Clark, 1980), 28.

21. Perkins, *Visions of the Future*, 4, 178–180.

22. Ibid., 14.

23. Ibid., 180–181.

24. Leo Marx, *The Machine in the Garden: Technology and the Pastoral Ideal in America*

(New York: Oxford University Press, 1967), 6; on the visual connotations of landscape, see John R. Stilgoe, *Common Landscape of America, 1580–1845* (New Haven, CT: Yale University Press, 1982), 25.

25. Robert H. Taylor, ed., *Marysville Herald*, February 25, 1851, 2.

26. Lawrence J. Jelinek, *Harvest Empire: A History of California Agriculture* (San Francisco: Boyd & Fraser, 1979), 33–35.

27. Jen Huntley-Smith, "'Such Is Change in California': James Mason Hutchings and the Print Metropolis, 1854–1862," *Proceedings of the American Antiquarian Society* 114, pt. 1 (2004): 35–86. Cover, *Hutchings' California Magazine* 16 (October, 1857).

28. Gary Kurutz, "Popular Culture on the Golden Shore," in *Rooted in Barbarous Soil: People, Culture, and Community in Gold Rush California*, eds. Kevin Starr and Richard J. Orsi (Berkeley: University of California Press, 2000), 298; Gerard Hurley "Reading in the Gold Rush," *Book Club of California Quarterly News-Letter* 15 (Fall 1950): 90.

29. Brechin, *Imperial San Francisco*, xxiv–xxv.

30. Bruce L. Johnson, "Nevada Imprints Produced in San Francisco: The Role of Towne & Bacon," *Kemble Occasional* 19 (June 1978), 1–6; Towne & Bacon, "Correspondence," Kemble Manuscript Collection, California Historical Society, San Francisco.

31. Advertisement, inside cover; E. A. Taylor, *The California Register and Statistical Reporter . . .* (San Francisco: Eureka Office, 1856).

32. *California Pictorial Almanac for 1859* (San Francisco: Hutchings & Rosenfield, 1859), advertisement.

33. Bruce L. Johnson, "Printing in Nineteenth-Century San Francisco: A Flame before the Fire," *Book Club of California Quarterly Newsletter* 46 (Summer 1981), 91. "California Stereotype Foundry, J. M. Burke & Co., 75 Davis" (advertisement), *The Illustrated California Almanac* (San Francisco: R. H. Vance, 1855), 49; Jen Huntley-Smith, "'The Genius of Civilization': The Material Culture of Print Technology in the Nineteenth-Century American West," in *Western Technological Landscapes*, Nevada Humanities Committee, *Halcyon* series, 20 (Reno: University of Nevada Press, 1998): 44; Barbara Cloud, *The Business of Newspapers on the Western Frontier* (Reno: University of Nevada Press, 1992), 137.

34. Sister Julie Bellefeuille, S.N.D., "Printing in California, 1831–1930," *Pacific Historian* 19 (Fall 1975): 264.

35. Martha A. Sandweiss, *Print the Legend: Photography and the American West* (New Haven, CT: Yale University Press, 2002), 83–85.

36. "Yo-Ham-I-Te Valley," *Hutchings' California Magazine* 2 (July 1857): 2; "The Great Yo-Semite Valley," 4 (October 1858–January 1859), 145, 193, 241, 335; "Trip to Walker's River and Carson Valley," 2 (May, June 1858), 489–496, 529–538; "The Farallone Islands," 1 (August 1856), 49–57; "Our Chowder Party," in Hutchings, *Scenes of Wonder and Curiosity from Hutchings' California Magazine, 1856–1861*, ed. R. R. Olmsted (Berkeley, CA: Howell-North, 1962), 20–22.

37. "The Great Yo-Semite Valley," *Hutchings' California Magazine* 4 (October 1859), in Hutchings, *Scenes of Wonder and Curiosity*, 284.

38. John F. Sears, *Sacred Places: American Tourist Attractions in the Nineteenth Century* (New York: Oxford University Press, 1989), 4–5; see also Ann Farrar Hyde, *An American Vision: Far Western Landscape and National Culture, 1820–1920* (New York: New York University Press, 1990).

39. "Notes and Sketches of the Washoe Country," Hutchings, *Scenes of Wonder and Curiosity*, 309.

40. Ibid., 310. Ronald M. James, "The Setting," in *The Roar and the Silence: A History of*

Virginia City and the Comstock Lode (Reno and Las Vegas: University of Nevada Press, 1998), 1–21.

41. "Notes and Sketches of the Washoe Country," Hutchings, *Scenes of Wonder and Curiosity*, 316.

42. Brechin, *Imperial San Francisco*, 44.

43. George L. Henderson, *California and the Fictions of Capital* (New York: Oxford University Press, 1998), x–xii.

44. Hutchings, "The Great Yo-Semite Valley," *Hutchings' California Magazine* 4, no. 4 (October 1859).

45. Hutchings, *Scenes of Wonder*, 286.

46. Hank Johnston, *The Yosemite Grant, 1864–1906: A Pictorial History* (Yosemite National Park, CA: Yosemite Association, 1995), 30–31.

47. Johnston, *Yosemite Grant*, 29, 38–40.

PART III. YOSEMITE AND THE NATIONAL SUBLIME

1. U.S. Statutes at Large, vol. 13, ch. 184, p. 325, "An Act Authorizing a Grant to the State of California of 'the Yo-Semite Valley,' and of the Land Embracing 'the Mariposa Big Tree Grove'" [S. 203; Public Act No. 159].

2. Malcolm Gladwell, *The Tipping Point: How Little Things Can Make a Big Difference* (Boston: Little, Brown, 2000).

CHAPTER 5. YOSEMITE AND THE CRUCIBLE OF WAR

1. Frederick Law Olmsted, *Yosemite and the Mariposa Grove: A Preliminary Report, 1865* (Yosemite National Park, CA: Yosemite Association, 1995), 12, http://www.yosemite.ca .us/library/olmsted/report.html.

2. U.S. Statutes at Large, vol. 13, ch. 184, p. 325, "An Act Authorizing a Grant to the State of California of 'the Yo-Semite Valley,' and of the Land Embracing 'the Mariposa Big Tree Grove'" [S. 203; Public Act No. 159].

3. Hans Huth, *Yosemite: The Story of an Idea* (Yosemite National Park, CA: Yosemite Natural History Association, 1984), 29.

4. Quoted in Huth, *Yosemite: The Story of an Idea*, 29.

5. Adam W. Sweeting, "Writers and Dilettantes: Central Park and the Literary Origins of Antebellum Urban Nature," in *The Nature of Cities: Ecocriticism and Urban Environments*, eds. Michael Bennet and David W. Teague (Tucson: University of Arizona Press), 93–110, 95.

6. Frederick Law Olmsted, "Yosemite and the Mariposa Grove: A Preliminary Report, 1865."

7. Olmsted, "Yosemite and the Mariposa Grove"; Scott Herring, *Lines on the Land: Writers, Art, and the National Parks* (Charlottesville: University of Virginia Press, 2004), 19, quoted in William Deverell, "'Niagara Magnified': Finding Emerson, Muir, and Adams in Yosemite," in *Yosemite: Art of an American Icon*, ed. Amy Scott (Berkeley: University of California Press, 2005), 12.

8. Amerindians suffering from the devastating effects of mining, lumbering, and genocidal campaigns may well have perceived their own homelands as "torn asunder." William Deverell, "'Niagara Magnified'" 12; Metropolitan Museum of Art, "Carleton Watkins (1829–1916) and the West: 1860s–1870s," http://www.metmuseum.org/toah/ hd/phws/hd_phws.htm#ixzzosZaSDXDQ.

9. Kevin Starr, *Americans and the California Dream, 1850–1915* (New York: Oxford University Press, 1973), 103. Arthur Quinn, *The Rivals: William Gwin, David Broderick, and the Birth of California* (Lincoln: University of Nebraska Press, 1994).

10. King's articles were later published as *A Vacation among the Sierras: Yosemite in 1860*, ed. John A. Hussey (San Francisco: Book Club of California, 1962), cited in John Sears, *Sacred Places: American Tourist Attractions in the Nineteenth Century* (New York: Oxford University Press, 1989), 127.

11. Starr, *Americans and the California Dream*, 103.

12. Thomas Starr King to James T. Fields, January 31, 1862, and October 19, 1862, cited in Jeffrey D. Groves, "'Ticknor-and-Fields-ism of All Kinds': Thomas Starr King, Literary Promotion, and Canon Formation," *New England Quarterly* (June 1995): 213; Starr, *Americans and the California Dream*, 103–104.

13. Starr, *Americans and the California Dream*, 103, 108.

14. Rosenfield continued to publish a few pieces in the years after Hutchings left, including *California Pictorial Almanac* for 1862 and a *California War Almanac* in 1863. A. Rosenfield, *California Pictorial Almanac* (San Francisco: C. F. Robbins, printer, 1862); *California War Almanac* (San Francisco: Chas F. Robbins & Co., printers, 1863).

15. James Mason Hutchings, *In the Heart of the Sierras, the Yo Semite Valley, Both Historical and Descriptive: And Scenes by the Way . . .* (Oakland: Pacific Press Publishing House, 1888), 103.

16. Hutchings, *In the Heart of the Sierras*, 101, 105–107, 118.

17. Ibid., 105.

18. W. A. Chalfant, *The Story of Inyo*, rev. ed. (Bishop, CA: Pinon Book Store, 1933), 170; James M. Hutchings, "A Close 'New Year's Call' in 1862 [1863]," mss Yosemite National Park Museum cat. no. 30, 156.

19. James Mason Hutchings, "Letter from San Carlos," *Alta California*, July 31, 1863, p. 1, col. 5, cited in James B. Snyder, ed. "James Mason Hutchings, *A Photographic Expedition to Fisherman's Peak and Kings Canyon in 1875*," unpublished ms, 2007, 13–14, 17.

20. "The Yosemite Grant Act, as legislated by Congress, consisted of two parts: Section I (called the Yosemite Valley Grant) comprised 36,111.14 acres . . . in and around the Valley itself; Section 2 (called the Mariposa Grove Grant), a noncontiguous area of 2,589.26 acres about twelve and one-half air miles to the south, contained the Mariposa Big Trees. The total reserved territory was 38,700.4 acres in all, or more than sixty square miles." Hank Johnston, *The Yosemite Grant 1864–1906: A Pictorial History* (Yosemite National Park, CA: Yosemite Association, 1995), 55. "Yosemite Grant Act," 1864.

21. Alfred Runte, *Yosemite: The Embattled Wilderness* (Lincoln: University of Nebraska Press, 1990); Johnston, *Yosemite Grant*, 54.

22. "America's Best Idea" is the subtitle for Ken Burns' 2009 documentary series on the national parks. Ken Burns, director, *The National Parks: America's Best Idea*, 2009.

23. Huth, *Yosemite: The Story of an Idea*, 30.

24. Raymond to Conness, in ibid., 37.

25. Ibid., 32; Sears, *Sacred Places*, 125–132; Victoria Post Ranney, editor of the Frederick Law Olmsted papers, disagrees that he could have been involved prior to his appointment as chair of the commissioners in the fall of 1864. Frederick Law Olmsted, *The Papers of Frederick Law Olmsted, Volume V, The California Frontier, 1863–65*, ed. Victoria Post Ranney (Baltimore, MD: Johns Hopkins University Press, 1990), 513.

26. Hank Johnston, *Yosemite Grant*, 30.

27. "Yosemite Grant Act," 1864.

28. Olmsted, "Yosemite and the Mariposa Grove," 10.

29. In some ways, Hutchings' career at this point resembles the "glass ceiling" experienced

by creole pioneers in Latin American colonies as described in Benedict Anderson, *Imagined Communities: Reflections on the Origin and Spread of Nationalism* (London: Verso, 1994), 56–65.

30. Hutchings, *In the Heart of the Sierras*, 149–153.

31. Ibid., 154; Justice Stephen J. Field, "Opinion of the Court," *Hutchings v. Low*, U.S. Supreme Court Case no. 435, January 6, 1873, 87; *Frederick F. Low, Governor, Henry W. Cleaveland, J. D. Whitney, William Ashburner, J. W. Raymond, E. S. Holden, Alexander Deering, George W. Coulter, and Galen W. Clark, Constituting and Known in Law as "The Commissioners to Manage the Yosemite Valley and the Mariposa Big Tree Grove," v. J. M. Hutchings*, California Supreme Court no. 2,723 (July 1871), 639.

32. *Hutchings v. Low*, 85.

33. Josiah Dwight Whitney, *The Yosemite Guide-Book* (Cambridge, MA: Welch, Bigelow, 1870), 22–23, cited in Michael Smith, *Pacific Visions: California Scientists and the Environment* (New Haven, CT: Yale University Press, 1987), 69.

34. Alfred Runte, "The National Park Idea: Origins and Paradox of the American Experience," *Journal of Forest History* 21, no. 2 (1977): 66; see also Patrick McGreevy, *Imagining Niagara: The Meaning and Making of Niagara Falls* (Amherst: University of Massachusetts Press, 1994); Sears, *Sacred Places*, 130.

35. Runte, "National Park Idea," 70–71.

36. Peter Blodgett, "Visiting the 'Realm of Wonder': Yosemite and the Business of Tourism, 1855–1916," *Yosemite and Sequoia: A Century of California National Parks*, eds. Richard J. Orsi, Alfred Runte, and Marlene Smith-Baranzini (Berkeley: University of California Press, 1993), 34–38; Runte, *Yosemite: The Embattled Wilderness*, 23.

37. Runte, *Yosemite: The Embattled Wilderness*, 23; Huth, *Yosemite: The Story of an Idea*, 29; Johnston, *Yosemite Grant*, 68–81.

38. Hans Huth, *Yosemite: The Story of an Idea*, 29.

39. Carl Parcher Russell, *One Hundred Years in Yosemite: The Story of a Great Park and Its Friends* (Yosemite National Park, CA: Yosemite Natural History Association, 1968), 151.

40. *Hutchings v. Low*, 85.

41. Hutchings, *In the Heart of the Sierras*, 130.

42. Alan Trachtenberg, *The Incorporation of America: Culture and Society in the Gilded Age* (New York: Hill and Wang, 1982).

43. Although Field's decision in this case may seem to be an anomaly in a long career promoting his theory that private property rights were so powerful as to be almost inalienable, the emphasis on the power of Congress and the context of incorporation indicates that the property rights of Congress and corporations superseded the more legally tentative claims of preemption holders. "Stephen Johnson Field," in Kermit L. Hall, ed., *The Oxford Companion to the Supreme Court of the United States* (New York: Oxford University Press, 1992), 290–291. For a discussion of the Reconstruction politics surrounding Congressional land grants to railroad corporations, see Eric Foner, *Reconstruction: America's Unfinished Revolution, 1863–1877* (New York: Harper & Row, 1988), 466–469; Alan Trachtenberg, *Incorporation of America*, 22–23.

44. Richard Maxwell Brown, "Violence," in *The Oxford History of the American West*, eds. Clyde A. Milner II, Carol A. O'Connor, and Martha Sandweiss (New York: Oxford University Press, 1994), 393–426.

45. Olmsted, "Yosemite and the Mariposa Grove."

46. Dennis Kruska, *James Mason Hutchings of Yo Semite: A Biography and Bibliography* (San Francisco: Book Club of California, 2009), 93, 103.

47. Ibid., 94; Russell, *One Hundred Years in Yosemite*, 153.

48. James Mason Hutchings, *Yosemite and the Big Trees of California, Hutchings' Guide and Souvenir* (San Francisco: J. M. Hutchings, 1894), 56, in Kruska, *James Mason Hutchings of Yo Semite*, 96.

49. Kruska, *James Mason Hutchings of Yo Semite*, 102.

50. J. W. Boddam-Whetham, *Western Wanderings, A Record of Travel in the Evening Land* (London, 1874), 123, quoted in Kruska, *James Mason Hutchings of Yo Semite*, 102.

51. Hutchings, *Scenes of Wonder and Curiosity* . . . (San Francisco: Hutchings & Rosenfield, 1860, 1861); Hutchings, *Scenes of Wonder and Curiosity* . . . (San Francisco: J. M. Hutchings & Co., 1861, 1862); Hutchings, *Scenes of Wonder and Curiosity* . . . (London: Chapman and Hall, 1865); Hutchings, *Scenes of Wonder and Curiosity* . . . (New York and San Francisco: A. Roman & Co., 1870, 1871, 1872, and 1876). See Lloyd W. Currey and Dennis G. Kruska, *Bibliography of Yosemite, the Central and Southern High Sierra and the Big Trees, 1839–1900* (Los Angeles: Dawson's Book Shop, 1992), 84–87.

52. Hutchings, *Scenes of Wonder and Curiosity in California*, 128, 156; Frank Brookman, "Park Naturalists and the Evolution of National Park Service Interpretation through World War II," *Journal of Forest History* 22 (January 1978), 26; Russell, *One Hundred Years in Yosemite*, 48–58.

53. Hutchings, *Scenes of Wonder and Curiosity*, 112, 116, 150, 147.

54. Hank Johnston, *Yosemite Grant*, 140.

55. Ibid., 141.

CHAPTER 6. HUTCHINGS, MUIR, AND THE MODERN PARADOX
OF WILDERNESS

1. Frederick Law Olmsted, *Yosemite and the Mariposa Grove: A Preliminary Report, 1865* (Yosemite National Park, CA; Yosemite Association, 1995).

2. James Mason Hutchings, *In the Heart of the Sierras, the Yo Semite Valley, Both Historical and Descriptive: And Scenes by the Way* . . . . (Oakland: Pacific Press Publishing House, 1888), 130.

3. William Hahn, *Yosemite Valley from Glacier Point*. 1874, oil on canvas 27.25 × 46.25 inches. Collection of the California Historical Society. Reproduced in *From Exploration to Conservation: Picturing the Sierra Nevada* (Reno, NV: Nevada Museum of Art, 1988), cover and Plate 1; Wikipedia Online Encyclopedia, "Claude Glass" http://en.wikipedia.org/wiki/Claude_glass.

4. Martha A. Sandweiss, *Print the Legend: Photography and the American West* (New Haven, CT: Yale University Press, 2002), 20. The discussion that follows is based primarily on Gary F. Kurutz's essay "Yosemite on Glass" in *Yosemite: Art of an American Icon*, ed. Amy Scott (Berkeley: University of California Press, 2007), 55–90.

5. Josiah Dwight Whitney, *The Yosemite Guide-Book* (Cambridge, MA: Welch, Bigelow, 1870), cited in Kevin DeLuca and Anne Demo, "Imagining Nature and Erasing Class and Race: Carleton Watkins, John Muir and the Construction of Wilderness," *Environmental History* 6, no. 4 (October 2001): 546.

6. Kurutz, "Yosemite on Glass," 68–69.

7. David C. Miller, "Introduction," in *American Iconology: New Approaches to Nineteenth-Century Art and Literature*, ed. David C. Miller (New Haven, CT: Yale University Press, 1993), 7.

8. Ibid., 5.

9. Alan Wallach, "A Picture of Mount Holyoke" in *American Iconology*, ed. Miller, 83.

10. William Cronon, "The Trouble with Wilderness, or Getting Back to the Wrong Na-

ture," in *Uncommon Ground: Rethinking the Human Place in Nature*, ed. William Cronon (New York: W. W. Norton, 1996), 69.

11. DeLuca and Demo, "Imagining Nature and Erasing Class and Race: Carleton Watkins, John Muir, and the Construction of Wilderness," *Environmental History* 5, no. 4 (October 2001), 541–560.

12. John P. Cowan, *"Forked Lightning" or, Gonza the Brigand. A Wild Tale of the Yosemite Valley* (New York: Ornum and Company, 1872), 1.

13. Dennis Kruska, *James Mason Hutchings of Yo Semite: A Biography and Bibliography* (San Francisco: Book Club of California, 2009), 134; Gaylen Lee, *Walking Where We Lived: Memoirs of a Mono Indian Family* (Norman: University of Oklahoma Press, 1998).

14. Samuel Bowles, *The Parks and Mountains of Colorado: A Summer Vacation in the Switzerland of America*, cited in DeLuca and Demo, "Imagining Nature," 544.

15. A. L. Bancroft, *Bancroft's Tourist Guide. Yosemite, San Francisco and around the Bay* (San Francisco: A. L. Bancroft & Co., 1871), 13, quoted in Jen Huntley-Smith, "Nature and Progress in Yosemite," *Nevada Historical Society Quarterly* 46, no. 3 (Fall 2003): 103. Dorothea Dix was a prominent activist for the mentally insane, and Anna Dickinson was an abolitionist and woman's suffrage advocate. Wikipedia: The Online Encyclopedia, http://en.wikipedia.org/wiki/Anna_Elizabeth_Dickinson.

16. Hank Johnston, *The Yosemite Grant 1864–1906: A Pictorial History* (Yosemite National Park, CA: Yosemite Association, 1995), 89. This discussion draws upon material published previously in Huntley-Smith, "Nature and Progress in Yosemite."

17. Kruska, *James Mason Hutchings of Yo Semite*, 106; Donald Worster, *A Passion for Nature: The Life of John Muir* (Oxford: Oxford University Press, 2008); the following discussion of the relationship between Elvira Hutchings and John Muir is drawn from the chronology of events compiled by Yosemite historian James B. Snyder in December 2010. Snyder, "Hutchings Chronology," personal email correspondence, December 15, 2010.

18. John Muir to Jeanne Carr, July 27, 1872, cited in Bonnie Johanna Gisel, ed., *Kindred and Related Spirits: The Letters of John Muir and Jeanne C. Carr* (Salt Lake City: University of Utah Press, 2001), 182.

19. Frank Buske, "Love Is Painful," *John Muir Newsletter* (Spring 1997): 4–5.

20. Letter from a private collection is transcribed in Buske, "Love Is Painful," 5.

21. Ibid.

22. Kruska, *James Mason Hutchings of Yo Semite*, 129–130.

23. James Mason Hutchings, "The Hutchings Expedition to the Top of Inyo Dome, Now Mt. Whitney, with the First Photographs," ms, 1875, James Mason Hutchings Papers, Yosemite Museum. Cited in Kruska, *James Mason Hutchings of Yo Semite*, 128.

24. Whitney, *Yosemite Guide-Book.*

25. John Muir, *Our National Parks* (Boston and New York: Houghton Mifflin & Co., 1901).

26. Dr. A. Kellogg, "New Species of California Plants," *Hutchings' California Magazine* 4 (September 1860): 101.

27. Kruska, *James Mason Hutchings of Yo Semite*, 132–133.

28. James Mason Hutchings, "The Geology and Scenery of the High Sierra," mss fragment, Shirley Sargent Collection of the Papers of James Mason Hutchings, Yosemite Research Library, 1–9.

29. Stephen J. Pyne, *Fire in America: A Cultural History of Wildland and Rural Fire* (Princeton, NJ: Princeton University Press, 1982), 100–102.

30. James B. Snyder, "Putting 'Hoofed Locusts' Out to Pasture," *Nevada Historical Society Quarterly* 46, no. 2 (Fall 2003): 139–172, 139.

31. Karl Jacoby, "Class and Environmental History: Lessons from 'the War in the Adirondacks,'" *Environmental History* 2, no. 3 (July 1997): 328–356.

32. Allen Kelly, "Restoration of Yosemite Waterfalls," *Harper's Weekly* (July 16, 1892); Michael Smith, *Pacific Visions: California Scientists and the Environment* (New Haven, CT: Yale University Press, 1987).

33. Worster, *A Passion for Nature*, 214–215.

34. Therese Yelverton (Viscountess Avonmore), *Zanita: A Tale of the Yo-semite* (Cambridge, MA: Riverside Press, 1872).

35. Thurman Wilkins, *John Muir: Apostle of Nature* (Norman: University of Oklahoma Press, 1995), 70–71; Worster, *Passion for Nature*, 171.

36. T. J. Jackson Lears, *No Place of Grace*, p. 25.

37. Arno Dosch, "The Mystery of John Muir's Money; a Simple Naturalist's Studies in the Temple of Mammon," San Francisco *Chronicle*, January 19, 1915. Cited in Worster, *A Passion for Nature*, p. 463.

38. Donald Worster, *A Passion for Nature*, 464.

39. Cronon, "Trouble with Wilderness," 78.

40. Thomas R. Vale and Geraldine R. Vale, *Walking with Muir across Yosemite* (Madison: University of Wisconsin Press, 1998), 120; on the class bias of environmental historians, see Jacoby, "Class and Environmental History," 325.

41. Martin V. Melosi, "Equity, Eco-racism, and Environmental History," *Environmental History Review* 4, no. 3 (Fall 1995): 5; Frederick H. Buttel and William L. Flinn, "Social Class and Mass Environmental Beliefs: A Reconsideration" *Environment and Behavior* 10 (September 1978): 433–450.

42. Cronon, "Trouble with Wilderness," 78.

CONCLUSION: DISCOVERING OUR PLACE IN NATURE

1. William Cronon, "The Trouble with Wilderness, or Getting Back to the Wrong Nature," in *Uncommon Ground: Rethinking the Human Place in Nature*, ed. William Cronon (New York: W. W. Norton, 1996), 77.

2. Amy Scott, "Introduction: Yosemite Calls," in *Yosemite: Art of an American Icon*, ed. Amy Scott (Berkeley: University of California Press, 2007), 1.

3. David Leeming and Margaret Leeming, *A Dictionary of Creation Myths* (New York: Oxford University Press, 1994) vii, cited in Paul Schullery and Lee Whittlesey, *Myth and History in the Creation of Yellowstone National Park* (Lincoln: University of Nebraska Press) 87.

4. Ibid.

5. Cronon, "Trouble with Wilderness," 81.

6. Ibid.

7. Ibid.

BIBLIOGRAPHY

ARCHIVES AND MANUSCRIPT COLLECTIONS
California State Library, Sacramento
   Anton Rosenfield Biographical File
California State Archives, Sacramento
   Frederick F. Low, Governor, Henry W. Cleaveland, J. D. Whitney, William Ashburner,
   J. W. Raymond, E. S. Holden, Alexander Deering, George W. Coulter, and Galen W.
   Clark, Constituting and Known in Law as "The Commissioners to Manage the Yosemite
   Valley and the Mariposa Big Tree Grove," v. J. M. Hutchings, California Supreme Court
   no. 2,723 (July 1871): 637–639.
California Historical Society, San Francisco
   Kemble Manuscript Collection
   Towne & Bacon, "Correspondence."
Huntington Library, San Marino, California
Private Collection of Dennis Kruska, Sherman Oaks, California
   "Chronological List of Hutchings' Publications." Unpublished mss, 1995.
Bancroft Library, University of California, Berkeley
   Archives/Manuscripts
      James M. Hutchings Diary, ms, 1841–1850
      James M. Hutchings Overland Diary of 1849 from New Orleans to the Carson
         River, and '49er Guide, microfilm
      The Honeyman Collection—Objects
         Hutchings & Rosenfield. "Inkwell with label: News-letter for writing home,"
            ca. 1856.
Library of Congress, Washington, DC
   Manuscripts Division
      J. M. Hutchings Papers, 1848–1855, LC control: mm 81026963, "Original Diary,
         1854–5."
Yosemite National Park, California: Yosemite Research Library
   James Mason Hutchings Biographical File
      Hazel M. Call to Emil F. Ernst, September 6, 1949.
      Rodney Hutchings to Shirley Sargent, March 6, 1986.
   J. M. Hutchings & Co., . . . Collectors and Dealers in Forest Tree, Shrub and Other
      Seeds, Bulbs, Etc., From all parts of California and the Pacific Coast" Advertise-
      ment offprint.
   J. M. Hutchings Diaries; ms May 1848–October 1849; 1855; photocopy of typed tran
      scripts by Gertrude Hutchings Mills.
   James M. Hutchings, "A Close 'New Year's Call' in 1862 [1863]," mss Yosemite Na-
      tional Park Museum cat. no. 30, 156.
   James Mason Hutchings. "Scrapbook, 1853–1855," Yosemite National Park Museum
      accession no. 6429.

Ayres, Thomas A. "General View of the Great Yo-Semite Valley, Mariposa County, California." San Francisco: Hutchings & Rosenfield, 1859. Lithograph.

———. "The Yo-Hamite Falls." San Francisco: Hutchings & Rosenfield, 1855, Lithograph.

De Groot, Henry. *De Groot's Map of the Washoe Mines.* San Francisco: Hutchings & Rosenfield, 1860.

———. *Sketches of the Washoe Silver Mines: With a Description of the Soil, Climate and Mineral Resources, of the Country East of the Sierra.* San Francisco: Hutchings & Rosenfield, 1860.

Hutchings, James Mason. "Articles in a Miner's Creed." Letter sheet. San Francisco: James Mason Hutchings, 1855.

———. "Autobiographical Statement." *Autobiographies and Reminiscences of Members.* San Francisco: Society of California Pioneers, n.d. 2: 5–11.

———. "Commandments to California Wives." Letter sheet. San Francisco: J. F. Larrabee, 1855.

———. "Editor's Table—More Water Wanted." *Hutchings' California Magazine* 2 (August 1857): 91.

———. *Hutchings' California Magazine,* volumes 1–5. San Francisco: Hutchings & Rosenfield, July 1856–June 1861.

———. "Hutchings' Panoramic Scenes: California Indians." Letter sheet. San Francisco: James Mason Hutchings, 1855.

———. "Hutchings' Panoramic Scenes: The Mammoth Trees of California." Letter sheet. San Francisco: James Mason Hutchings, 1855.

———. "Hutching's [*sic*] Panoramic Scenes—Northern California." Letter sheet. San Francisco: W. C. Butler, 1855.

———. *The Illustrated California Almanac.* San Francisco: R. H. Vance, 1855.

———. *In the Heart of the Sierras: The Yo Semite Valley, Both Historical and Descriptive: And Scenes by the Way . . .* Oakland, CA: Pacific Press Publishing House, 1888.

———. "'Miner's Ten Commandments.'" H. Eastman DEL, Anthony & Baker. San Francisco: Sun Print, 1853.

———. "A New Commandment." *Placerville Herald,* v1, n16 (August 13, 1853), 2.

———. "Our Introductory." *Hutchings' California Magazine* 1 (July 1856): 1.

———. "Saw Mill Railroad." *Hutchings' California Magazine* 2 (August 1857): 62–64.

———. "A Saw—One of 'em." *Placerville Herald,* v1, n7 (June 11, 1853), 2.

———. *Scenes of Wonder and Curiosity from Hutchings' California Magazine, 1856–1861,* ed. R. R. Olmsted. Berkeley, CA: Howell-North, 1962.

———. *Scenes of Wonder and Curiosity in California, Illustrated by Upwards of 100 Engravings.* London: Chapman and Hall, 1865.

———. *Seeking the Elephant, 1849: James Mason Hutchings' Journal of His Overland Trek to California, Including His Voyage to America, 1848 and Letters from the Mother Lode,* ed. Shirley Sargent. Glendale, CA: Arthur H. Clark, 1980.

———. "Way-Side Scenes in California." Letter sheet. NP: Anthony & Baker S.C., C. Nahl, Del, 1855.

[James Mason Hutchings]. *The Miners' Own Book: Containing Correct Illustrations and Descriptions of the Various Modes of California Mining, Including all the Improvements Introduced from the Earliest Day to the Present Time.* San Francisco: Hutchings & Rosenfield, 1858.

Hutchings & Rosenfield. *California Pictorial Almanac for 1859.* San Francisco: Hutchings & Rosenfield, 1859.

————. *California Pictorial Almanac for 1860*. San Francisco: Hutchings & Rosenfield, 1860.

————. *San Francisco, 1860*. San Francisco: Hutchings & Rosenfield, 1860. Lithograph.

San Francisco Committee of Vigilance. "Proclamation of the Vigilance Committee of San Francisco. June 9th, 1856." Broadside. San Francisco: Hutchings & Co., 1856.

Scott, Rev. William Anderson. *Pavilion Palace of Industry: California Industrial Exhibition, San Francisco 1857*. San Francisco: Hutchings & Rosenfield, 1857.

Taylor, E. A. *The California Register and Statistical Reporter* . . . San Francisco: Eureka Office, 1856.

PUBLISHED PRIMARY SOURCES

Bancroft, A. L. *Bancroft's Tourist's Guide. Yosemite, San Francisco and around the Bay*. San Francisco: A. L. Bancroft & Co., 1871.

[Bausman, William]. "The Idle and Industrious Miner." Sacramento: J. Anthony, 1854.

Bowles, Samuel. *Our New West: Records of Travel between the Mississippi River and the Pacific Ocean . . . Including a Full Description of the Pacific Railroad; and of the Life of the Mormons, Indians and Chinese*. Hartford, CT: Hartford Publishing Co., 1869.

Browne, J. Ross. *Mineral Resources of Nevada Territory* . . . . Washington, DC: U.S. Government Printing Office, 1863.

————. *Report of J. Ross Browne on the Mineral Resources of the States and Territories West of the Rocky Mountains*. Washington, DC: U.S. Government Printing Office, 1868.

————. *Reports upon the Mineral Resources of the United States*. Washington, DC: U.S. Government Printing Office, 1867.

Bunnell, Lafayette H. *Discovery of the Yosemite and the Indian War Which Led to That Event*, 3rd ed. New York: Fleming H. Revell, 1880.

California State Automobile Association. "Bay and Mountain Section" map. 1997.

Carmany, John H. *A Review of the Mining, Agricultural, and Commercial Interests of the Pacific States, for the year 1866 . . . Prepared for the Mercantile Gazette under the Supervision of Titus F. Cronise, Esq*. San Francisco: H. H. Bancroft and Company, 1867.

Carrie & Damon's California Almanac. San Francisco: Carrie & Damon, 1856.

Clappe, Louise A. K. S. *The Shirley Letters: Being Letters Written in 1851–1852 from the California Mines*. Salt Lake City: Peregrine Smith, 1970.

Geological Survey of California. *The Yosemite Guide Book: A Description of the Yosemite Valley and the Adjacent Region of the Sierra Nevada* . . . Cambridge, MA: Welch, Bigelow & Co., 1871.

Greenwood, Grace. *New Life in New Lands, Notes of Travel*. New York: J. B. Ford, 1873.

Kelly, Allen. "Restoration of Yosemite Waterfalls," *Harper's Weekly* (July 16, 1892): 678.

Leslie, Miriam. *California: A Pleasure Trip from Gotham to the Golden Gate (April, May, June, 1877)*. New York: G. W. Carleton, 1877.

Olmsted, Frederick Law. *Yosemite and the Mariposa Grove: A Preliminary Report, 1865*. Yosemite National Park, CA: Yosemite Association, 1995.

Raymond, Rossiter. *Mineral Resources of the States and Territories West of the Rocky Mountains*. Washington, DC: U.S. Government Printing Office, 1868.

Robinson, Fayette. *California and Its Gold Regions; with a Geographical and Topographical View of the Country, Its Mineral and Agricultural Resources, Prepared from Official and Other Authentic Documents; with a Map of the U. States and California, Showing the Routes of the U.S. Mail Steam Packets to California, also the Various Overland Routes*. New York: Stringer & Townsend, 1849. Reprinted in *The Gold Mines of California; Two Guidebooks*. New York: Promontory Press, 1974.

Rosenfield, Anton. *The California Pictorial Almanac*. San Francisco: A. Rosenfield, 1862.

A Statement by the President and Board of Trustees of the Silver Series Mining Company, at Geneva, Smoky Valley, Lander Co., State of Nevada . . . New York: Raymond & Caulon, 1866.

Taylor, E. A. The California Register and Statistical Reporter . . . San Francisco: The Eureka Office, 1856.

U.S. Government. Reports of Explorations and Surveys, to Ascertain the Most Practicable and Economical Route for a Railroad from the Mississippi River to the Pacific Ocean, vol. 9. Washington, DC: A.O.P. Nicholson, 1855.

U.S. Statutes at Large, vol. 13, ch. 184, p. 325. "An Act Authorizing a Grant to the State of California of 'the Yo-Semite Valley,' and of the Land Embracing 'the Mariposa Big Tree Grove'" [S. 203; Public Act No. 159].

U.S. Supreme Court, Justice Stephen J. Field, "Opinion of the Court," Hutchings v. Low, U.S. Supreme Court Case no. 435, January 6, 1873.

Vance, R. H. The Illustrated California Almanac. San Francisco: R. H. Vance, 1855.

Whitney, Josiah Dwight. The Yosemite Guide-Book. Cambridge, MA: Welch, Bigelow, 1870.

Yelverton, Therese (Viscountess Avonmore). Zanita: A Tale of the Yo-semite. New York: Hurd and Houghton, Cambridge, MA: Riverside Press, 1872.

SECONDARY SOURCES

Anderson, Benedict. Imagined Communities: Reflections on the Origin and Spread of Nationalism. London: Verso, 1994.

Anderson, M. Kat. Tending the Wild: Native American Knowledge and the Management of California's Natural Resources. Berkeley: University of California Press, 2006.

Anderson, Patricia. The Printed Image and the Transformation of Popular Culture 1790–1860. Oxford: Clarendon Press, 1994.

Avery, B. P. "Art Beginnings on the Pacific" (part 1). Overland Monthly 1, no. 2 (August 1868): 28–34.

Baird, Joseph Armstrong. California's Pictorial Letter Sheets 1849–1869. San Francisco: David Magee, 1967.

Bakken, Gordon Morris. "American Mining Law and the Environment: The Western Experience." Western Legal History 1, no. 2 (Summer/Fall 1988): 211–236.

Bancroft, Hubert Howe. History of California, v. VI: 1848–1859. The Works of Hubert Howe Bancroft, Volume 23. San Francisco: The History Company, 1888.

———. Literary Industries: A Memoir. New York: Harper & Brothers, 1891.

Barth, Gunther. Instant Cities: Urbanization and the Rise of San Francisco and Denver. New York: Oxford University Press, 1975.

Bean, Walton, and James J. Rawls. California: An Interpretive History. New York: McGrawHill, 1988.

Beck, Warren A., and Ynez D. Hasse. "California and the Indian Wars: Mariposa Indian War, 1851," in California State Military Museum: A United States Army Museum Activity Preserving California's Military Heritage, http://www.militarymuseum.org/Mariposa.html.

Bedell, Rebecca. "Thomas Cole and the Fashionable Science." Huntington Library Quarterly 59 (1997): 348–378.

Beesley, David. Crow's Range: An Environmental History of the Sierra Nevada. Reno: University of Nevada Press, 2004.

Bellefeuille, Sister Julie, S.N.D. "Printing in California, 1831–1930." Pacific Historian 19 (Fall 1975): 261–270.

Berger, Peter L., and Thomas Luckmann. *The Social Construction of Reality: A Treatise in the Sociology of Knowledge.* Garden City, NY: Doubleday, 1966.

Bermingham, Ann. "System, Order, and Abstraction: The Politics of English Landscape Drawing around 1795." In *Landscape and Power,* ed. W. J. T. Mitchell. Chicago: University of Chicago Press, 1994: 77–102.

Billinge, Mark. "Hegemony, Class and Power in Late Georgian and Early Victorian England: Towards a Cultural Geography." In *Explorations in Historical Geography: Interpretive Essays,* eds. Alan R. Baker and Derek Gregory. Cambridge, UK: Cambridge University Press, 1984: 28–67.

Black, Fiona A., Bertrum MacDonald, and J. Malcolm W. Black. "Geographic Information Systems: A New Research Method for Book History." *Book History* 1 (1998): 11–31.

Blodgett, Peter. *Land of Golden Dreams: California in the Gold Rush Decade, 1848–1858.* San Marino, CA: Huntington Library, 1999.

———. "Visiting 'the Realm of Wonder': Yosemite and the Business of Tourism, 1855–1916." In *Yosemite and Sequoia: A Century of California National Park,* eds. Richard J. Orsi, Alfred Runte, and Marlene Smith-Baranzini. Berkeley: University of California Press, 1993: 33–47.

Blumin, Stuart M. *The Emergence of the Middle Class: Social Experience in the American City, 1760–1900.* New York: Cambridge University Press, 1989.

Brechin, Gray. *Imperial San Francisco: Urban Power, Earthly Ruin.* Berkeley: University of California Press, 1999.

Bromell, Nicholas K. *By the Sweat of the Brow: Literature and Labor in Antebellum America.* Chicago: University of Chicago Press, 1993.

Brookman, Frank. "Park Naturalists and the Evolution of National Park Service Interpretation through World War II." *Journal of Forest History* 22 (January 1978).

Brown, Richard Maxwell. "Violence." In *The Oxford History of the American West,* eds. Clyde A. Milner II, Carol A. O'Connor, and Martha Sandweiss. New York: Oxford University Press, 1994: 393–426.

Bruce, Robert V. "A Statistical Profile of American Scientists, 1846–1876." In *Nineteenth-Century American Science: A Reappraisal,* ed. George H. Daniels. Evanston, IL: Northwestern University Press, 1972: 63–94.

Buchanan, B. J. "The Evolution of the English Turnpike Trusts: Lessons from a Case Study." *Economic History Review* 39, no. 2 (1986): 223–243.

Burns, Ken. *The National Parks: America's Best Idea.* Documentary film, 2009.

Burns, Rex. *Success in America: The Yeoman Dream and the Industrial Revolution.* Amherst: University of Massachusetts Press, 1976.

Buske, Frank. "Love Is Painful." *John Muir Newsletter* (Spring 1997).

Buttel, Frederick H., and William L. Flinn. "Social Class and Mass Environmental Beliefs: A Reconsideration." *Environment and Behavior* 10 (September 1978): 433–450.

Chalfant, W. A. *The Story of Inyo,* rev. ed. (Bishop, CA: Pinon Book Store, 1933).

Chan, Sucheng. "A People of Exceptional Character: Ethnic Diversity, Nativism, and Racism in the California Gold Rush." In *Rooted in Barbarous Soil: People, Culture, and Community in Gold Rush California,* eds. Kevin Starr and Richard J. Orsi. Berkeley: University of California Press, 2000: 44–85.

Chandler, Robert J. "A Stereotype Emerges." *Western States Jewish History* 21, no. 4 (July 1989): 310–313.

Charvat, William. *Literary Publishing in America, 1790–1850.* 1959 reprint, Amherst: University of Massachusetts Press, 1993.

Cloud, Barbara. *The Business of Newspapers on the Western Frontier.* Reno: University of Nevada Press, 1992.

Cohen, Michael P. *The Pathless Way: John Muir and American Wilderness.* Madison: University of Wisconsin Press, 1984.

Cornford, Daniel. "'We All Live More Like Brutes than Humans': Labor and Capital in the Gold Rush." In *A Golden State: Mining and Economic Development in Gold Rush California*, eds. James J. Rawls and Richard J. Orsi. Berkeley: University of California Press, 1997: 78–103.

Cronon, William. *Changes in the Land: Indians, Colonists, and the Ecology of New England.* New York: Hill and Wang, 1983.

———. "Introduction: In Search of Nature." In *Uncommon Ground: Rethinking the Human Place in Nature*, ed. William Cronon. New York: W. W. Norton, 1996: 23–68.

———. *Nature's Metropolis: Chicago and the Great West.* New York: W. W. Norton, 1991.

———. "The Trouble with Wilderness; or Getting Back to the Wrong Nature." In *Uncommon Ground: Rethinking the Human Place in Nature*, ed. William Cronon. New York: W. W. Norton, 1996: 69–90.

———, ed. *Uncommon Ground: Rethinking the Human Place in Nature.* New York: W. W. Norton, 1996.

Currey, Lloyd W., and Dennis G. Kruska. *Bibliography of Yosemite, the Central and Southern High Sierra, and the Big Trees, 1839–1900.* Los Angeles: Dawson's Book Shop, 1992.

Daniels, George H., ed. *Nineteenth-Century American Science: A Reappraisal.* Evanston, IL: Northwestern University Press, 1972.

Danky, James P., and Wayne A. Wiegand, eds. *Print Culture in a Diverse America.* Urbana: University of Illinois Press, 1998.

Dann, Kevin, and Gregg Mitman. "Essay Review: Exploring the Borders of Environmental History and the History of Ecology." *Journal of the History of Biology* 30 (1997): 291–302.

Darnton, Robert. "What Is the History of Books?" In *Reading in America: Literature and Social History*, ed. Cathy N. Davidson. Baltimore, MD: Johns Hopkins University Press, 1989: 27–52.

Davidoff, Leonore, and Catherine Hall. *Family Fortunes: Men and Women of the English Middle Class, 1780–1850.* Chicago: University of Chicago Press, 1987.

Davidson, Cathy N., ed. *Reading in America: Literature and Social History.* Baltimore: Johns Hopkins University Press, 1989.

DeLuca, Kevin, and Anne Demo. "Imagining Nature and Erasing Class and Race: Carleton Watkins, John Muir, and the Construction of Wilderness." *Environmental History* 5, no. 4 (October 2001): 541–560.

DeLuca, Kevin Michael. "Trains in the Wilderness: The Corporate Roots of Environmentalism." *Rhetoric and Public Affairs* 4, no. 4 (2001): 633–652.

Deverell, William. "'Niagara Magnified': Finding Emerson, Muir, and Adams in Yosemite." In *Yosemite: Art of an American Icon*, ed. Amy Scott. Berkeley: University of California Press, 2007: 9–22.

Dickens, Charles. *The Posthumous Papers of the Pickwick Club, Including Three Little-Remembered Chapters from Master Humphrey's Clock, in which Mr. Pickwick, Sam Weller & Other Pickwickians Reappear.* The Inner Sanctum Edition, ed. Clifton Fadiman. New York: Simon and Schuster, 1949.

Dodgshon, R. A., and R. A. Butlin, eds. *An Historical Geography of England and Wales.* London: Academic Press, 1978.

Dorman, Robert L. *A Word for Nature: Four Pioneering Environmental Advocates, 1845–1913.* Chapel Hill: University of North Carolina Press, 1998.

Dosch, Arno. "The Mystery of John Muir's Money." *Sunset* 36 (February 1916): 61–63.

Douglas, Ann. *The Feminization of American Culture.* New York: Knopf, 1977.

Driesbach, Janice T., Harvey L. Jones, and Katherine Church Holland. *Art of the Gold Rush.* Berkeley: University of California Press, 1998.

Drury, Clifford Merrill. *William Anderson Scott: No Ordinary Man.* Glendale, CA: Arthur H. Clark, 1967.

Duane, Timothy P. *Shaping the Sierra: Nature, Culture and Conflict in the Changing West.* Berkeley: University of California Press, 1998.

Dunlap, Thomas R. *Nature and the English Diaspora: Environment and History in the United States, Canada, Australia and New Zealand.* Cambridge, UK: Cambridge University Press, 1999.

Eisenstein, Elizabeth. *The Printing Press as an Agent of Change: Communications and Cultural Transformations in Early Modern Europe.* Cambridge, UK: Cambridge University Press, 1979.

Everett, Nigel. *The Tory View of Landscape.* New Haven, CT: Yale University Press, 1994.

Evernden, Neil. *The Social Creation of Nature.* Baltimore, MD: Johns Hopkins University Press, 1992.

Farquhar, Francis P. *Yosemite, the Big Trees and the High Sierra: A Selective Bibliography.* Berkeley: University of California Press, 1948.

Foner, Eric. *Reconstruction: America's Unfinished Revolution, 1863–1877.* New York: Harper & Row, 1988.

Gates, Paul W. *The Jeffersonian Dream: Studies in the History of American Land Policy and Development,* eds. Allan G. and Margaret Beattie Bogue. Albuquerque: University of New Mexico Press, 1996.

Gifford, Terry, ed. *John Muir: His Life and Letters and Other Writings.* Seattle: Mountaineers, 1996.

Gisel, Bonnie Johanna, ed. *Kindred and Related Spirits: The Letters of John Muir and Jeanne C. Carr.* Salt Lake City: University of Utah Press, 2001.

Gladwell, Malcolm. *The Tipping Point: How Little Things Can Make a Big Difference.* Boston: Little, Brown, 2000.

Glanz, Rudolf. *The Jews of California: From the Discovery of Gold until 1880.* New York: Southern California Jewish Historical Society, 1960.

Goodman, David. *Gold Seeking: Victoria and California in the 1850's.* Stanford, CA: Stanford University Press, 1994.

Gramsci, Antonio. *Selections from the Prison Notebooks,* ed. and trans. Quintin Hoare and Geoffrey Nowell Smith. London: Lawrence & Wishart, 1988.

Greenwood, Robert, ed. *California Imprints, 1833–1862: A Bibliography.* Seiko June Suzuki and Marjorie Pulliam, comps. Los Gatos, CA: Talisman Press, 1961.

Gregory, Derek. *Geographical Imaginations.* Cambridge, UK: Blackwell, 1994.

Groves, Jeffrey D. "'Ticknor-and-Fields-ism of All Kinds': Thomas Starr King, Literary Promotion, and Canon Formation." *New England Quarterly* (June 1995).

Grusin, Richard. *Culture, Technology, and the Creation of America's National Parks.* Cambridge, UK: Cambridge University Press, 2004.

Hackenberg, Michael, ed. *Getting the Books Out: Papers of the Chicago Conference on the Book in 19th-Century America.* Washington, DC: Library of Congress, 1987.

Hahn, Steven. *The Roots of Southern Populism: Yeoman Farmers and the Transformation of the Georgia Upcountry 1850–1890.* New York: Oxford University Press, 1983.

———. "The 'Unmaking' of the Southern Yeomanry: The Transformation of the Georgia Upcountry, 1860–1890." In *The Countryside in the Age of Capitalist Transforma-*

tion: *Essays in the Social History of Rural America*, eds. Steven Hahn and Jonathan Prude. Chapel Hill: University of North Carolina Press, 1985: 179–204.

———, and Jonathan Prude, eds. *The Countryside in the Age of Capitalist Transformation: Essays in the Social History of Rural America*. Chapel Hill: University of North Carolina Press, 1985.

Hall, David D. *Cultures of Print: Essays in the History of the Book*. Amherst: University of Massachusetts Press, 1996.

———. "The Uses of Literacy in New England, 1600–1850." In *Printing and Society in Early America*, eds. William L. Joyce, David D. Hall, Richard D. Brown, and John B. Hench. Worcester, MA: American Antiquarian Society, 1983.

———. *Worlds of Wonder, Days of Judgment: Popular Religious Belief in Early New England*. New York: Knopf, 1989.

Hall, Kermit L., ed. *The Oxford Companion to the Supreme Court of the United States*. New York: Oxford University Press, 1992.

Harlan, Robert D. "Printing for the Instant City: San Francisco at Mid-Century." In *Getting the Books Out: Papers of the Chicago Conference on the Book in 19th-Century America*, ed. Michael Hackenberg. Washington, DC: Library of Congress, 1987: 137–164.

Harrison, Charles. "The Effects of Landscape." In *Landscape and Power*, ed. W. J. T. Mitchell. Chicago: University of Chicago Press, 1994: 203–239.

Hays, Samuel P. *Explorations in Environmental History: Essays by Samuel P. Hays*. Pittsburgh: University of Pittsburgh Press, 1998.

Henderson, George L. *California and the Fictions of Capital*. New York: Oxford University Press, 1998.

Hewitt, Martin. "The Travails of Domestic Visiting, 1830–1870." *Historical Research* 71, no. 175 (1998): 196–228.

Heyck, T. W. *The Transformation of Intellectual Life in Victorian England*. New York: St. Martin's Press, 1982.

Hill, Mary. *Gold: The California Story*. Berkeley: University of California Press, 1999.

Hobsbawm, Eric J. *The Age of Capital 1848–1875*. New York: Charles Scribner's Sons, 1975.

———. *The Age of Revolution, Europe 1789–1848*. New York: New American Library, 1962.

Holland, Katherine Church. "Biographies of the Artists." In *Art of the Gold Rush*, eds. Janis T. Dreisbach, Harvey L. Jones, and Katharine Church Holland. Berkeley: University of California Press, 1998: 117–118.

Holliday, J. S. *The World Rushed In: The California Gold Rush Experience*. New York: Simon & Schuster, 1983.

Huntley-Smith, Jen. "'The Genius of Civilization': The Material Culture of Print Technology in the Nineteenth-Century American West." In *Western Technological Landscapes*, Nevada Humanities Committee, *Halcyon* series, 20. Reno: University of Nevada Press, 1998: 37–50.

———. "Nature and Progress in Yosemite." *Nevada Historical Society Quarterly* 46, no. 3 (Fall 2003): 173–192.

———. "Publishing the 'Sealed Book': James Mason Hutchings and the Landscapes of California Print Culture, 1853–1886." Ph.D. diss., University of Nevada, Reno, 2000.

———. "'Such Is Change in California': James Mason Hutchings and the Print Metropolis, 1854–1862." *Proceedings of the American Antiquarian Society* 114, pt. 1 (2004): 35–85.

———. "Territorial Enterprises: Print Culture and the West." In *Perspectives on American Book History: Artifacts and Commentary*, eds. Scott E. Casper, Joanne D. Chaison, and Jeffrey D. Groves. Amherst: University of Massachusetts Press, 2002: 276–278.

———. "Water in Print: Nature and Artifice." *Agricultural History* 76, no. 2. Agricultural History Society, Berkeley: University of California Press, Spring 2002: 354–363.

Hurley, Gerard. "Reading in the Gold Rush." *Book Club of California Quarterly News-Letter* 15 (Fall 1950): 90.

Hurtado, Albert L. *Indian Survival on the California Frontier.* New Haven, CT: Yale University Press, 1988.

Huth, Hans. *Yosemite: The Story of an Idea.* Yosemite National Park, CA: Yosemite Natural History Association, 1984.

Hyde, Ann Farrar. *An American Vision: Far Western Landscape and National Culture, 1820–1920.* New York: New York University Press, 1990.

Igler, David. "When Is a River Not a River? Reclaiming Nature's Disorder in *Lux v. Haggin.*" *Environmental History* 1, no. 2 (April 1996): 52–69.

Jacoby, Karl. "Class and Environmental History: Lessons from 'the War in the Adirondacks.'" *Environmental History* 2, no. 3 (July 1997): 328–336.

James, Ronald M. *The Roar and the Silence: A History of Virginia City and the Comstock Lode.* Reno: University of Nevada Press, 1998.

Jelinek, Lawrence J. *Harvest Empire: A History of California Agriculture.* San Francisco: Boyd & Fraser, 1979.

Johnson, Bruce L. "California on Stone, 1880–1906: A Proposed Sequel to Harry Peters's Pioneering Study." In *Getting the Books Out: Papers of the Chicago Conference on the Book in 19th-Century America,* ed. Michael Hackenberg. Washington, DC: Library of Congress, 1987: 165–174.

———. *James Weld Towne: Pioneer San Francisco Printer, Publisher & Paper Purveyor.* San Francisco: Book Club of California, 2008.

———. "Nevada Imprints Produced in San Francisco: The Role of Towne & Bacon." *Kemble Occasional* 19 (June 1978): 1–6.

———. "Printing in Nineteenth-Century San Francisco: A Flame before the Fire." *Book Club of California Quarterly Newsletter* 46 (Summer 1981).

Johnson, Paul E. *A Shopkeeper's Millennium: Society and Revivals in Rochester, New York, 1815–1837.* New York: Hill and Wang, 1984.

Johnson, Susan Lee. *Roaring Camp: The Social World of the California Gold Rush.* New York: W. W. Norton, 2000.

Johnston, Hank. *The Yosemite Grant, 1864–1906: A Pictorial History.* Yosemite National Park, CA: Yosemite Association, 1995.

———. *Yosemite's Yesterday,* vol. 2. Yosemite: Flying Spur Press, 1991.

Johnston-Dodds, Kimberly. "The California Militia and Expeditions against the Indians, 1850–1859." In *Early California Laws and Policies Related to California Indians.* Sacramento, CA: California State Library California Research Bureau, September 2002, http://www.militarymuseum.org/MilitiaandIndians.html.

Jones, Harvey L. "The Hessian Party: Charles Christian Nahl, Arthur Nahl, and August Wenderoth." In *Art of the Gold Rush,* eds. Janice T. Driesbach, Harvey L. Jones, and Katherine Church Holland. Berkeley: University of California Press, 1998, 47–64.

Jung, Maureen A. "Capitalism Comes to the Diggings; From Gold-Rush Adventure to Corporate Enterprise." In *A Golden State: Mining and Economic Development in Gold Rush California,* eds. James J. Rawls and Richard J. Orsi. Berkeley: University of California Press, 1997: 52–77.

Kelley, Robert. *Battling the Inland Sea: American Political Culture, Public Policy, and the Sacramento Valley 1850–1986.* Berkeley: University of California Press, 1989.

———. *Gold versus Grain: The Hydraulic Mining Controversy in California's Sacramento Valley.* Glendale, CA: Arthur H. Clark, 1959.

Kemble, Edward C. *A History of California Newspapers, 1846–1858.* Reprinted from the Supplement to the Sacramento *Union* of December 25, 1858, ed. Helen Harding Brentnor. Los Gatos, CA: Talisman Press, 1962.

Klancher, Jon P. *The Making of English Reading Audiences, 1790–1832.* Madison: University of Wisconsin Press, 1987.

Knobloch, Frieda. *The Culture of Wilderness: Agriculture as Colonization in the American West.* Chapel Hill: University of North Carolina Press, 1996.

Kowalewski, Michael. "Imagining the California Gold Rush: The Visual and Verbal Legacy." *California History* 71 (Spring 1992): 60–73.

Kruska, Dennis. "Hutchings' Letter Sheets." *Hoja Volante* 192. Los Angeles: Zamorano Club, 1996: 9–11.

———. *James Mason Hutchings of Yo Semite: A Biography and Bibliography.* San Francisco: Book Club of California, 2009.

Kurutz, Gary F. "Popular Culture on the Golden Shore." In *Rooted in Barbarous Soil: People, Culture, and Community in Gold Rush California,* eds. Kevin Starr and Richard J. Orsi. Berkeley: University of California Press, 2000: 280–315.

———. "Yosemite on Glass." In *Yosemite: Art of an American Icon,* ed. Amy Scott. Berkeley: University of California Press, 2007: 55–90.

Latour, Bruno. *We Have Never Been Modern,* trans. Catherine Porter. Cambridge, MA: Harvard University Press, 1993.

Laurie, Bruce. *Artisans into Workers: Labor in Nineteenth-Century America.* New York: Hill and Wang, 1989.

Lears, T. J. Jackson. *No Place of Grace: Antimodernism and the Transformation of American Culture 1880–1920.* Chicago: University of Chicago Press, 1981.

Lee, Gaylen D. *Walking Where We Lived: Memoirs of a Mono Indian Family.* Norman: University of Oklahoma Press, 1998.

Lerman, Nina. "From 'Useful Knowledge' to 'Habits of Industry': Gender, Race and Class in Nineteenth-Century Technical Education." Ph.D. diss., University of Pennsylvania, 1993.

Mann, Ralph. *After the Gold Rush: Society in Grass Valley and Nevada City, California, 1849–1870.* Stanford, CA: Stanford University Press, 1982.

Marx, Leo. *The Machine in the Garden: Technology and the Pastoral Ideal in America.* New York: Oxford University Press, 1967.

McCurry, Stephanie. *Masters of Small Worlds: Yeoman Households, Gender Relations, and the Political Culture of the Antebellum South Carolina Low Country.* New York: Oxford University Press, 1995.

McGreevy, Patrick. *Imagining Niagara: The Meaning and Making of Niagara Falls.* Amherst: University of Massachusetts Press, 1994.

McMurtrie, Douglas C. *A History of Printing in the United States: The Story of the Introduction of the Press and of Its History and Influence during the Pioneer Period in Each State of the Union.* New York: Bowker, 1936.

Melosi, Martin V. "Equity, Eco-racism, and Environmental History." *Environmental History Review* 4, no. 3 (Fall 1995): 1–16.

Metropolitan Museum of Art. "Carleton Watkins (1829–1916) and the West: 1860s–1870s." http://www.metmuseum.org/toah/hd/phws/hd_phws.htm#ixzz0sZaSDXDQ, accessed January 12, 2011.

Miller, Angela. *The Empire of the Eye: Landscape Representation and American Cultural Politics, 1825–1875.* Ithaca, NY: Cornell University Press, 1993.

Miller, David C. "Introduction." In *American Iconology: New Approaches to Nineteenth-Century Art and Literature,* ed. David C. Miller. New Haven, CT: Yale University Press, 1993.

Miller, Howard S. "The Political Economy of Science." In *Nineteenth-Century American Science: A Reappraisal,* ed. George H. Daniels. Evanston, IL: Northwestern University Press, 1972: 95–114.

Mitchell, W. J. T. "Imperial Landscape." In *Landscape and Power,* ed. W. J. T. Mitchell. Chicago: University of Chicago Press, 1994: 5–34.

———, ed. *Landscape and Power.* Chicago: University of Chicago Press, 1994.

Mossinger, Rosemarie. *Woodleaf Legacy: The Story of a Gold Rush Town.* Nevada City, CA: Carl Mautz Publishing, 1995.

Mott, Frank Luther. *A History of American Magazines, 1850–1865.* Cambridge, MA: Harvard University Press, 1938.

Moylan, Michele, and Lane Stiles, eds. *Reading Books: Essays on the Material Text and Literature in America.* Amherst: University of Massachusetts Press, 1996.

Muir, John. "Nevada's Dead Towns." *San Francisco Evening Bulletin,* January 15, 1879.

———. *Steep Trails, California—Utah—Nevada—Washington—Oregon—The Grand Canyon,* ed. William Frederic Bade. Boston: Houghton Mifflin, 1918.

Nash, Linda. *Inescapable Ecologies: A History of Environment, Disease, and Knowledge.* Berkeley: University of California Press, 2006.

Nicolson, Marjorie Hope. *Mountain Gloom and Mountain Glory: The Development of the Aesthetics of the Infinite.* Ithaca, NY: Cornell University Press, 1959.

Novak, Barbara. *Nature and Culture: American Landscape and Painting, 1825–1875.* New York: Oxford University Press, 1980.

Ogden, Kate Nearpass. "Sublime Vistas and Scenic Backdrops; Nineteenth-Century Painters and Photographers at Yosemite." In *Yosemite and Sequoia: A Century of California National Parks,* eds. Richard J. Orsi, Alfred Runte, and Marlene Smith-Baranzini. Berkeley: University of California Press, 1993: 49–67.

Olmsted, Frederick Law. *The Papers of Frederick Law Olmsted, Volume 5: The California Frontier, 1863–65,* ed. Victoria Post Ranney. Baltimore, MD: Johns Hopkins University Press, 1990.

Orsi, Richard J. "'Wilderness Saint' and 'Robber Baron': The Anomalous Partnership of John Muir and the Southern Pacific Company for Preservation of Yosemite National Park." *Pacific Historian* 29 (1985): 136–156.

———, Alfred Runte, and Marlene Smith-Baranzini, eds. *Yosemite and Sequoia: A Century of California National Parks.* Berkeley: University of California Press, 1993.

Palmquist, Peter E. "California's Peripatetic Photographer, Charles Leander Weed." *California History* 58 (Fall 1979): 194–219.

———. *Carleton E. Watkins: Photographer of the American West.* Albuquerque: University of New Mexico Press, 1983.

———. "Discovering Yosemite." *Timeline* 14 (Fall 1997): 40–54.

Paul, Rodman. *California Gold: The Beginning of Mining in the Far West.* Cambridge, MA: Harvard University Press, 1947.

Perkins, Maureen. *Visions of the Future: Almanacs, Time, and Cultural Change 1775–1870.* Oxford, UK: Clarendon Press, 1996.

Pisani, Donald J. "'I Am Resolved Not to Interfere, but Permit All to Work Freely': The

Gold Rush and American Resource Law." In *A Golden State: Mining and Economic Development in Gold Rush California*, eds. James J. Rawls and Richard J. Orsi. Berkeley: University of California Press, 1997: 123–173.

———. "The Origins of Western Water Law: Case Studies from Two California Mining Districts." *California History* 70 (Fall 1991): 242–257.

Pitt, Leonard. *The Decline of the Californios: A Social History of the Spanish-Speaking Californians, 1846–1890.* 1966; reprint, Berkeley: University of California Press, 1998.

Pomeroy, Earl. *The Pacific Slope: A History of California, Oregon, Washington, Idaho, Utah and Nevada.* Lincoln: University of Nebraska Press, 1965.

Poovey, Mary. *Making a Social Body: British Cultural Formation 1830–1864.* Chicago: University of Chicago Press, 1995.

Prude, Jonathan. "Town-Factory Conflicts in Antebellum Rural Massachusetts." In *The Countryside in the Age of Capitalist Transformation: Essays in the Social History of Rural America*, eds. Steven Hahn and Jonathan Prude. Chapel Hill: University of North Carolina Press, 1985: 71–102.

Pyne, Stephen J. *Fire in America: A Cultural History of Wildland and Rural Fire.* Princeton, NJ: Princeton University Press, 1982.

Quinn, Arthur. *The Rivals: William Gwin, David Broderick, and the Birth of California.* New York: Crown Publishers, 1994.

Rawls, James J., and Richard J. Orsi, eds. *A Golden State: Mining and Economic Development in Gold Rush California.* Berkeley: University of California Press, 1997.

Rawls, Walton. *The Great Book of Currier & Ives' America.* New York: Abbeville Press, 1979.

Raymond, C. Elizabeth. "Outside the Frame: Landscape, Art, and Experience in the Sierra Nevada." In *From Exploration to Conservation: Picturing the Sierra Nevada.* Reno: Nevada Museum of Art, 1998: 17–32.

Reingold, Nathan. *Science in Nineteenth-Century America: A Documentary History.* New York: Hill and Wang, 1964.

Reps, John W. *Views and Viewmakers of Urban America: Lithographs of Towns and Cities in the United States and Canada, Notes on the Artists and Publishers, and a Union Catalog of their Work, 1825–1925.* Columbia: University of Missouri Press, 1984.

Rice, Stephen P. "Minding the Machine: Languages of Class in Early Industrial America, 1820–1860." Ph.D. diss., Yale University, 1996.

Roberts, Brian. *American Alchemy: The California Gold Rush and Middle-Class Culture.* Chapel Hill: University of North Carolina Press, 2000.

Rohe, Rand E. "Man as Geomorphic Agent: Hydraulic Mining in the American West," *Pacific Historian* 27 (Spring 1983): 5–16.

Rohrbough, Malcolm. *Days of Gold: The California Gold Rush and the American Nation.* Berkeley: University of California Press, 1997.

Royce, Josiah. *California from the Conquest in 1846 to the Second Vigilance Committee in San Francisco: A Study of American Character.* 1886 Reprint, New York: Alfred A. Knopf, 1948.

Runte, Alfred. "The National Park Idea: Origins and Paradox of the American Experience." *Journal of Forest History* 21, no. 2 (1977).

———. *Yosemite: The Embattled Wilderness.* Lincoln: University of Nebraska Press, 1990.

Russell, Carl Parcher. *One Hundred Years in Yosemite: The Story of a Great Park and Its Friends.* Yosemite National Park, CA: Yosemite Natural History Association, 1968.

Ryan, Mary P. *Cradle of the Middle Class: The Family in Oneida County, New York, 1790–1865.* Cambridge, MA: Cambridge University Press, 1981.

Sagendorph, Robb. *America and Her Almanacs: Wit, Wisdom and Weather 1639–1970*. Boston: Little, Brown, 1970.

St. Clair, David J. "The Gold Rush and the Beginnings of California Industry." In *A Golden State: Mining and Economic Development in Gold Rush California*, eds. James J. Rawls and Richard J. Orsi. Berkeley: University of California Press, 1997: 185–208.

Sandweiss, Martha A. *Print the Legend: Photography and the American West*. New Haven, CT: Yale University Press, 2002.

Sargent, Shirley. *Pioneers in Petticoats: Yosemite's Early Women, 1856–1900*. Yosemite, CA: Flying Spur Press, 1966.

Scharnhorst, Gary. "Introduction." In Bret Harte, *The Luck of Roaring Camp and Other Writings*. New York: Penguin Books, 2001.

Schullery, Paul, and Lee Whittlesey. *Myth and History in the Creation of Yellowstone National Park*. Lincoln: University of Nebraska Press, 2003.

Schweikart, Larry, and Lynne Pierson Doti. "From Hard Money to Branch Banking: California Banking in the Gold Rush Economy." In *A Golden State: Mining and Economic Development in Gold Rush California*, eds. James J. Rawls and Richard J. Orsi. Berkeley: University of California Press, 1997: 209–232.

Scott, Amy. "Introduction: Yosemite Calls." In *Yosemite: Art of an American Icon*, ed. Amy Scott. Berkeley: University of California Press, 2007: 1–8.

Sears, John. *Sacred Places: American Tourist Attractions in the Nineteenth Century*. New York: Oxford University Press, 1989.

Shackel, Paul A. *Culture Change and the New Technology: An Archaeology of the Early American Industrial Era*. New York: Plenum Press, 1996.

Sheldon, Francis E. "Pioneer Illustration in California." *Overland Monthly*, 2nd series, 11 (April 1888): 337–355.

Shinn, Charles Howard. "Early Books, Magazines, and Book-Making." *Overland Monthly*, 2nd series, 12 (October 1888): 337–352.

———. *Mining Camps: A Study in American Frontier Government*. 1884 reprint. New York: Alfred A Knopf, 1948.

Silverman, James A. "Uncovering the Snow Storm: Rescuing California's First Children's Poem from Obscurity." *California History* 63 (Spring 1984): 172–176.

Sklar, Kathryn Kish. *Catharine Beecher: A Study in American Domesticity*. New Haven, CT: Yale University Press, 1974.

Smith, Henry Nash. *Virgin Land: The American West as Symbol and Myth*. New York: Vintage Books, 1950.

Smith, Michael. *Pacific Visions: California Scientists and the Environment*. New Haven, CT: Yale University Press, 1987.

Snyder, James, ed. "James Mason Hutchings, *A Photographic Expedition to Fisherman's Peak and Kings Canyon in 1875*," unpublished ms, 2007.

———. "Putting 'Hoofed Locusts' Out to Pasture." *Nevada Historical Society Quarterly* 46, no. 3 (Fall 2003): 139–172.

Solnit, Rebecca. *River of Shadows: Eadweard Muybridge and the Technological Wild West*. New York: Penguin, 2003.

———. *Savage Dreams: A Journey into the Hidden Wars of the American West*. San Francisco: Sierra Club Books, 1994.

Spence, Mark David. *Dispossessing the Wilderness: Indian Removal and the Making of the National Parks*. Oxford: Oxford University Press, 1999.

Starr, Kevin. *Americans and the California Dream 1850–1915*. New York: Oxford University Press, 1973.

Starrs, Paul. "Work in the Sierra Nevada: Picturing Productivity." In *From Exploration to Conservation: Picturing the Sierra Nevada*. Reno: Nevada Museum of Art, 1998, 49–64.

Stedman Jones, Gareth. *Outcast London: A Study of the Relationship between Classes in Victorian Society*. Oxford: Clarendon, 1971.

Steiner, Michael C., and David M. Wrobel. "Many Wests: Discovering a Dynamic Western Regionalism." In *Many Wests: Place, Culture & Regional Identity*, eds. Michael C. Steiner and David M. Wrobel. Lawrence: University Press of Kansas, 1997: 1–30.

Stern, Madeleine B. "Dissemination of Popular Books in the Midwest and Far West during the Nineteenth Century." In *Getting the Books Out: Papers of the Chicago Conference on the Book in 19th-Century America*, ed. Michael Hackenberg. Washington: The Center for the Book, 1987: 76–97.

———. *Publishers for Mass Entertainment in Nineteenth-Century America*. Boston: G. K. Hall, 1980.

Stilgoe, John R. *Common Landscape of America, 1580–1845*. New Haven, CT: Yale University Press, 1982.

Stoll, Mark. "Milton in Yosemite: *Paradise Lost* and the National Parks Idea." *Environmental History* 13, no. 2 (April 2008): 237–274.

Storer, Tracy I., and Lloyd P. Tevis, Jr. *California Grizzly*. Lincoln, NE: Bison Books, 1978.

Sunderland, John, and Margaret Webb, comps. and eds. *Towcester: The Story of an English Country Town: The Celebration of 2000 Years of History*. Towcester, UK: Towcester Local History Society, 1995.

Sweeting, Adam W. "Writers and Dilettantes: Central Park and the Literary Origins of Antebellum Urban Nature." In *The Nature of Cities: Ecocriticism and Urban Environments*, eds. Michael Bennet and David W. Teague. Tucson: University of Arizona Press, 1999: 93–110.

Terrie, Philip G. *Contested Terrain: A New History of Nature and People in the Adirondacks*. Syracuse: The Adirondack Museum/Syracuse University Press, 1997.

Trachtenberg, Alan. *The Incorporation of America: Culture and Society in the Gilded Age*. New York: Hill and Wang, 1982.

———. *Reading American Photographs: Images as History, Mathew Brady to Walker Evans*. New York: Hill and Wang, 1989.

Twain, Mark. *Roughing It*. 1872 reprint. Pleasantville, NY: The Reader's Digest Association, 1994.

Vale, Thomas R., and Geraldine R. Vale. *Walking with Muir across Yosemite*. Madison: University of Wisconsin Press, 1998.

Warner, Michael. *The Letters of the Republic: Publication and the Public Sphere in Eighteenth-Century America*. Cambridge, MA: Harvard University Press, 1990.

Watkins, T. H. "The Idle and Industrious Miner; a Tale of California Life." *The American West* 13 (May/June 1976): 39–45.

Wikipedia Online Encyclopedia. "Claude Glass." http://en.wikipedia.org/wiki/Claude_glass, accessed 7 January 2011.

Wilentz, Sean. *Chants Democratic: New York City and the Rise of the American Working Class, 1788–1850*. New York: Oxford University Press, 1984.

Wilkins, Thurman. *John Muir: Apostle of Nature*. Norman: University of Oklahoma Press, 1995.

Williams, Raymond. *The Country and the City*. New York: Oxford University Press, 1973.

———. *Culture and Society: 1780–1950*. New York: Harper and Row, 1966.

———. *Marxism and Literature*. Oxford: Oxford University Press, 1977.

Winship, Michael. *American Literary Publishing in the Mid-Nineteenth Century: The Business of Ticknor and Fields.* Cambridge, MA: Cambridge University Press, 1995.

Wolfe, Linnie Marsh. *Son of the Wilderness: The Life of John Muir.* New York: Knopf, 1947.

Worster, Donald. *Nature's Economy: A History of Ecological Ideas,* 2nd ed. New York: Cambridge University Press, 1994.

———. *A Passion for Nature: The Life of John Muir.* Oxford: Oxford University Press, 2008.

———. "Transformations of the Earth: Toward an Agroecological Perspective in History." *Journal of American History* 76, no. 4 (March 1990): 1087–1106.

Wrobel, David M. *Promised Lands: Promotion, Memory, and the Creation of the American West.* Lawrence: University Press of Kansas, 2002.

INDEX

A. Roman and Company, 135
"act for the government and protection of
Indians," 55
act of Congress, 122
Adams & Co., 83
Adirondacks, 163
agriculture, cash-crop, 85
Ahwahneechee (California Indian), 58. *See
also* Amerindians; *and under*
California Indian
albumen print photograph. *See under*
photography
alcohol, 36
almanacs, 68, 90, 93–94
agriculture and, 93
colonization and, 93
cultural function of, 93
history of, 92
See also California Pictorial Almanac
Alta California (newspaper), 92
amateur scientist, the, 159
American Civil War, 5–7. *See also* Civil War,
U.S.
American conservation policy, origin of,
120–121
American environmental history, 9, 112, 132,
169–170
irony of, 172
American environmentalism, 132
elitism and, 169
twentieth century, 107
American environmental philosophy, 2, 8–9,
169
American icons
national parks as, 173
value of, 176
American identity. *See* American national
identity; national identity
American national identity, 9, 169
American Revolution, 18
American River, 22, 87
American society, contradictions of, 141

American West, 61
Civil War impact on, 130
incorporation of, 125
industrial capitalism in, 130
reconstruction in, 130
Amerindians, 141, 161
in Yosemite, 150–151
women, in Yosemite, 153–154
See also Ahwahneechee; California
Indians; California indigenes;
Chowchilla; Miwok; Mono; Yokuts;
Yosemite
Anderson, George, 160
Anglo (as ethnic group), 24, 31
Anglo American, 62
authority, 26, 36, 39
civilization, 89
colonization, 90
cultural empire, 94
culture, 59, 68
culture-makers, 59
economic power, 4
print culture, 89
republicanism, 35
values, 27
violence, 26, 55
Anglo California, 47, 97
anti-Black sentiment, 140
anti-Irish sentiment, 140
Archer, Frederick Scott, 144
Argonauts, gold rush. *See under* California
gold rush
Arizona, 85
armchair
tourist, 76, 104
travel, 81, 99–100
See also under tourism
Armory Hall, 66
Armstrong, Anthony (engraver), 49
"Articles in a Miners' Creed" (letter sheet),
47
artist-engraver, 46

Ashburner, William, 122, 123
Atlantic Monthly (magazine), 117
Atlantic world, 6, 53, 24, 100
    institutions, 59
Awahneechee, 150
Ayres, Thomas (artist), xii, 45, 60, 65, 67, 70,
        76–77, 97, 103, 145
    biographical information, 45n6
    "General View of the Great Yo-Semite
        Valley," xii (illus.), 5, 65
    Golden Gate (sketch), 70
    Harper's Weekly commission, 45n6
    "Yo-Hamite Falls, The" (lithographic
        print) 5, 60, 65, 76–77, 79, 81, 83, 145
        (*see also* Hutchings, James Mason;
        "Yo-Hamite Falls, The")

Baker, George, 46
    biographical information, 46n8
Bank of California, 88
Barber and Baker, engravers, 45
barley, 93
Barth, Gunther, 85
basin and range, 79
Basque, 161, 163
Bates, Anna, 73
Bavaria, 124
bear-and-bull fight, 39
    arena, Placerville, 39
Bedford, Edmund, 157
Bee, A. W., 37
Belmont (Ralston Estate), 88, 105, 173
Benecia, 82
Bierstadt, Albert, Yosemite paintings, 111, 115
bighorn sheep, native populations of, 162
Big Oak Flat, 103, 104
    road, 153
Big Tree Grove. *See* Mariposa Big Tree
        Grove
big tree room, 134
bird's-eye view, 44, 77
Birmingham (England), 16, 21
Blodgett, Peter, 128
Boddam Wetham, J. W., 135
Boericke, Mr., 158
bonanza wheat, 88
booster, boosterism, 51, 77. *See also under*
        Hutchings
Boston, 115
    elite networks of, 125

Boston Evening Transcript, 113. *See also* King,
        Thomas Starr
bourgeoisie (middle class), 76
Bowles, Samuel, 114
    attitude toward Indians, 151
Brady, Matthew (studio of), 116
Brannan, Samuel, 22, 91
Brayton, A. P., 37
Brayton, I. P. (*Pacific* editor), 37, 44, 70
Brechin, Gray, 85
Brewer, William, 168
Britton and Rey, 46, 76
Broderick, Mount, 143, 146
Bunnell, Lafayette, 57
Burke, Edmund, 18
Burke, J. M., & Co., 97
Burnett, Peter H. (California governor), 56
Burns, Ken, 2
Butler, W. C., 46, 75

Calaveras Grove Hotel, 165
Calaveras mammoth trees, 44
California, 1, 11, 13
    Academy of Science, 70, 73, 159
    admission to union of, 116
    agriculture, 68, 88
    Anglos, 35
    Central Valley of, 1, 15, 87, 119
    chivalry party of, 116
    Civil War and, 115–116, 131
    culture makers, 43
    economic depression in, 130
    economic diversification, 84
    environment of, 36
    environmental damage, 85
    ethnic diversity of, 150
    geologic survey, 157, 158, 159
    governor of, 127
    history, 93
    identity of, 119
    incorporation and, 130
    industrialization, 43, 68, 84
    intermarriage in, 151
    legislature, 55
    mining communities, 43, 144
    Mexican era, 22, 151
    mining, industrialization of, 84
    missions, 26
    mission novice, 22
    natural scenery, 68

post gold rush, 41
post gold-rush economy, 84
publishing, 41
resources, 77
race in, 51
Sabbatarian movement, 36–37 (*see also*
    Sabbatarianism)
sense of place, 28, 68, 178
social reality, contradictions in, 105
society, 4, 10, 17, 43–44
Spanish colonies, 22
state constitution, 160
Supreme Court, 122
Thomas Starr King in, 117
urbanization, 68
working class, 74
See also California gold mining;
    California gold rush; California
    identity; California Indians;
    California indigenes; California
    landscapes; California print culture;
    California State Legislature;
    Sacramento; San Francisco; Sierra
    Nevada; Yosemite
California, State of, 111, 120, 125, 132, 137, 145,
    163. *See also* California; California
    state legislature
California gold mining, 33
    environmental impact of, 36
    industrialization of, 43
California gold rush, 4–6, 10–12, 17, 83, 151
    Argonauts, 25, 97
    demographics, uncertainty of data,
        25n22
    economic volatility of, 28
    entertainment, 29
    Chinese in, 27
    cost of living, 25
    disease in, 25
    ethnic diversity of, 89
    international quality of, 24
    miners, 35
    northern mines, 44
    poverty in, 25
    religion, 31
    social instability, 27
    start of, 22, 25
    violence, 26, 33, 36
California identity, 48, 73, 93
    middle class, 105

California Indians, 13, 26, 44, 53
    Ahwahneechee, 58
    coastal, 24
    Chowchilla, 56
    demographic disaster, 26
    illustrations of, 51, 53
    kidnapping, 56
    laborers, 56
    Miwok, 83, 55, 57, 150, 154
    Mono, 55, 59, 150
    rancheria(s), 56, 58–59 (*see also*
        rancheria[s])
    violence against, 93
    Wiyot tribe massacre, 27
    Yokuts, 55–57, 83
    See also Amerindians, Ahwahneechee,
        California indigenes, Chowchilla,
        Miwok, Mono, Yokuts, Yosemite
California indigenes, 55–56, 61. *See also*
    individual tribes
California landscape(s), 19, 44, 74, 105
    in illustration, 44
California Pictorial Almanac, 80, 88–90,
    91–93
    advertising in, 91
    illustrations in, 91
    See also almanacs; Hutchings, James
        Mason
California print culture, 36
    ethnicity, 51
    race, 51
California Star (newspaper), 91
California state legislature, 113, 124–125
    memorial to U.S. Congress, 127
California Steam Navigation Company, 45
Californio, 22, 68, 89–90, 94, 149, 151
    miners, 31
    economy of, 24
Calvary Church. *See under* San Francisco
Camp Independence, California, 157
Cape Horn, California, 88
capitalism
    gold rush expression of, 25
    imperial, 18
    industrial, 18
    laissez-faire, 20
    urban-industrial, 171
capitalist, 101
    gilded age, 173
capitalization, 43

See also Muir, John, and James Mason Hutchings

Hutchings, Tom, 59, 150, 160
 adoption of, 164
Hutchings & Rosenfield, 65, 68, 70, 90, 94, 135
 California Pictorial Almanac, 91, 93
 office and shop, 65
 publishing firm, 66
 publications, 74
Hutchings children, 2, 148. *See also individual children*
Hutchings lawsuit (*Hutchings v. Low; Low v. Hutchings*), 108, 113, 122, 125
 public relations, 107, 128
 ruling, 113, 128
Hutchings travel guides
 advice to tourists, 135
 Yosemite descriptions, 135
Hutchings, William (father), 15
Hutchings, Willie Yo Semite, 152, 156, 160
Hutchings' almanac. *See California Pictorial Almanac*
Hutchings' California Magazine, 5, 12, 48, 57, 70, 71–73, 78–80, 91, 99–101, 119, 130, 135, 159
 contributors to, 72
 end of, 118
 engravings in, 70
 illustrations in, 70
 tourism in, 97
Hutchings' House (Yosemite hotel), 120, 122, 130
 cooking in, 134
 Coulter & Murphy lease, 137
 destination resort as, 134
 guests, 135
 improvements to, 134
Hutchings' Illustrated California Magazine. See Hutchings' California Magazine
"Hutchings' Panoramic Scenes: Northern California and Oregon," 44–45
Huth, Hans, 113, 122, 129
hybrid, 169. *See also* Latour, Bruno
hydraulic mines, 87
hydraulic mining, 36, 47, 49, 85, 87–88, 105, 164, 172
 appearance of, 88
 capitalization of, 50

environmental impact of, 49
industrialization of, 50
legal end of, 86
slickens, 86
technology, 43, 47, 84

iconography
 landscape, 114
 national, 108
Idaho, 85, 96
imagined communities, 20
immigrants
 eastern European, 140
 southern European, 140
immigration, 140
imperialism, 67, 89
incorporation, 5, 127, 131
 Hutchings and, 130
 postbellum, 123
 railroads and, 131
 war of, 113
 western, 127, 130
independence, 58
Indian removals, 26–27, 79
 forced marches, 56
 Yosemite, 56
Indian Tom, 150. *See also* Hutchings, Tom
industrial capitalism, 73
industrial capitalism, American west, 130
industrialization, 12, 19, 140, 173
 Civil War and, 6
 social organization, 43, 51
 romantic critique of, 20
industrial lumbering, 156
industrial manufacturing, 84
industrial revolution
 environmental impact of, 172–173
 Second, 5 (*see also* Second Industrial Revolution)
industrial society, 41
industrial technology, enthusiasm for, 163
industry
 captains of, 123, 171 (*see also* robber barons)
 environmental responsibility of, 178
Inspiration Point (Yosemite), xii, 65
intentional fire, ecological impact of, 162
In the Heart of the Sierras, 59, 126–127, 151, 154, 159, 164, 168
Ione valley, 44